Chronicles of My Life with a Blonde

Written by Jax Hix

Cover Art by Sarah Steever

Dreaming Dragon Publishing LLC
3840 A St SE, Ste 105, PMB 34
Auburn, WA 98002

Copyright © 2011 Dreaming Dragon Publishing LLC
All rights reserved.
ISBN: 978-0615475936
ISBN-13: 0615475930
Library of Congress Control Number: 2011929558

ACKNOWLEDGMENTS

JC, beloved Blonde-Spouse, without whom this book would not be possible.

Bryan,Brunette-Teenage-Son-And-Self-Designated-Peanut-Gallery-Of-Sarcastic-Commentary, without whom this book would not be possible.

Aryana,Blonde-Spouse-Dimiutive-Duplicate, without whom this book would not be possible.

Glorious Proofreader extroidinaires: Alessandra D'Angelo, Stanley McAdams, and Adrienne Alton-Gust, without whom this book would be one run-on sentence.

Cover Design: Sarah Steever, Thank you for capturing the true Blonde-Spouse's spirit.

For the loved ones who are lost.

For the lifetime of wisdom gained.

For the dream that is dared to dream.

For the Indigo Dancer in the Rain.

DEDICATION

It began as a blog outlet to vent frustration without killing my newlywed Blonde husband. After a few years, it evolved into a record for potential divorce court...until I realized that leaving my muse would be akin to leaving the movie theater during the part in the horror movie where the blonde coed is the last one left in the house in the woods in the middle of the night in the dark in the storm after all of her friends went to the cellar to check on the fuse box but did not return so she doesn't know they've all been slaughtered by the homicidal maniac waiting in the cellar after having cut the power so she goes to investigate...*breath*...so you know how it's going to end but you just can't tear your eyes away all the while screaming at the blonde coed on the screen to run away as fast as she can but knowing she can't hear you and will continue anyway to meet her violent end and you are frozen to the spot waiting with baited breath. Life with him was just too fun not to stick around for the ending! And I have learned his greatest gift to teach was that we should all embrace the Blonde within us, and the reminder that life is too precious to be so serious with ourselves...instead our mistakes should be an opportunity to laugh while we learn, so our journey is enriched with adventures in the making of the palettes of our souls complete.

This book is dedicated to the Blonde in all of us, with laughter and joy I give you, Chronicles of My Life with a Blonde!

Jax Hix

CONTENTS

1 IN THE BEGINNING

1-1: Running Errands

"So you're gonna go to the grocery store after you pick up the kids from school?" Brunette-Self asked, turning to Blonde-Spouse.

"Of course, what else would I be doing at this hour?" Blonde-Spouse replied with a slightly bitter tone to his voice.

"Do you have your wallet?" she inquired skeptically of him.

"Of course, duh, Dear." Blonde-Spouse looked emotionally injured at the suggestion he would forget such a thing.

"Are you sure?" Brunette-Self pushed, as she did not buy into his assurances.

"Of course, DEAR. Geesh," he said and rolled his eyes over and over at her.

"Ok, drive safe," she conceded, knowing he'd be back and secretly betting herself on how long it would be before he was.

"Of course," Blonde-Spouse replied automatically.

(Pitter patter of Blonde-Spouse feet down the front steps, followed by a car door slamming and the sound of the car backing out the driveway. Puppy petting commenced. 5 minutes later the sound of a car could be heard pulling into the driveway, followed by a car door slamming and stomping up the steps).

"What did you forget?" she asked. Blonde-Spouse looked highly annoyed, "Oh, nothing."

"Seriously, what did you forget?" Brunette-Self asked again, undaunted.

"My wallet, okay?" he retorted.

1-2: Paying Bills

Brunette-Self directed toward Blonde Spouse "The check to pay the hardware store bill is laying right by the door."

"Ok, Darling," Blonde-Spouse replied, distracted by something shiny across the room.

"Do you have your store card?" she prodded, knowing full well he didn't.

"S***!" he grumbled as he wandered about the bedroom, bathroom and kitchen and ripped them to shreds in his search.

"Found it," and he held it up like a trophy.

"See you in about an hour" offered Brunette-Self, rather amused.

"Ok." He shot out over his shoulder before the door closed behind him.

Brunette-Self discovered the check still laying next to door about 25 minutes after blonde departed. Grinning, she called his cell phone.

"Hi, Honey. Where are you?" she asked as she picked up the check and looked at it and smirking to herself . She decided to set him up, to see if he had yet remembered.

"Hardware store," Blonde-Spouse said "You know, where you sent me to pay the bill?"

"So, are you missing anything?" Brunette-Self queried.

"Nope. Got my card, my id, my wallet, my car keys, my cell phone." Blonde-Spouse verbally checked off his list of items.

Laughing inside, Brunette-Self reminded him "How about a check to pay the bill?" Silence. "You still there?" she prodded.

"I'll be home in 30 minutes."

1-3: Drunk Driver

On the freeway, Blonde-Spouse was driving and Brunette-Self noticed they were now weaving back and forth in their lane.

She looked over at Blonde-Spouse, who was gleefully chugging a Henry Weinart's Root Beer. Brunette-Self also noticed several other drivers reaching for cell phones to report 'root beer' drunk driver.

Brunette-Self mentioned to Blonde-Spouse that chugging a beverage that looks like beer may not be the wisest of choices while driving and weaving. Blonde-Spouse could not fathom why, and stated if the other drivers were so concerned they could buy their own.

Brunette-Self mentally smacked her forehead.

1-4: Fashion

Blonde-Spouse-Diminutive-Duplicate (aka the couple's blonde daughter who was more like a little female clone of Blonde-Spouse) presented herself in a pink plaid Hello Kitty shirt with hot Blonde-Spouse-Diminutive-Duplicate pink camoflauge shorts, and gleefully informed Brunette-Self that Blonde-Spouse had selected this outfit for her.

Brunette-Self wandered into the room where Blonde-Spouse was diligently surfing the internet and asked, "What were you thinking?" and pointed at the child. Blonde-Spouse glanced at their daughter, looked at Brunette-Self and replied, "But they match...they're pink!"

Blonde-Spouse was sporting a tee-shirt on inside-out and backward, mismatched socks with a hole in the toe on one and a rainbow toe-sock on the other, and a pair of boxer shorts on backwards and also, apparently, inside-out.

Brunette-Self gave up and stopped arguing, she knew it was futile.

1-5: Banned from Power tools

Blonde-Spouse, "I think I'll change that bulb in the bedroom light fixture."
Brunette-Self mumbled, "Let me make sure we're current on the health insurance."

Blonde-Spouse disappeared into the bedroom. Cussing and swearing floated back down the hallway to her waiting ears--followed by hammering — wait, HAMMERING?!? and..."Hooneeey, I need your help!"

Brunette-Self wandered down the hall and into the bedroom, where Blonde-Spouse stood on a stepladder, holding entire light fixture (now with short in the wiring) dangling ON between his arms..."ouch-ouch-ouch-ouch! It's hot!" Blonde-Spouse whined while he juggled.

Brunette-Self counted to 10, and then asked Blonde-Spouse why he didn't turn off the light first and then unscrew the glass covers, followed by unscrewing of the light bulb from the socket leading to screwing in a new bulb.

"THEY UNSCREW?!?"

Three trips to the hardware store to fix wire short, buy new mount screw for fixture: $25.

Two hours of swearing under breath while fixing light fixture: exhausting.

Being married to a walking blonde joke: definitely priceless frustration.

1-6: Baby Barricades

Each night Brunette-Self would come home unable to open the door. She would knock and wait 5 minutes while a great racket arouse on the other side of the door.

Blonde-Spouse, decided baby fences were not 'enough.' Instead, he created the ever growing "baby barricade." Blonde-Spouse "Baby Barricades" were an arrangement of furniture (usually end tables and chairs), with pillows and blankets shoved underneath them and pots and pans along the top...an alarm system of sorts.

They soon found "Baby Barricades" also made exceptional "Catch the Teens Sneaking Outs" or "Crooks Sneaking Ins" alarm systems, not to mention the ever popular "Blow out the discs in your back taking a midnight trip to the fridge" diet coaches as well.

1-7: The Jenga Fire

Blonde + Lamp Oil + "Fire From Space!" = Chronicle 1-7, of Chronicles of My Life with a Blonde: "The Jenga Fire."

Whilst the family went camping, Brunette-Self pondered the sanity of what she was about to ask of Blondus-Spousus-Of-The-Leo-Signus-Pyronus, but decided to risk it..."Would you please start a cooking fire in the fire pit while I get the rest of dinner ready to go?"

Blonde-Spouse began banging wood on a rock with hatchet to make a large pile of kindling. Brunette-Self swore she heard a faint series of "ughs" drifting on the wind and wondered if her social network site friend, Sasquatch, had decided to crash the party.

Blonde-Spouse began to erect large tower of kindling in an infinity style Jenga pattern, until the tower was nearly 8 inches high. Brunette-Self -- torn -- between the satiating with inquiry the morbid curiosity on why Blonde-Spouse was making a tower with no coals beneath it to start the kindling on fire, and watching to see the rationale of Blondus-Spousus-Of-The-Leo-Signus-Pyronus of building the campfire upside down, wondering if at any moment he would stand up and declare "JENGA!"

Alas, morbid curiosity won. "Honey," Brunette-Self mustered her courage.

"Yes, dear." Blondus-Spousus-Of-The-Leo-Signus-Pyronus

"Um, so why are you building the campfire upside down?" she asked.

"So the coals are higher up and closer to the cooking grill" he responded, "Duh."

Brunette-Self gulped and hid the oil.

1-8: Laundry Logic

Blonde-Spouse began to throw all colors of laundry and white into washer. He only filled it 1/4 full and proceeded to turn the wash water to large load.

Brunette-Self, water conscious, asked what in the world was he thinking and doing.

Blonde-Spouse looked at Brunette-Self like she was a moron, "Adding more water will keep the reds from staining the whites."

1-9: Urinal Soap

They went camping for their friend Oponn's "21 again" birthday, but discovered when they arrived that their usual campsite had been closed. They found ourselves, begrudgingly, at a new site hosting no water or flushing toilets, but one that did contain a porta-potty.

As Oponn and Brunette-Self journeyed to town to purchase water, they left their daughters (Oponn'sNemo and Blonde-Spouse-Diminutive-Duplicate) in the care of the Blondus-Spousus-Dingle-Dorfus.

Upon their return, they discovered Blonde-Spouse-Diminutive-Duplicate had a terrible bout of diarrhea. When Brunette-Self took Blonde-Spouse-Diminutive-Duplicate to the port-a-potty for her third trip of the afternoon, she stayed to keep her company while she finished.

Blonde-Spouse-Diminutive-Duplicate pointed to the urinal on the side of the porta-potty and asked Brunette-Self what the pink 'soap' was for. Brunette-Self looked at her and told her, "Ew, that's where boys pee!"

Blonde-Spouse-Diminutive-Duplicate, looked quite mortified and exclaimed angrily, "But Daddy (Blondus-Spousus-Dingle-Dorfus) said it was soap! He did!"

Brunette-Self sighed and turned to yell down the hill to Blondus-Spousus-Dingle-Dorfus to ask him if he did, indeed, advise the girls the urinal cake was "soap." Blondus Dorkus yelled back that he had, and cited that he felt it was safer than referring to it as "cake."

Blonde-Spouse-Diminutive-Duplicate began to cry, "Daddy said it was soap, so Nemo and I washed our hands with it!" Aha! No wonder the child experienced diarrhea.

Oponn and Brunette-Self dunked the girls in the river and then sprayed down both children in Lysol. Blondus-Dorkus was then placed in charge of their diarrhea the rest of the weekend.

1-10: Painting the Fence

A few years ago they installed a 6 foot tall wooden privacy fence in their back-yard and drowned it in clear sealer. Sadly, only two years later, it needed to be re-sealed.

The original sealer did a lousy job of keeping its beautiful cedar color quality, so they opted to stain it this time in addition to sealing the wood. They only had enough redwood stain to do one side of the fence, and enough red mahogany stain to do the other side.

Brunette-Self, "Hon, why don't we mix the two stains together?"

Blonde-Spouse, "Why would we do that? We might run out of color!"

Brunette-Self, taking deep breath, "Hon, wouldn't we run out regardless of whether or not we mixed them, since we have equal parts of both?"

Blonde-Spouse, "No way! I'm going to paint the outside redwood and the inside mahogany!" Result? Two toned fence.

Brunette-Self abandoned ill-logical debate and wondered if Blonde-Spouse shouldn't run for president.

1-11: Ordering Take-Out

Sometimes Brunette-Self was afraid to order anything with Blonde-Spouse, for fear Disgruntled-Food-Service- Workers would spit in her food in frustration with the order.

The two rolled up to the order menu, "May I take your order."

Blonde-Spouse yelled into the speaker, "I'll take a cheeseburger, please. No ketchup but mustard, no tomato but onion, no pickles but mayonnaise."

Disgruntled-Food-Service-Worker, "So, you want a cheeseburger with pickles and mayonnaise?"

Blonde-Spouse, "No! No pickles but mayonnaise, with onions but no tomato and no ketchup but mustard."

Disgruntled-Food-Service-Worker, "So you want a cheeseburger plain?"

Angry Blonde-Spouse, "NO! Mayonnaise no ketchup, mustard no pickles, onions no tomato!"

Brunette-Self, "I'll just a #3, please. Surprise me on the drink."

Angry-Blonde-Spouse, "Did you get all of that?"

Disgruntled-Food-Service-Worker with an audible sigh of annoyance, "Please pull forward to the first window."

Brunette-Self turned to Blonde-Spouse, "Why don't you just order a cheeseburger with mayonnaise, onion and mustard?"

Blonde-Spouse, "Because that would be too complicated."

1-12: "Dis-Organization"

Brunette-Self had come to realize that her Blonde-Spouse had some pretty odd habits when it came to organization.

He would look at a box of random items, select the biggest thing in the box (say, "a pan") and determine it is all kitchen stuff. They had lived in their house for over four years now, and she still couldn't find everything he "organized."

Yet, Blonde-Spouse was surprisingly anal about the weirdest things: his pillows had to be arranged perfectly perpendicular to each other in order to sleep, toilet paper had to be folded and not bunched, just to name a few.

Her Brunette-Self-Valiant-Virgo had begun to wear off on her Blonde-Spouse, the last time he packed for a camping trip, he proudly announced, "I have made a list."

Her Brunette Virgo heart jumped with joy and promptly fell to her shoes when he so proudly presented her with "The List."

"The List" consisted of a complex drawing with arrows, curved lines connecting items and the occasional "Uh, oh, I don't know where that is" comment. There were bubbles connected to other bubbles, big X's over duplicate items, etc.

Blonde-Spouse determined that they required six rolls of toilet paper (for a two day trip) and replacement flashlight bulbs, but plates and silverware were not important items--neither was propane or the tent. Brunette-Self attempted to point this out but angered Blonde-Spouse, who stated "I can do this!"

They arrived at said campsite to discover: he had packed the tent (after she'd suggested it), but forgot the poles; three replacement light bulbs but no batteries for the flashlights; six rolls of toilet paper but no biodegradable chemical for the porta-potty; tarps but no rope to hang them; and had directional signs to the campsite to post but no ties to post them. *sigh*

Brunette-Self-Valiant-Virgo took over the packing lists, and has resigned herself to composing a "secret" list to assure it never happens again.

1-13: The UnHandy Handyman

On Wednesday of last week, the Blonde-Spouse and Brunette-Self agreed that the main bathroom shower/tub unit needed to be recaulked. Blonde-Spouse heartily agreed to take on the task. Brunette-Self felt a sense of foreboding and shuddered.

"Hon?" Brunette-Self ventured, knowing disaster was imminent.

"Yea, babe." Blonde-Spouse

"Do you know where you put the caulking gun and supplies?" queried Brunette-Self, (reader is directed to refer to chronicle 1-12: Dis-Organization for further details) "We cannot afford to get more caulking and a new caulking gun right now, the County wants their blood--er, TAX money on the 31st."

Blonde-Spouse diligently removed the trim around top of tub/base of shower surround and treated area with mildew preventer. Blonde-Spouse placed the trim (with nails still in it and pointing upward) on the base of the tub. Brunette-Self asked why the nail points were pointing up (and figured explaining REMOVING NAILS FROM TRIM WAS THE SAFEST OPTION was too difficult and lengthy to get into at the moment), and Blonde-Spouse snappingly replied it's so the nails don't scratch the tub. *BRUNETTE-SELF BIT HER TONGUE*

Blonde-Spouse forgot to remove remaining tidbits of caulking prior to using mildew preventer. Tidbits of Napalm like caulking hung dripping with mildew preventer (that Brunette-Self was highly allergic to) around the shower surround. Blonde-Spouse also forgot to take into account drying time of mildew preventer, thus extending the project back into his work week. Brunette-Self, several eye rolls later and pondered if they can budget in anti-histamines to combat the welts and swelling, offered to complete the project if Blonde-Spouse would locate caulking and caulking gun.

Blonde-Spouse stated "They're behind the door in the master bathroom."

Brunette-Self simply ignored the nagging need to try to rationalize why

Blondus Spousus Dis-Organizedous would consider this the most prime location for home maintenance supplies, and simply replied, "Ok."

By Sunday, Brunette-Self had managed to remove napalm-dripping caulk tidbits from unit without putting herself into the hospital. Brunette-Self looked behind the doors in master bathroom for caulking supplies and gun and--no caulking supplies and gun.

Brunette-Self mustered up the courage to educate Blonde-Spousus-Of-The-Work-Week-Grumpus on Monday evening, "Hon, the caulking stuff wasn't where you said it would be. Are you sure you didn't move it?"

Blonde-Spousus-Of-The-Work-Week-Grumpus pretended not to hear Brunette-Self. This told Brunette-Self that Blonde-Spousus-Of-The-Work-Week-Grumpus had dis-organized these items so far that even he did not know where they were.

Having a family of four share one bathroom for the next two weeks awaiting Blonde Spousus Dis-Organizedous' next paycheck in order to purchase new caulking supplies and gun--ANNOYING. Getting that annoyance out by writing another Chronicles episode—THERAPY.

1-14: "HAMMERTIME"

Blonde-Spouse had long since been banned from power tools. There entailed a long story in why he was banned that involved blood--lots of blood--the reader is asked to leave it at that for the sake of their sanity.

They were putting in a new shelving unit in their bedroom, and Brunette-Self had just completed cutting the shelf to size. Brunette-Self assigned the task of removing the nails from the top shelving piece (reclaimed wood) to Blonde-Spouse, as she had wrongly assumed safety due to Blonde-Spouse's banned status from power tools.

Brunette-Self watched in horror as Blonde-Spouse leaned the wood piece against the kitchen sink, and proceeded to attempt to knock out the nails by hitting the tips of the nails. The wood had been propped so that the nail tip side faced Blonde-Spouse--so he could "obtain better leverage." Blonde-Spouse began to hammer the nail tips and bent them in the process. Brunette-Self pleaded with Blonde-Spouse to stop "before you hurt yourself." Blonde-Spouse was offended Brunette-Self could not be more supportive. Blonde-Spouse then proceeded to whack one of the nail tips at the top of the board, and drove the bottom row of nail tips into said Blonde-Spouse's foot. Brunette-Self fought the urge to mutter "I told you so."

Brunette-Self placed new shelf down into shelf unit and on top of the support brackets of wood already mounted on the inside of the unit.

Brunette-Self thought Blonde-Spouse would be safer driving in nails rather than pulling them out, and offered to have Blonde-Spouse nail the shelf in. Thinking Blonde-Spouse will drive a few nails attaching the board to the support, Brunette-Self handed Blonde-Spouse the hammer and a box of nails and proceeded to sit down and play Word Search games.

Brunette-Self got highly involved in finding words in the puzzles and tuned out the hammering coming from the bedroom. Brunette-Self snapped out of it at the end of puzzle 1 and then realized Blonde-Spouse had been hammering for quite some time. Brunette-Self, feeling much like a horror movie victim about to discover the first body in the other room, wandered into the bedroom to check on the status of shelf nailing. Brunette-Self was greeted with dozens of nails hammered one half inch apart down the length of the shelf.

1-15: Medication Mismanagement

With the turn of the seasons always came the rounds of colds and flu in their home, and this year was no exception.

Blonde-Spouse-Diminutive-Duplicate and Blonde-Spouse-Sniffleupagus caught the nasties first, immediately going into massive snot production and dry cough hacking the bug all over the home.

Blonde-Spouse-Sniffleupagus ventured out to the market to buy cough drops to help with the hacking that threatened to leave them both paralyzed in fits and waves of continuous coughing.

Most of this first day, Blonde-Spouse-Sniffleupagus diligently gave Blonde-Spouse-Diminutive-Duplicate and himself a cough drop every 2 hours. Oddly, the hacking was unabated. She was overly willing to take a cough drop, something she usually despised as it "tastes funny."

Brunette-Self began to wonder if the cold was now a "super bug" and investigated the medication Blonde-Spouse-Sniffleupagus brought home from the market, now tucked in on the back of the counter. She discovered he had purchased hard candy by mistake.

"Aha!" thought Brunette-Self "No wonder the child was so eager for her cough drop!"

Brunette-Self departed for the store in search of real cough drops, leaving the two hacky blondes at home.

1-16: How many Blondes are needed to use an Easy Bake Oven?

Q: How many Blondes would it take to use an Easy Bake Oven?
A: 2 Blondes--and a Brunette to walk them through it.

Thus began another Chronicles of My Life with a Blonde to definitely put the "irony" in "easy."

The little one said, "Momma, I wanna play with my Easy Bake Oven."

"Honey, how about you ask Daddy to play with you with your Easy Bake Oven? The two of you haven't played with it together yet!" replied Brunette-Self as she thought to herself that both she and Brunette-Older-Brother had been suckered into playing the munchkin and her Easy Bake oven twice over, when it was Blonde-Spousus-Santa-Clausus who purchased said Easy Bake Oven for ages 8 and up for said munchkin, aged 5. Aha--revenge time! BWAHAHAA!

Blonde-Spouse-Diminutive-Duplicate replied, "What a great idea!"

Fast forward two days to unsuspecting Blonde-Spousus-Santa-Clausus' next day off from work. Heh. Brunette-Self mentally rubbed her hands together in anticipation of getting him good.

Blonde-Spouse-Diminutive-Duplicate said to Blonde-Spousus-Santa-Clausus, "Daddy, will you please play with me and play Easy Bake Oven?"

Blonde-Spousus-Santa-Clausus, trying to 'fast step' in avoidance replied, "Perhaps another time, Daddy is really busy right now."

Her beautiful little eyes teared up. Big-Mean-Brunette-Self jumped in and reminded Blonde-Spousus-Santa-Clausus that Kind-Brunette-Older-Brother and Weary-Brunette-Momma had already played twice with her and that Blonde-Spousus-Santa-Clausus' first turn was overdue.

Realizing he'd been bamboozled, he laughingly agreed.

Alas, revenge was HIS [plot twist]. It began with a frustrating 15 minutes while he struggled with the picture instructions--upside down. Brunette-Self began to feel incredibly guilty.

Blonde-Spousus-Santa-Clausus then started poking things into the Easy Bake

Oven, trying to figure out "how to get the #*&$^*&#^(*&^#$! cake pan IN there! There's no door!"

Brunette realized immediately the impending shock hazard and spent the next 15 minutes guiding Blonde-Spousus-Santa-Clausus and Blonde-Spouse-Diminutive-Duplicate like Wolfgang Puck through the process of preparing the better, pans and how to slide the cake pan through the oven without ripping the oven apart.

By end of process, Sneaky-Blonde-Spouse-Santa-Claus and Blonde-Spouse-Diminutive-Duplicate had retired from the kitchen, leaving Brunette-Self to complete the rest of the cake.

1-17: First Grader Fashion Faux Pas

NOTE: Chronicles of My life with a Blonde came to an abrupt end at the creation of "1-16, How many blondes would be needed to use an easy bake oven?" Blonde-Spousus-Apparently-No-Sense-Of-Humorous
threatened gigantus divorcus, so Chronicles of My Life with a Blonde saw a brutal and abrupt end. Brunette-Self decided THIS INCIDENT warranted an exception. So without further ado and at the risk of her marriage...

"1-17: 1st Grader Fashion Faux Pas."

Monday morning was a wonderful treat, Blonde-Spouse had the day off and so kindly allowed Brunette-Self to leisurely sleep in and then woke her up with a cup of coffee in hand around 10 am. He had already seen 1st-Grader-Blonde-Child off to school, fed the dogs and taken them out, and all of the usual morning riff raff. Because Brunette-Self had put out 1st-Grader-Blonde-Child clothes on the dresser the night before, it seemed she had nothing to worry about and went about enjoying the rest of their day alone together.

At 3 pm, Brunette-Self discovered just how wrong that sense of security turned out to be, when 1st-Grader-Child got home from school. Blonde-Spouse was a gifted master of many creations that come out of his kitchen that are unique and delightful. Alas, that magical combination ability ceased (and apparently curled up and died a horrible death) when he replaced food ingredients with pieces of clothing: he sure knew how to dress a turkey but not necessarily the 1st-Grader-Child. Now, Brunette-Self was no fashion connoisseur and wouldn't claim to be, but even her eyeballs had some limits.

The door opened to reveal her 1st-Grader-Child, magically transformed from mummy's lil princess to a banjo playing, spitting through her proverbial missing front teeth, um, daughter. She was dressed in a long sleeved flannel, with a short sleeve tee-shirt two sizes to small over the top of the flannel. The late spring attire was punctuated in a clash of seasons, with the flannel sporting snowflakes in reds and greens and the tee-shirt was a glaringly bright orange flower print.

Brunette- Self was about to comment on the attire, when she noted for the first time that day that Blonde-Spouse was currently wearing a purple long sleeved flannel underneath a Spider Man silk dress shirt in comic colors.

Brunette-Self spent the next hour programming the 1st-Grader-Child to "Just Say No" to Blonde-Spouse fashion faux pas and to tell him anytime he approaches her with clothing in hand, "Nooooo! We must go find the color coordinator, the Virgo-Brunette-Self, to check the ensemble against her color clash meter."

1-18: Pimp Daddy Drop Off in HookerLand

"All rise for the Honorable Justice McWhines-A-lot."

"Please be seated." gavel strike "We call to order the Superior Court in the matter of the State of Washington versus Brunette-Self, attempted murder in the first degree. Prosecuting Attorney, you may proceed with your opening remarks."

"Thank you, Your Honor. Ladies and Gentlemen of the jury, the State intends to show that Brunette-Self, on the evening of May 16th, did indeed and with malice attempt to murder Blonde-Spouse by telling him he could light the BBQ propane directly in the canister with a blow torch. We intend to show that the Blonde-Spouse was incapable of understanding this would have explosive results." The Prosecutor sat down.

"We intend to show that the Defendant, Brunette-Self, was driven mad by the constant and consistent torment of "We intend to show that the Defendant, Brunette-Self, was driven mad by the constant and consistent torment of having to clean up the disaster wake created by Blonde-Spouse through his-- ah, how shall I put this—blondeness.

"I present into evidence exhibits 1-17, Chronicles of my Life with a Blonde. This provides rock solid evidence that any normal, Brunette individual would be driven to temporary insanity by these antics. And now, to the day at hand. Let me preface this by imbuing the court with the knowledge that this was NOT the best day for my client, Defendant Brunette-Self. In sum, her entire day was a disaster, or, the Universe screamed "YOU SHOULD HAVE STAYED IN BED ALL DAY" and she failed to listen.

"She was to work a shift as security dispatch for a local science fiction convention. She'd packed a backpack with a change of clothes, two thermoses of coffee and hardboiled eggs for her pregnant friend who was craving eggs.

While getting ready to go she locked herself in the closet (the doorknob came off in her hand). This was immediately followed by finding her favorite shirt and the discovery that, somehow, most likely assisted by her disgruntled teen forced to do chores, had avoided both the wash and dry cycles and was hanging, soiled, in the closet. Her Plan B was then put into action…another outfit was located and procured.

"Her 'infinitely helpful' Blonde-Spouse offered to look up the hotel address for her while she was in the shower and put it in the GPS. She provided said Blonde-Spouse with the convention url where he could then obtain the proper address. She was unaware at the time that he would not follow this sound advice and instead procure the address from 'the thin air of his memories.'

"They left with plenty of time to arrive at the hotel and locate the office before the beginning of her shift. However, Blonde-Spouse determined the GPS was 'just clueless' and took his own route, thereby cutting down her arrival time from 20 minutes early to 13 minutes early. Blonde-Spouse then drove her to the wrong hotel and dumped her off there.

"I would like to call attention to the fact that the hotel was located in a seedy part of town, Hooker Land. I would also like to mention that Brunette-Self is disabled and has difficulty walking without a cane and was carrying a large backpack full of eggs, coffee and clothes, and no working cell phone.

"She had to walk 2 miles to find the nearest payphone and call her mother-in-law to come and rescue her. Because of her disability this process took an exceptionally long amount of time as she can only walk approximately 50 feet before having to sit and rest.

Along the way, she had a grand misadventure in Hooker Land. She was tormented by a gaggle of seagulls moving in on the hardboiled eggs and suffered what the Defense is coining as 'Roaming McDonalds Breakfast' trauma, or 'RMcDB' for short. 'RMcDB' is a chronic state to which the patient suffers extreme traumatic reaction when exposed to all breakfast goods. To this date she still suffers panic when confronted with egg McMuffins.

"Moreover, she was almost beat up by two hookers for 'working their block' and nearly got recruited by a pimp who mistook her for an 'independent.' She was only able to free herself from the pimp's grasp by throwing the eggs into the shrubbery and pointing out some 'new chicks' had arrived on the scene. This distraction turned the pimps attention away from her long enough for her to serve him a double tall along the side of the face with a thermos of coffee and free herself from his grasp. This caught the attention of a nearby homeless man, who began fighting with the pimp for the ejected eggs and provided my client a chance to eggs-scape."

"Objection—this is just a bunch of clucking" said the Prosecuting Attorney.

"Over-ruled. However, the Defense is advised to stop fluffing feathers with the bad egg puns" replied the Honorable Justice McWhines-A-Lot.

"Of course, Your Honor. I will scratch this line of commentary going forward" crowed the Defense Attorney, proceeding, "Upon her rescue and return to home, her friend attempted to cheer her up by taking for a bowl of Pho. While there, Brunette-Self rubbed her eyes after handling the jalapenos, effectively tear gassing herself. The next several hours were spent in a significant amount of burning agony.

"She also discovered, after talking with another friend, that Blonde-Spouse had dropped her off less than one block away from the correct hotel.

"These factors, coupled with a past riddled with these types of events, drove my client into a fury that she, understandably, unleashed upon Blonde-Spouse when she directed him to the BBQ. The prosecution has no basis for this charge, the Brunette-Self did not murder Blonde-Spouse, he simply blew himself up in an unfortunate situation, being the victim of his own Blondeness, a terminal condition."

...

"Has the jury reached a verdict?" declared the Honorable Justice McWhines-A-Lot.

"We have, Your Honor" said the Jury-Foreperson.

He replied "What say you?"

"We find the Defendant, Brunette-Self, not guilty of all charges of attempted murder and determine the explosion resulted from simple blondeness. The jury hereby recommends the Defendant immediately be released on her own recognizance immediately."

"Thank you, Ladies and Gentlemen of the jury, you are excused. Brunette-Self, you are released from custody."

"This is Fox 13 News, standing here with the Prosecuting Attorney on the Blonde-Spouse attempted murder case. How does the prosecution feel about the verdict today?"

"There is still substantial evidence that Brunette-Self is guilty of murder, Blondes everywhere must be protected. However, she was found innocent of all charges by a jury of her peers-consisting solely of brunettes."

"And there you have it folks, this has been Fox 13 News, and now a word from our sponors."

1-19: How many paramedics are needed to put a band-aid on a child's finger?

Repressed Memory Flashback: Chronicle 1-19 was remembered.

Brunette-Self had gone to work, leaving Blonde-Spouse-First-Time-Parentus in charge. Because Brunette-Self still reeled from the home improvement fiasco in the changing of the light bulb, so she put Blonde Mother-In-Law in charge of watching the protective Blonde-Spouse-First-Time- Parentus with Blonde-Spouse-Diminutive-Duplicate, hoping between the two adult blondes the little One would stand a chance. Brunette-Self would soon discover how *wrong* that assumption could be!

Brunette-Self received the following text message: "The ambulances have just left, please call me on your next break." PANIC! MAYHEM! WHAT THE @#($(*&%#$@!) WAS WRONG WITH HER BABY?!?!? Brunette-Self 'power walked/ran' out of the building to call and thought the worst: the baby was dead, she fell, he dropped her on her head, he locked himself out of the house with her alone inside--PANIC, PANIC, PANIC, PANIC!

"Hi, Honey, what happened? Is everyone okay? What ambulances?" She rambled, concerned.

"Oh, Grandma was cutting her fingernails, clipped a bit of skin on the top of
her finger and it started bleeding" stated
the silly Blonde-Spouse-First-Time-
Parentus.

Brunette-Self paused with an imper-
ceptible intake of breath and fought the
urge to freak out "So, why 911?"

"Because her finger was bleeding" he
answered matter-of-factly.

She counted to 10, counted to 10 again
and took a deep breath "So, you called
911 because she cut her finger?"

"Yes, it was bleeding" he again
acknowledged.

She fought back anger "Did you try
putting a clean cloth on it and applying
pressure?"

"Well, we wiped off the blood but it
kept coming back" Blonde-Spouse-First-
Time-Parentus developed an edge in his
voice.

She gave herself a silent face-palm
"And you called 911 for that?"

"Yes. Three ambulances and a fire
truck came out. One paramedic held her,
one wrapped the bandage and the other
put it on her finger."

"You're kidding me?" demanded Highly-Annoyed-Brunette-Self.

"No, they all wanted to help her out" Shot back the Equally-Annoyed-Blonde-Spouse-First-Time-Parentus.

WOW. Of course all of the paramedics wanted to help out, then all three of the ambulance companies could bill her for the service, covered by insurance at 80%.

Very annoyed with herself, Brunette-Self sighed and mentally noted to herself that three blondes put together do not a brunette make.

Upon returning home, she observed that the poor tiny baby Blonde-Spouse-Diminutive-Duplicate's finger had a small piece of skin from the top with a small cut, where Blonde Mother-in-Law had clipped her nail down a bit too far. Brunette-Self hid every nail clipper in the house hoping to afford daycare once the ambulance bills were paid. At the date of writing this chronicle in response to the repressed memory coming up again, Brunette-Self was still making payments on the ambulance bills.

1-20: The Danger of Cooking Shows

One of the following DOES NOT belong on the following list, can you guess which one?

Food Network
High quality Angus T-Bone Steak
Beer & Coffee
Blonde-Spouse

If you guessed Blonde-Spouse, you are completely correct! Thus began another Chronicles of My Life with a Blonde, "The Danger of Cooking Shows."

Brunette-Self returned from work one evening to see Blonde-Spouse, standing so adorably in his frilly apron, waiting with a spatula in one hand and a steak on a plate in the other. Gleefully, she helped Blonde-Spouse finish setting out dinner. They all gathered around the table and sat down, barely containing their drool as their tummies rumbled and their minds fantasized over each delectable bite of lean Angus meat fresh off the BBQ, still beading with juicy anticipation.

As they cut into their steaks, Blonde-Spouse announced he had tried a new recipe from a cooking show he caught on Food Network. Brunette-Self glanced down in terror at her plate, but saw nothing out of the ordinary save for a highly textured peppery appearance on the surface of the steak, of which she immediately mistook for peppercorn.

Admiring how the steak was cooked just to the brink of well done, Brunette-Self
brought the first morsel to her lips--and thus began the largest assault on her taste buds ever launched since the
invention of pumpkin pie filling in a can and Blonde-Spouse's initial inability to glean from its instructional labeling the need to include additional ingredients such as sugar and spice.

After the initial wave of nausea passed, she was alarmed to discover the projectile phase was not aborted in time-- the morsel shot out of her mouth and across the dining room. Upon landing on the carpet, the morsel was pounced on by a waiting housecat who then sneezed and repeated the morsel launch scenario from its own mouth.

Apparently, the peppered tex-ture was NOT PEPPER. No. The texture was coffee grounds. The coffee ground "paste" that coated the steak was created with the assistance of mixing said grounds with beer.

As they waited for the pizza to arrive, Blonde-Spouse apologized and then confessesed he did not actually watch the entire episode of the cooking show but had only watched a small part of the beginning of the show.

It took a full two days to remove all the grounds from their teeth, and the kids were exceptionally hyper during that time.

1-21: Car Maintenance Mistakes

Every six months they performed some general car maintenance. This used to be a chore designated to the Blonde-Spousus-Mr.-Midas-Touch until closer observation by Brunette-Self revealed he was to be immediately removed from this duty. Blonde-Spousus-Mr.-Midas-Touch announced he would perform some car maintenance and promptly disap-peard. Brunette-Self continued working on dusting the pantry shelves, pausing whenever she heard splashing on the windows. After an hour or so, Blonde-Spouse-Mr.-Midas-Touch returned with puffed up chest and requested "Come see what I did!"

Gulping, Brunette-Self slipped on shoes and followed Blonde-Spouse-Mr.-Midas-Touch out to the driveway. Upon first glance she noted both cars were "exceptionally shiny." Brunette-Self also noted that the windshields also appeared "exceptionally shiny."

Afraid to ask, but compelled to, she managed "So, you used the Turtle Car Wax on the cars, right? You must have buffed them quite a bit to get them so shiny and bright."

Blonde-Spouse-Mr.-Midas-Touch smile fell, "Um, well--no."

Brunette-Self was truly concerned and asked "Well, what did you use, then?"

Blonde-Spouse-Mr.-Midas-Touch replied hopefully, "Future Floor Wax, it shines and protects!"

Brunette-Self began to cry inside and balled up her firsts to fight the urge to deck him.

Blonde-Spouse-Mr.-Midas-Touch, now not quite as confident, ventured that he had also refilled the windshield wipers. As he saw the panic develop in her eyes, he blurted that he noticed the windshield fluid had not cleared all of the bug guts properly off of the windshield and that Windex said it would cut grease, so it had to be able to clean bug guts off the windshield and it would "leave a streak-free shine with a refreshingly clean scent."

An audible groan escaped from Brunette-Self's lips.

Sensing her discomfort, Blonde-Spouse-Mr.-Midas-Touch immediately moved to stand in front of the drivers side mirror.

"What's wrong with the mirror?" she asked, as she tried to peer over his shoulder.

"Um, well, the glue I used last year didn't work well so I rigged together a way to hold the mirror up and on the door." *Note to Reader: The glue not only fail to hold the mirror on the door, it expanded, exploded and spattered the entire driver's Indigo Blue side of the van with Yellow blobs of what appeared to be Puffy Styrofoam.*

Blonde-Spouse-Mr.-Midas-Touch quickly stepped to the side to reveal a complicated web of miniature bungee cords and rope twine tied in knots around the driver door mirror, looped through the open window and door frame and then back to the web of cords and twine surrounding the mirror, which made it appear as if the mirror was a fly ensnared in the web of a Bungee cord spider of doom.

Dejected, Brunette-Self finally fielded the inevitable question, "Anything else?"

In a grand finale flourish, Blonde-Spouse-Mr.-Midas-Touch flung open the hood to reveal that he had welded--yes, WELDED--the battery cable to the top of the battery.

"This way it won't fall off again."

Thus ended yet another Chronicle of My Life with a Blonde, Car Maintenance Mistakes or "How to Cut in Half the Kelly Blue Book Value of your Personal Vehicle in Approximately One Hour or Less."

1-22: How Not to Set Up a Job Interview

Blonde-Spouse-Of-The-How-Not-To could make a career out of showing people the perils of not following instructions. Because You Tube and Americas Funniest Home Videos have cornered this market, Blonde-Spouse-Of-The-How-Not-To must resort to finding actual work.

Blonde-Spouse-Of-The-How-Not-To would like to offer up the following example, however on 'How Not To Set Up' A Job Interview:

Blonde-Spouse-Of-The-How-Not-To was on the phone with a prospective employer and had charmed the Prospective employer in his initial intake enough to obtain scheduling for an interview.

When asked by the prospective employer if next Tuesday at 11 a.m. would be agreeable, Blonde-Spouse-Of-The-How-Not-To asked the employer to hold while he checked his calendar and set the phone down without hitting the mute button first.

"Wifey? Do I have anything on my calendar for next Tuesday at 11?"

Brunette-Self, whispered, "Did you hit the mute button first?"

Blonde-Spouse-Of-The-How-Not-To, pales and hits the redial button, "Well, do I?"

Brunette-Self, realizing the damage could not be undone, "No."

As expected, Blonde-Spouse-Of-The-How-Not-To did not get the job.

1-23: When combining chores can be disastrous

She thought her instructions should have been simple enough, given there were only two steps involed in the list of chores to do:

Honey Do List:

Spray/clean dead moss off roof with hose/broom

Clean gutters with hand and hose

Because the moss killing products contained some nasty chemicals, Brunette-Self had donned appropriate safety gear and sprayed the roof to kill the moss. The hard part was done, or so she thought. All Brunette-Self needed now was for her Blonde-Spouse-Gadget-Greenhorn to come along behind and remove the dead moss and clean the gutters. Repeat, Brunette-Self thought her instructions were simple enough. Blonde-Spouse-Gadget-Greenhorn was about to prove her horribly wrong.

Brunette-Self, "So, honey, I just need you to get up on the roof and spray off the dead moss. Use the broom for the tough stuff, just sweep it and it should come loose. Then clean out the gutters, please. Scoop out any moss with your hands and then run the hose down them to clean out any silt built up, please? Ok? Thanks, honey."

Brunette-Self went back inside and spent the next hour or so playing with her home music studio and lost track of the time. Had Brunette-Self not plugged into earphones, she may have noticed it was taking her Blonde-Spouse-Gadget-Greenhorn quite a long amount of time to get up onto the roof and then to get back down.

Brunette-Self decided to take a coffee break. When she took off the headset she faintly heard Blonde-Spouse-Gadget-Greenhorn calling for help. Rushing outside, Brunette-Self discovered Blonde-Spouse-Gadget-Greenhorn had stranded himself on the roof when he climbed up the ladder by accidentally knocking the ladder with his foot and sending it crashing down to the ground.

Brunette-Self apologized profusely and admitted she was plugged in to earphones and couldn't hear his cries for help. She choked back laughter in her throat as to appear believable and righted the ladder so Blonde-Spouse-Gadget-Greenhorn could climb down.

As the embarassed Blonde-Spouse-Gadget-Greenhorn scurried down the ladder, Brunette-Self fought another wave of laughter as she realized her Leo Blonde-Spouse-Gadget-Greenhorn (who had indeed treed himself) was just like his Leo cousin the housecat. Brunette-Self was distracted by that thought and didn't notice the gutters full of dead moss.

A usual spring in the Pacific Northwest, the beautiful sun gave way a day or two later to heavy rains, and Brunette-Self stood in front of the kitchen sink doing dishes and gazing out at the rain pouring down. After a few minutes of gazing, Brunette-Self jumped as she realized that an actual sheet of water was coming down past the window. Wait a minute--a sheet of water?

Brunette-Self ran outside to see the gutters of the house bowing under the weight of the water and waterlogged swollen dead moss, overflowing in sheets of water that cascaded like a mountain waterfall down the front and back of the house.

Running back in, Brunette-Self confronted a startled Blonde-Spouse-Gadget-Greenhorn about the gutters. Blonde-Spouse-Gadget-Greenhorn indignantly replied that he did clean the gutters, he cleaned them before he cleared off all of the moss.

Brunette-Self exploded in anger "Did it ever occur to you that I put 'clean gutters' LAST on the list because you were cleaning the roof FIRST?"

Blonde-Spouse-Gadget-Greenhorn responded bitingly "No, I cleaned the gutters first because I had to climb over them to get to the roof, so I cleaned in the order in which I came to them."

The gutters gave way in two areas due to the weight of the moss soup and had to be replaced. Needless to say, Blonde-

Spouse-Gadget-Greenhorn was not hired to do the job, instead Brunette-Self wisely opted to go with Boyfriend-Of-The-Neighbors–Daughter-And-Sometimes-Handyman-Dan.

Brunette-Self chalked up the experience into the realization that alpha numeric's would be required in future chore lists for Blonde-Spouse-Gadget-Greenhorn, and that she would also need to keep him away from the ladder.

1-24: Technology FAIL: electronic chaos

When they moved the entertainment center, Brunette-Self had asked Blonde-Spouse-Captain-Chaos to take care of reconnecting the components. Brunette-Self's first cause of concern was when Blonde-Spouse-Captain-Chaos had so expeditiously disappeared behind the console and she could faintly hear his twisted rendition of "Dry Bones."

Muffled Blonde-Spouse-Captain-Chaos, "The DVRs connected to the router box, the router box's connected to the TV, the TV's connected to the VCR, now where does this cord go?"

Brunette-Self's second cause of concern came with she remembered that Blonde-Spouse-Captain-Chaos had repeatedly failed in the past to set the time on the digital alarm clock, the stove, the microwave and the VCR.

Brunette-Self's third cause of concern came with the occasional shout of "SHIT!" from behind the console, punctuated with increasing dread the muffled ongoing rendition of twisted "Dry Bones," "The Game Cube's connected to this thingy. That thingy's connected to those thingies. And I don't even know what that plug is for, so I guess I'll toss it aside."

Brunette-Self nonchalantly snuck back to the fuse box and turned off circuit breakers and returned to living room "Need any help?" she ventured.

"Nah, I got it" he remarked as he fought with the wires.

She waited for Blonde-Spouse-Captain-Chaos to complete his version of "Dry Bones" and to plug his creation into the wall, then distracted Blonde-Spouse-Captain-Chaos with a reward cup of coffee while Brunette-Teenage-Son-And-Self-Designated-Peanut-Gallery-Of-Sarcastic-Commentary snuck quickly to turn the circuit breakers back on.

Blonde-Spouse-Captain-Chaos began his explanation of operation of his "Dry Bones" twisted maze of wires, "To watch satellite, you'll need to turn on the TV, have the router set to GAMES, and have both the DVR and the VCR on.

"I'm not sure if you'll need the Game Cube on, too, but I know you'll need the VCR. Now, to play the PlayStation, set the router to VIDEO, turn off the VCR, turn on the DVR and the TV, but make sure the Game Cube is off.

"To play the Game Cube, set the router to TV and turn off the Play station and VCR and turn on the TV and DVR. If you want to watch the DVR you will have to unplug the router and plug the DVR directly into the TV. Got it?"

Brunette-Self ignored the urge to mention that he had forgotten the X-Box, and the DVD player. She waited for Blonde-Spouse-Captain-Chaos to go to bed for the night.

Brunette-Self unwound twisted "Dry Bones" and reconnected the entertainment center, first color coding the masking tape and taping small tags onto each cord to coordinate with the proper component. Mr. Blonde-Spouse-Captain-Chaos snottily informed Brunette-Self the next day that "I told you I could do it" when the components work properly. Thus ended the beginning of Technology FAIL, electronic wire chaos, Chronicles of My Life with a Blonde.

1-25: Technology FAIL: MP3 Madness

"I can't get this MP3 player to work, it won't turn on! Would you fix it, please?" Blonde-Spouse thrusted MP3 player into Brunette-Self's hands, "I charged it on the computer, it (*&(*&$#@)(*@#$!^&**$ doesn't work! It's brand new!"

Brunette-Self opened the back of MP3 player, pulled out the AAA battery and removed plastic shrink wrap. Brunette-Self replaced AAA battery and cover and turned on MP3 player. Handing it back to Blonde-Spouse, she inquired, "What did we learn?"

Blonde-Spouse responded "Oh, that's the power button?"

1-26: Technology FAIL: DVR Conspiracy

Blonde-Spouse-Conspiracy-Theorist informed Brunette-Self that the networks had plotted to force higher ratings for certain shows in their lineups that are not doing as well.

"How?" Brunette-Self inquired, her curiousity piqued.

"Well, it's like this" Blonde-Spouse–Conspiracy-Theorist began, rubbing his hands together, "The satellite company sells higher cost advertising space based on higher scores than those that people record to watch later. So the networks that had shows that people recorded and watched later tried to boost their ratings by buying show start and stop times that are a minute before or a minute behind the hour or half hour, so people with DVRs can't record their show and watch another one at the same time on another channel."

"Ah," she replied "You might be on to something there! Except, I think I set the DVR to start a minute before and end a minute later on a few shows by mistake."

"Aha!" Blonde-Spouse Conspiracy Theorist shouted, "You see? You've already bought into their conspiracy!"

1-27: Technology FAIL: 3D

Blonde-Spouse and Brunette-Self sat to watch a movie trailer when Blonde-Spouse declared, "I just don't understand what all the hubbub is about 3D? How in the world do they think they are going to fit an entire movie set in the living room or even in a movie theater?"

Brunette-Self just blinked at him.

1-28: Toasting Marshmallows

Brunette-Self Mistake #1: Staying up too late the night before.

Brunette-Self Mistake #2: Not drinking enough coffee to stay awake during the next day.

Brunette-Self Mistake #3: Deciding that an afternoon nap was in order.

Brunette-Self Mistake #4: Taking such a nap leaving the fuses in the fuse box on.

Brunette-Self Mistake #5: FATAL ERROR. Leaving Blonde-Spouse unattended in the home with fuse box on.

Brunette-Self's blissful afternoon nap dream was cut rudely short by the screeching of the fire alarms in the living room, supplemented by the howls of a tortured Scottie dog.

Brunette-Self sprung out of bed in reaction only to be knocked immediately back into it by the thick, nauseous haze of smoke and scorched corn syrup.

Regaining composure, Brunette-Self covered her mouth with a pillow case. Eyes stinging, she wandered out into the living room to investigate.

Brunette-Self was immediately greeted by a panicked Blonde-Spouse-Diminutive-Duplicate, who was now rambling hysterically and incoherently interjected only by gasps for air and sobs. Brunette-Self allowed her smoke teared gaze to find a sheepish Blonde-Spouse, covered head to toe in what appeared to be powdered sugar. Thinking he'd make a lovely ghost, Brunette-Self brushed on past Blonde-Spouse-The-Sheepish-Ghost as he used his body as a shield trying to hide whatever was behind him.

Their once lovely white stovetop now sported so many flame marks that it would rival even the coolest painted motorcycle, reminiscent of the skies in Vincent Van Gogh paintings. The burners were each the center of rays of flame marks, looking like charcoal covered suns with their spiral coils covered in miniature mountain ranges of charred black food.

Every available surface of the kitchen, including everything in the pantry and in the cupboards was coated in the same mysterious white powdered sugar as Blonde-Spouse-The-Sheepish-Ghost — yes, EVERY AVAILABLE SURFACE. She still could not fathom how one human being could be capable of such damage on such a consistence basis.

"Count to 10 - Count to 10 - Count to 10 - Consider 25 to life - Count to 10 - Count to 10" she muttered to herself before she turned to him "WTF?"

Blonde-Spouse-The-Sheepish-Ghost started "Um…"

Brunette-Self, now raising her voice to a scream, "SERIOUSLY, WTF?!?"

"Well, Blonde-Spouse-Mini-Me wanted toasted marshmallows."

Brunette-Self prompted sharply "And?…"

Blonde-Spouse-The-Sheepish-Ghost rambled "Well, so I didn't want to get the tongs all gooey because there's no way to burn off the marshmallow on them inside and plus it takes forever, so I just turned all the burners on low and set the marshmallows on them to toast--then I went to the bathroom. I must have left them on too long or something."

Result of these Brunette-Self mistakes? Two solid weeks of scrubbing each and every millimeter of the kitchen, four new range burner coils, one half gallon of white appliance paint, three new paint brushes to apply it, an emergency room visit to deal with the fumes because Blonde-Spouse shut the windows, a new fire extinguisher and yet another Chronicles of My Life with a Blonde: Toasting Marshmallows.

1-29: Fire Safety

After the Marshmallow-Toast-Ghost incident, Blonde-Spouse began to take Fire Safety very seriously. Blonde-Spouse's vigorous interest could be attributed to being on Brunette-Self's bad side for two weeks while they cleaned the entire kitchen of fire extinguisher debris (for further details, reader should refer to part 28: Toasting Marshmallows.) However, Blonde-Spouse's vigorous interest would soon be found disastrous.

It began one afternoon when Brunette-Self noticed half of the house smoke detectors on the walls had been turned upside down. Knowing the Blonde-Spouse-Diminutive-Duplicate was too short to have reached them and that her Brunette-Teenage-Son-And-Self-Designated-Peanut-Gallery-Of-Sarcastic-Commentary knew better, Brunette-Self deducted it was the result of efforts of the Blonde-Spouse and cornered him in the laundry room.

Brunette-Self, "Hon, why are half the smoke detectors upside down?"

Blonde-Spouse-Smoke-Jumper replied in a condescending tone "Duh, so half of the smoke detectors can pick up smoke coming from the floor and the other half can detect the smoke that is coming from the ceiling!"

Brunette-Self realized this warning statement meant other disasters of this nature would be forthcoming or had already occurred around the home-- further investigation was warranted and required.

Thus, the search began:

1. Tin foil was taped to the cupboards immediately adjacent to the stove. Tin foil was also taped around the furnace and hot water heater and along the floor surrounding the heating registers.

Blonde-Spouse-Smoke-Jumper excitedly volunteered "The tin foil protects the wood from overheating and catching fire."

2. A route from each bed directed the person with arrows and "This way!" scrawled in permanent black marker was spaced a foot apart from each other to etch out a route to the window of each room, where it ended in a large "EMEGENCY EXOT HERE!" Yes, the word exit was misspelled and this irked Brunette-Self-Valiant-Virgo.

Blonde-Spouse-Smoke-Jumper advised "So we can escape in a fire without getting lost!"

Brunette-Self could not understand why this was necessary as the windows in the bedrooms of the home were within 5 feet of each bed or less.

3. In the middle of each room was a 5 gallon bucket full of soapy water.

Blonde-Spouse-Smoke-Jumper added with pride "Just in case, so we can pour it on a fire and clean at the same time!"

4. A smoke detector super glued to the handset of the phone.

Blonde-Spouse Smoke Jumper declared "So it will dial 911 if it senses smoke!"

5. WET FURNITURE, discovered when she attempted to sit down before she fainted of the shock of the past few fire safety discoveries. Blonde-Spouse-Smoke-Jumper had been very thorough and had drenched every single piece of fabric covered furniture, bed mattresses, towels, sheets, curtains, clothing and wood furniture. Thankfully, appliances and electronics were spared this precautionary wetting, however each now had a squirt gun full of water next to it.

Blonde-Spouse-Smoke-Jumper said with importance "Because fire can smolder for a long time, this way it will be smothered before it can smolder.

"There's more but I want to show you what I just got done doing outside!"

"No!" she screamed in her head.

6. The entire base of the house, from the ground to about 3 feet high, was covered in tin foil scotch taped onto the house.

Blonde-Spouse-Smoke-Jumper puffed up proudly, "It took me 6 rolls, but I got it done! Now the whole neighborhood could burn and we'd be protected!"

Upon this display of accomplishment, Blonde-Spouse Smoke Jumper was distracted by the shininess of the tin foil and decided to make mirrors with the pieces he had left on the ends of the rolls.

Brunette-Self was haunted by what else was lurking around the house just waiting until it could spring out in surprise and kill Brunette-Self—
with safety.

1-30: Gas Station Goofs

Blonde-Spouse was driving the family to go camping in the woods. Brunette-Self noticed the fuel light come on and advised Blonde-Spouse the car was low on gas and it needed to be refueled. The concept seemed straight forward enough, just locate the nearest gas station and refuel the car. However, Brunette-Self was merely a copilot in this misadventure, so simple became complicated immediately.

Blonde-Spouse took his hands off the wheel, picked up the GPS and started poking at it with his finger. The car began to veer into the next lane and the children screamed. Alarmed, Brunette-Self snapped at Blonde-Spouse and grabbed the wheel to straighten the car. Brunette-Self looked up just in time to see a gas station sign flash by her window.

Brunette-Self yelled "WHAT ARE YOU DOING?!?"

Blonde-Spouse responded "I'm looking for nearby gas stations on the GPS! And stop harping, it's looking for one now and your harping is distracting me from driving."

Brunette-Self realized arguing was pointless and bit her tongue.

Blonde-Spouse returned the GPS to its stand and then his hands to the wheel. An audible sigh of relief erupted in chorus in the car in response. The GPS directed them around the block and back to the gas station they'd just missed.

Blonde-Spouse was now "driving by GPS" and did not realize the 500 foot delay until they had again passed the gas station. Blonde-Spouse then missed the right turn they took previously to go around the block as the GPS was "recalculating." The GPS again directed them back to the gas station, and this time the children told Blonde-Spouse to turn. He made the turn this time and they finally pulled into the parking lot.

Blonde-Spouse pulled up to the pump to get gas with the pump on the passengers side. Brunette-Self gently reminded him the gas tank was on the drivers side. Blonde-Spouse pulled away and then up to the pump on the other side, again on the passengers side. This time Brunette-Self allowed Blonde-Spouse the discovery on his own. Grumbling, Blonde-Spouse returned to drivers seat after knocking on the window to be let back into the car as he'd locked himself out. The circle was repeated another two times. On the fifth try, the pump was successfully on the drivers side.

Once they were parked, Blonde-Spouse's captive car riding family was then able to glance around. They immediately realized the convenience store had been evacuated and there were fire engines pulling up around them and the store was billowing flame and smoke.

Fearfully, they turned their heads to see Blonde-Spouse, back leaning on the car and away from the scene, pumping gas into the car. Before Brunette-Self could get out to warn him to stop, Blonde-Spouse finished refueling, replaced the nozzle and began walking toward the convenience store. As he walked away he took out his wallet and approached the clerk in the parking lot, still completely oblivious to the fire.

Brunette-Self was unsure of what was said but it looked as though the clerk was rather upset with him. Blonde-Spouse returned to the car and again knocked on the window to be let back in. Blonde-Spouse put on his seatbelt, started the car and drove them away from the scene, all the while complaining that the pump ate his receipt and the clerk wouldn't give him a new one.

(armband of mourning for the author's common sense, please cut and tape to arm in a non-hairy location. For the reader not gifted with scissors, the author has provided a few second chances on the next pages.)

2 IN THE MIDDLE

2-1: Furniture Rearrangement Fiasco

They recently obtained a new computer desk for the home office, which prompted Blonde-Spouse-Shuffle-Stuff into action.

"Babe, we need to re arrange the living room so this new desk will fit in here. Now, I know your back is hurting, so you just take it easy there on the couch and I'll do all the work."

"Thanks, hon." Brunette-Self was relieved of duty and propped herself on the couch with a book to read. Content Blonde-Spouse-Shuffle-Stuff could handle the rearrangement once she observed him pre-measuring the furniture, Brunette-Self redirected her attention to her book and immediately tuned out the room.

After a chapter, Brunette-Self realized her coffee had gone cold and it was time to warm it in the microwave. She put the book down and stood up, took a step out and promptly tripped over a large pile of papers. She took flight across the room as waves of loose papers fluttered in her wake. Brunette-Self landed on an end table, narrowly missing the metal music stand.

The living room was now a muddle maze of mayhem, the only item missing in the maze was the couch Brunette-Self had so recently vacated in haphazard manner.

Blonde-Spouse-Shuffle-Stuff had left a path around the muddle maze of mayhem along each wall, but had failed to leave access out of the room. All of the furniture was stacked with stuff from around the room: books, piano rolls, knickknacks. Feeling a bit like Dorothy in the Land of Oz, Brunette-Self found herself nose to nose with her very confused Scottie dog, Toto. Poor Toto had been rudely awakened from her nap to a Brunette-Self falling into her face and realized she'd also been "relocated" while sleeping to a moon chair cocooned by end tables and bookshelves. After a stretch and a yawn, Toto went back to sleep.

Blonde-Spouse-Shuffle-Stuff was busy taking everything off of one book shelf and piling it high upon another, completely unaware of her harrowing journey. Blonde-Spouse-Shuffle-Stuff then moved the first empty bookshelf back to the exact location he'd removed it from earlier, and proceeded to put all of the stuff back onto it as well as the stuff that had already been on the other bookshelf. Blonde-Spouse-Shuffle-Stuff moved the newly emptied bookshelf and placed it right next to the one he had previously placed in it's exact original location. He then restocked that bookshelf.

Deciding this was far more entertaining than reading at the moment, Brunette-Self slowly and quietly made her way back to the couch.

She sat down and pretended to read her book, all the while watching Blonde-Spouse-Shuffle-Stuff work. Intently Blonde-Spouse-Shuffle-Stuff repeated his process for the remaining two bookshelves and placed them again in the original locations. Once he was satisfied with the arrangement on the bookshelves, he dusted them.

Blonde-Spouse-Shuffle-Stuff then turned his attention to the computer desk in question, unloaded the stuff he'd piled upon it onto the chair, and then slid it against the wall next to the bookshelves and where the original computer desk had been. Outside of finding a new location for the file cabinet, Brunette-Self knew instantly in which direction Blonde-Spouse Shuffle Stuff's process was going and choked back a laugh.

Blonde-Spouse-Shuffle-Stuff cleared the chair and reloaded the computer desk and moved the chair back to it's original location. Then he moved and repacked the steamer trucks in their original place.

Realizing Blonde-Spouse-Shuffle-Stuff only had three more pieces of furniture to go, Brunette could no longer quietly watch this and ventured, "Why don't you just box the stuff up, move the furniture and then unpack the boxes?"

Blonde-Spouse Shuffle Stuff, irritated, "Because that would be too much work!"

Not pleased with his nasty tone, Brunette-Self decided to not mention the fact to Blonde-Spouse-Shuffle-Stuff that it wasn't necessary to move all of the furniture in the room, he only needed to move the file cabinet and original computer desk.

2-2: Shaky Stack

Even when Blonde-Spouse got annoyed with Brunette-Self over her often-helpful-but-too-late-to-be-helpful advice, he did on occasion take it to heart. And on those occasions, the aftermath could be quite precarious. The Shaky Stack incident was an excellent example.

Blonde-Spouse-Shuffle-Stuff had adopted some of these pieces of "helpful Brunette-Self Advice" at the end of the "Furniture Rearrangement Fiasco," and had implemented it while cleaning up the kitchen. Instead of putting the dishes away straight from the dishwasher, the Blonde-Spouse-Shaky-Stack deduced that he could box the dishes, do the other load of dishes and then pack those as well, and then move each box of dishes to its cupboard to be unpacked and put away.

Blonde-Spouse-Shaky-Stack disappeared for 20 minutes and came back with the van full of empty boxes from the produce department of the local supermarket. Gleefully, Blonde-Spouse-Shaky-Stack unloaded silverware into one box, glasses into another, coffee cups into yet another and finally pots and pans into the final box. He so thoughtfully had picked boxes to scale with what he was putting in them, so the silverware box was the smallest and the pots and pans the biggest. What Blonde-Spouse-Shaky-Stack failed to take into account was the order in which he packed and then stacked the boxes on top of the kitchen table.

Brunette-Self entered the kitchen from the living room in time to see an upside down pyramid of boxes sway perilously to and fro. She also took in the back of Blonde-Spouse-Shaky-Stack's head bobbed along to his I-Pod as he rinsed and loaded the next load into the dishwasher, completely obvlious. Brunette-Self could not reach the upside down pyramid in time, the top heavy stack teetered over the edge of the table and crashed upon the floor sending a blizzard of glass shards, silverware and pots in every direction. The noise got the attention of Blonde-Spouse-Shaky-Stack, who took out his earphones as he turned around.

When confronted with his shaky stack failure, Blonde-Spouse-Shaky-Stack defended himself, "It had to be the wind blowing through the window that caused the stack to fall over, I told you those drafts were getting pretty fierce.

2-3: Attack of the Advertising Icons

Mr. Blonde-Spouse and Mrs. Brunette-Self were shopping at the local supermarket, when Mr. Blonde-Spouse steered them down the housecleaning aisle.

"Come on!" He squealed "They're here!"

"Who is here?" Mrs. Brunette-Self asked as she was shuffled quickly down the aisle.

"Mister Clean and the Scrubbing Bubbles!"

Somewhere on Ad Alley, a marketing executive viewed the footage from the supermarket video feed of Blonde-Spouse's childlike excitement and screamed "Yes! Yes!"

"Hon, why don't we just get the earth friendly generic cleaner? Or even better, some vinegar and baking soda?" Brunette-Self sadly pleaded, knowing the chemicals would wreak havoc with her allergies.

"No! No! No! It has to be THESE ONES!" he demanded, pouting and stomping his feet.

"Fiiiiiiiiiiiiiiiiiine." exasperation = Brunette-Self, clueless = Blonde-Spouse.

As soon as they got home, Blonde-Spouse raced through the house to the bathroom. After a brief pause, a faint hiss could be heard emanating from the open bathroom door. A sound of muffled human confusion--another pause--and more hissing. A long moment went by with no sound from the bathroom, followed by a very disappointed, "Awwwwwwwwww."

Brunette-Self walked into the bathroom to see her dejected Blonde-Spouse kneeling over foam on the inside of the bathtub.

Brunette-Self, "What's wrong?" patting him on the shoulder.

"There's no stinking Scrubby Bubbly guys! They lied on TV! Oh no!" sobbed Blonde-Spouse as he jumped up and bolted out of the bathroom with the bag down the hall and out into the kitchen.

Brunette-Self caught up just in time to see him pour Mister Clean onto the linoleum, "I'll bet you aren't going to come and scrub my #$%(*&&(*)#$@ floors, either!"

2-4: Bacteria Barriers

Every flu season, Blonde-Spouse-Bacteria-Buster would come to reign of power and unleash his arsenal of logic upon the primordial life forms. While the methods of Blonde-Spouse-Bacteria-Buster were seldom effective and frequently dangerous, they were always entertaining (writer refers reader to Chronicle 1-15: Medication Mismanagement for further background). Thus, this seasons adventures of Blonde-Spouse-Bacteria-Buster had begun!

Despite flu shot protection, Brunette-Self and Teenage-Brunette-Son-And-Self-Designated-Peanut-Gallery-Of-Sarcastic-Commentary were both highly susceptible to catching viruses and spent each winter sick. In addition to being cursed with a poor front line of defense to getting sick, they had the added burden of failure to build immunity from it and would catch the same flu two and sometimes three times in a season.

Unfortunately for them, many people in their lives did not respect this disability and exposed them quite often to the flu. That year was by far the worst, with a particularly nasty flu infecting their home repeatedly from November to

February. Two of their older pets--having caught it from them and promptly gave it back--succumbed to the virus and passed away within weeks of each other. Brunette-Self suffered with asthma (complicated by lost COBRA insurance coverage) and was on round three of this flu. She fought to avoid the ER while Blonde-Spouse-Bacteria-Buster attacked the problem with a vengeance.

They were combating it with constant cleaning and Lysol disinfections, but Brunette-Self believed because they altered being sick when the pets were well and being well when the pets were sick, that all the disinfection in the world couldn't have stopped it. Undaunted, Blonde-Spouse-Bacteria-Buster put his plan into action.

Blonde-Spouse-Bacteria-Buster came out of the bathroom holding three dripping handkerchiefs and wearing a fourth over his nose and face. He handed one to each of them and indicated that they should tie them over their faces. Brunette-Self immediately realized he had soaked them in Lysol and declined on behalf of herself and the children and recommended Blonde-Spouse-Bacteria-Buster remove his handkerchief before he asphyxiated himself.

Blonde-Spouse-Bacteria-Buster begrudgingly complied and immediately set to work on phase two of his Bacteria Buster annihilation plan.

Blonde-Spouse-Bacteria-Buster stripped the bedding in all of the bedrooms and started putting the first load in the wash. Brunette-Self stopped Blonde-Spouse-Bacteria-Buster when she realized he was pouring a half of bottle of Pine Sol into the washer along with the bedding to "clean and disinfect."

Blonde-Spouse-Bacteria-Buster moved on to the final phase, steam disinfection. Blonde-Spouse-Bacteria-Buster filled the 20-gallon pot with water and boiled it on the stove. Once a good steam billowed out, he put on his "Potholder Hands," lifted the pot and began to walk through the house with it holding it up to things. He returned it to the stove top and burned his hands while he held the car keys above the pot to disinfect it in the steam. He was relieved of further Bacteria Busting duties indefinitely.

Everyone recovered about a week after Blonde-Spouse-Bacteria-Buster's annihilation adventure, which he proudly attributed to his diligence in destroying the germs.

2-5: A Question of Suppositories

"In order to spare those readers who may be more of a delicate stomach; we have omitted this chronicle in entirety. We apologize for any inconvenience, sense of discontinuity or morbid curiosity peaks this may have caused within you, our esteemed reader."

Respectfully,

The Publisher and Editor of "Chronicles of My Life with a Blonde"

(Editors Note: No illustration is necessary for this chronicle, thank you.)

2-6: DIY Headlamp

Blonde-Spouse had completed everything on his "Honey Do" list for the day and was sitting back enjoying a beer as the sun slipped below the horizon. Once the darkness settled and the stars came out, Blonde-Spouse returned inside to tell Brunette-Self he'd completed his list. Brunette-Self--checking on the status of the "Honey Do" list--pointed out that Blonde-Spouse forgot to mow the lawn, that it was now dark and it was supposed to rain buckets for the next several days.

Not to be daunted by darkness, Blonde-Spouse disappeared into their bedroom closet for several minutes. After much rustling about and moving of items, Blonde-Spouse emerged from the closet. He had taken a pair of her nylons, placed the center of it under his chin and then tied a flashlight onto the top of his head (with the light bulb resting just above his forehead) into the nylon knot to hold it on to his head.

Blonde-Spouse reached up with great grandeur, turned on the flashlight and yelled "Ta Da! DIY headlamp!" The light did not come on.

"Maybe the batteries are dead?" Brunette-Self offered diabolically, even though she knew they possessed four separate fully functioning Coleman headlamps and exactly where they were tucked away for the next camping trip.

Blonde-Spouse located the appropriate battery size and proceeded onward to the bathroom, where he spent the next 30 minutes struggling with his reflection to change out the batteries on the flashlight tied onto his head. Again, he turned on the light with grandeur--this time it successfully lit. It was close to 10 pm, almost quiet time.

Blonde-Spouse rushed outside to mow the lawn in the dark with his new DIY headlamp strapped onto his head and completed mowing just moments before the 10 pm cutoff time. The next morning revealed he had missed so many spots in his mowing that he created something of a crop circle in the couple's backyard.

Blonde-Spouse swore by his DIY flashlight headlamp, donning it for late night gardening or for walking in the evening. Brunette-Self was content he looked crazy enough to the world that he was in no danger of being mugged-committed perhaps--but no one would dare mug him.

2-7: Appropriate Cooking Utensil Substitution

One evening their family decided to BBQ kabobs for dinner, and Brunette-Self diligently sent Blonde-Spouse to the store to pick up wooden skewers for the kabobs. While Blonde-Spouse was at the store, Brunette-Self cut and prepped all of the food for the kabobs then hopped into the bathtub for a nice soak while Blonde-Spouse skewered and cooked the kabobs for their dinner.

Brunette-Self fell asleep in the bathtub, and awoke with a shock to a tub of cold water. A shivering Brunette-Self--salivating in her anticipation of kabobs--quickly donned her bathrobe and joined the family in the kitchen for dinner, where she discovered them eating pizza instead of delicious kabobs.

"Dare I ask what happened?" Brunette-Self began, disappointed, as she sat down to join them

"We'll let Dad tell you about it," piped up Brunette-Teenage-Son-And-Self-Designated-Peanut-Gallery-Of-Sarcastic-Commentary.

"Dear, care to elaborate?" Brunette-Self turned her head to look at Blonde-Spouse.

Blonde-Spouse munched a slice of pizza and refused to meet her gaze, "Well, uh, you should try some of this pizza, I got your favorite."

I-Got-Your-Favorite = Something-Terrible-Happened-To-The-Kabobs.

Undaunted, Brunette-Self pushed on "What happened to the kabobs, Dear?"

Blonde-Spouse set down his pizza slice, took a sip of water and began, "Well, when I got to the store they were all out of those wooden skewer things and they only had those steel ones. You know, the ones we want to get but they're too expensive? So I substituted the skewers with something else."

"What?" she said, afraid of the answer.

"I said I substituted the skewers with something else" he hedged.

"Yes, I got that. What did you substitute the wooden skewers with?"

He muttered quickly into his hand "At first I was going to use # 2 pencils, but I thought the erasers might melt so I looked at the knitting needles. Then I remembered you telling me that knitting needles are made of aluminum and they would not survive the heat of the BBQ without melting, so I bought plastic pens instead and used those because I thought they'd withstand the heat better."

The College-Chemistry-Minor-Brunette-Self rationalized that the first substitution (minus the eraser and once the wood burned off) would contain graphite that might actually survive

BBQ temperatures but could not withstand the weight of cooking kabob pieces, still could not fathom why Blonde-Spouse would believe plastic a better substitute. College-Chemistry-Minor-Brunette-Self then followed the sequence of most logical events with the plastic pen scenario on the propane BBQ grill, and quickly lost her appetite.

"How bad is it?" she finally mustered aloud, again afraid of the answer.

Blonde-Spouse and Brunette-Self proceeded outside to the BBQ, where charred kabob ingredients were fused onto the grill by the once blue plastic of the pens.

"Did I tell you today that I love you?" Blonde-Spouse volunteered hopefully.

The next time Brunette-Self went to the hardware store, she picked up a replacement grill, propane parts and invested in a set of steel kabob skewers.

2-8: Color Coordinate & Dewey Decimal System

Brunette-Self had always been proud of her "Inner Librarian." She had mastered the true librarian talent of remembering exactly where information was within any given book in her library and where that book was to be found in her library. Brunette-Self delighted that her large personal library had been organized using the Dewey Decimal System. She had painstakingly labeled each and every volume binding with proper classifications and call numbers and coordinated them with a searchable Excel spread sheet on her home computer.

Brunette-Self and Blonde-Spouse were doing a thorough dusting of the living room shelves, when she received an invitation to go yard sale hopping with a friend she hadn't spoken with in a long time. Blonde-Spouse cheerfully agreed to finish dusting, so Brunette-Self took the afternoon off and enjoyed treasure hunting local yard sales.

When she returned, she was greeted in the driveway by Blonde-Spouse, who offered to carry in some of her newly found treasure and to show her "this great surprise I did for you, I worked on it for hours and hours and hours!"

Blonde-Spouse had Brunette-Self wait at the door while he put down the treasures and returned to her. Blonde-Spouse covered her eyes with his hands and slowly guided her into the living room. He removed his hands and shouted "Ta-da!"

Brunette-Self summarily discovered Blonde-Spouse had industriously rearranged the Brunette-Self-Private-Dewey-Decimal-Organized-Library into A RAINBOW by color coordinating the book bindings.

"Wow, honey, I'm...speechless." Brunette-Self mustered while fighting back tears.

"I knew you'd love it!" he exclaimed with glee as he jumped up and down.

To date, Brunette-Self still couldn't find several of her books and she was afraid to ask what the Blonde-Spouse did with the "those outside of the rainbow prism coordination scheme" volumes and collections.

2-9: Earth Orbit Error

Blonde-Spouse, being an amiable husband, had honestly attempted to learn more about Brunette-Self hobbies and interests, especially Astronomy, Geology and Physics. Blonde-Spouse had been devouring cable television scientific documentaries in hopes of better understanding these subjects so he could discuss them with Brunette-Self.

Yet sometimes a bit too much information without the right context can lead to confusion in any scientific inquiry, and Blonde-Spouse-Documentary-Scientist was not immune to this confusion.

Blonde-Spouse-Documentary-Scientist watched a two hour documentary on the Earth's Orbital path around the sun and periodically paused the documentary to ask Brunette-Self questions. Thus Blonde-Spouse-Documentary-Scientist's initial delve into confusion came when the scientist explained that the Earth rotated around the sun one full time in one year, and also rotated in a complete circle once each day, "thereby putting you, the human on Earth, on the other side of the world at night."

Blonde-Spouse-Documentary-Scientist then announced he would be performing his own astronomical observations in the middle of the night, because there was a full moon. Pleased Blonde-Spouse-Documentary-Scientist was so involved in a beloved hobby, Brunette-Self offered to get up with him.

Before retiring for the night, they set the alarm for 1 am and went to sleep. When the alarm went off, Brunette-Self stirred and found herself alone in bed. She could hear soft sobbing coming from the living room and went to scout the source. Blonde-Spouse-Documentary-Scientist was sitting in the windowsill under the light of the full moon, face buried in his hands.

"What's the matter, Sweetie?" Brunette-Self asked gently as she sat down next to Blonde-Spouse-Documentary-Scientist sobbing on the windowsill and hugged his shoulder.

"The scientist said at night, as a human on Earth, that would we find ourselves on the other side of the world. And I thought, if I got up, we would be in Europe and I've always wanted to go to Europe. But when I looked out the window, we were still in our neighborhood. The scientist was wrong!" he wailed.

"Well, I think his choice of words were a bit off, but he wasn't wrong. Let's make a model of the Earth orbit tomorrow and we'll see what happens in action, ok?"

"Ok" he responded, still dejected.

The next day they used a bare lamp bulb to

stand in for the sun and a baseball to represent Earth. Brunette-Self walked slowly around the bulb and spinned the baseball slowly counterclockwise from her path around the bulb. Mr. Blonde-Spouse-Documentary-Scientist quickly recognized the scientist had simply meant night.

2-10: Milk Crate Construction

They put off rebuilding the stair steps to their home as long as they possibly could. A couple of dear friends of theirs had helped construct the more difficult back steps earlier in the year. Fortune did not smile upon them for the front steps. It was a chore both of them feared, Brunette-Self had been shooed away from learning carpentry as a child. Blonde-Spouse was banned from power tools (reader referred to Chronicle 1-5: Banned from Power Tools for background.)

Brunette-Self painstakingly studied step building online and by visiting other homes that had steps that were not attached to the house. The steps had to be free standing Because of local building codes regarding flooding. The steps were also being placed on a slightly sloped driveway, so the base had to be built to accommodate the slope while keeping the top steps perfectly level to the door. Brunette-Self had taken quite a bit of math in college, so figuring out the angles, supports, screws and wood lengths required was the easy part. Carpentry, on the other hand, was the nemesis.

Because Blonde-Spouse was exceptionally gifted at destruction, so she gave him free reign in ripping out the old steps.

Outside of a few hairy moments with the chainsaw, he cleared the steps within the hour. Blonde-Spouse then took it upon himself to construct temporary front steps--by stacking plastic milk crates together into the shape of a staircase. Blonde-Spouse made the staircase three milk crates wide as well, to "make it easier to climb up the steps."

What Blonde-Spouse did not take into account, was that the height of his new milk crate staircase was 36 inches and the height required to reach the front door stoop was only 28 inches. In essence, three steps up to the door--each a foot in height--and three-fourths of a foot to step back down through the door and into the house. This would have been a tolerable solution except Brunette-Teenage-Son-And-Self-Designated-Peanut-Gallery-Of-Sarcastic-Commentary (BTSASDPGOSC) was over six feet tall and the clearance provided by the 'new' staircase was only five and a half feet.

Both Brunette-Self and BTSASDPGOSC realized Blonde-Spouse's temporary solution was going to have to be, indeed, very temporary.

After triple checking measurements and quadruple checking her math, Brunette-Self handed of the supply list to Brunette-Teenage-Son-And-Self-Designated-Peanut-Gallery-Of-Sarcastic-Commentary (BTSASDPGOSC). Blonde-Spouse was to drive him to the hardware store and pay for the items BTSASDPGOSC selected off of the list. BTSASDPGOSC succeeded--as expected--in locating nearly everything they needed to construct the steps. He failed when he allowed Blonde-Spouse to load the lumber. Blonde-Spouse jammed the first piece of lumber into the back door of the van and promptly rammed the other end of the lumber directly into the car stereo, pushing the stereo back into the dashboard and creating a short in the wiring that would later prove maddening.

When the boys returned from the hardware store, Brunette-Self began measuring out the lengths for cutting for the lumber with a double check before penciling in the cut lines.

Brunette-Self developed a sense of confidence that she could, indeed, construct these steps. Blonde-Spouse grabbed the first piece and went over to where he had placed two railroad ties--parallel to each other and about three feet apart on the ground--and set the lumber across the two ties. Blonde-Spouse then jumped on the board, picked up the circular saw and bent over the board to begin cutting it along the lines between his two feet.

BTSASDPGOSC immediately unplugged the saw and sent Blonde-Spouse on a wild goose chase to 'troubleshoot it." BTSASDPGOSC and Brunette-Self then used the other circular saw to properly cut the wood and spare all fingers and toes and other necessary body parts.

With Blonde-Spouse out of their way "troubleshooting," the two made fast progress cutting the lumber and laying out the step risers to be assembled with side supports. By the time the frustrated Blonde-Spouse returned to tell them it "just doesn't work anymore" they were ready to screw the entire staircase together and sand and stain.

"BTSASDPGOSC, where are the screws?" Brunette-Self asked, rummaging through the bag from the hardware store.

"Uh, oops." BTSASDPGOSC replied.

"Yeah, oops. I guess you two will need to head back down there to get those screws." BTSASDPGOSC tapped Blonde-Spouse on the shoulder. "Ok, Mom. Come on, Dad, should only take us 30 minutes."

"Hurry back, please?" offered Brunette-Self, a little dismayed at having to stop 'her groove' in getting this dreaded project done, which had been going incredibly well up until now.

This time BTSASDPGOSC got behind the wheel of the van and--nothing happened.

"Mom, the van won't turn over!" BTSASDPGOC yelled out the window to

Brunette-Self, even though she stood only 10 feet away.

"What? Are you kidding me?" she asked, a feeling of foreboding slipped over her.

"Yeah, won't even turn over. Hey, why is the radio smashed into the dashboard?"

Her skill set of automotive repair rivaled that of her carpentry skills, so removing the smashed dash radio became a two day ordeal. She couldn't identify which fuse went to the radio, Blonde-Spouse had lost the manual.

Once Brunette-Self was able to successfully remove the radio, it took another day to recharge the battery. Rather than risk any more delays, Brunette-Self purchased the screws at the hardware store herself that evening and vowed to finish those steps the very next morning.

The next morning--and the morning after that and the morning after that--gave way to a huge storm front moving in off of the Pacific Ocean and brought torrential downpours.

The 'temporary' milk crate stairway had stood to greet their guests for nearly a week and elicited some humorous critique from the neighbor's tongues. A gentlemen down the street even threatened to submit a photo of it to **www.thereifixedit.com** (*author note, prompted by publisher's legal department: author does not have any opinion whatsoever regarding this website, however if they paid for submissions, a certain someone with dark hair would be RICH*).

Brunette-Self was able to finish the construction of the stairs on the seventh day, and stain and seal the wood. By sunset, the temporary staircase was removed and relocated both in and outside of Blonde-Spouse-Diminutive-Duplicate inflatable pool so she would have a "ladder." The completed staircase was then put into its place.

A project that should have taken at most two days was drawn into a week long ordeal, but it brought their neighbors together and provided Brunette-Self with yet another entry into Chronicles of My Life with a Blonde.

2-11: Potting Soil and Bathtubs Do Not Equal Rivers and Soil Deposits

Blonde-Spouse and Brunette-Self were walking by the river. Blonde-Spouse asked Brunette-Self-Geologist why the soil ended up in certain areas along the river. Brunette-Self-Geologist briefly explained that the water currents of the river carried soil and rocks from the mountains to the ocean. In areas of the river where the water current wasn't as strong, the rocks and soil would settle to the bottom of the channel.

After such a lovely walk in the sunshine, Blonde-Spouse decided it was time to get back to the house and repot the houseplants before the kids got home from school. Brunette-Self decided to plant some seedlings outside. When

Blonde-Spouse had repotted the plants, he came outside to help finish planting the seedlings. Somewhere in the middle of the tomatoes, the sound of a waterfall broke the serene silence of the backyard. Turning to investigate the source, Brunette-Self noted the backdoor steps had become a waterfall.

"Oh $^&*^$#(@)!" yelled Blonde-Spouse as he ran for the door, Brunette-Self right on his heels. They followed the indoor river upstream and into the master bathroom, where they waded through the water and floating shampoo bottles to the bathtub faucet and turned it off.

Apparently, Blonde-Spouse had opted to re-pot the plants in the master bathroom bathtub--for easier cleanup. Blonde-Spouse had not put in the removable shower drain to catch any soil spillage. Instead, he'd decided to rinse out the bathtub by turning on the faucet as high as it would go and then came out to help Brunette-Self and had forgotten he'd left the faucet on.

"But you said the river current would move the soil! I figured the faucet current would wash the soil down the drain!" he whined.

"Possibly a small amount," Brunette-Self admitted, "But it would not carry out the pea gravel in the bottom of each pot or the larger chunks of soil because those are larger than the drain. And again, only a SMALL AMOUNT of particulate. How much soil did you have in there anyway?"

"Um, well, I decided to dump out the old pots of soil into the bathtub." He replied.

"THE WHOLE POT?" she screamed.

"Yeah. All of them. So next time maybe you should be more specific on how much current one would need to move that amount of soil."

Brunette-Self had to admit he had a point.

2-12: Bike Chain Security

Poor Little Miss Blonde-Spouse-Diminutive-Duplicate had her bike stolen, the nasty little thieves cut through the security chain with wire cutters and made off with her freedom. Blonde-Spouse-Diminutive-Duplicate was emotionally destroyed by the event and was terrified of getting a new bike and having it also stolen.

To encourage a sense of safety again in little Blonde-Spouse-Diminutive-Duplicate, Blonde-Spouse decided to make her an uncuttable bike security chain with an even more secure lock. Rummaging through the tool drawer, Blonde-Spouse located their strongest pin shape lock left over from the old shed door and began building an indestructible bike chain. Blonde-Spouse took the chandelier chain from one of the living room lights because it was 'just the right length' he needed, and "that cord should hold that chandelier up anyway, the chain is redundant." Brunette-Self made a mental note to start a betting pool on how long that chandelier cord would hold.

Blonde-Spouse disappeared out the back door for several hours, presumed toiling away in the tool shed. Later, Blonde-Spouse returned triumphantly sporting his new and improved homemade bike security chain, which consisted of the chain and pin lock, with a broken necklace chain wound around the ends of each chandelier chain and around the pin lock.

"See the pin lock wouldn't fit through the chain link, so I made some of my own chain link to wrap around the lock" he explained.

"Why is it knotted?" Blonde-Spouse-Diminutive-Duplicate inquired.

"Oh, to hold the two chain types together" he replied.

Blonde-Spouse-Diminutive-Duplicate picked up the modified bike security chain and the lock slipped right out of the Blonde-Spouse-made chain link and fell onto the ground at her feet. Blonde-Spouse spent the rest of the evening attempting to sauder the jewelry metal chain link he made to the stainless steel lock, while Brunette-Self took Blonde-Spouse-Diminutive-Duplicate shopping for a bike security chain.

2-13: Google Earth: You Are Here!

Blonde-Spouse-Documentary-Scientist became ecstatic (Chronicle 2-39: Earth Orbit Error) when he discovered Google Earth and he could use Google Earth to check out anything and everything! From outer space to street level,

Blonde-Spouse-Documentary-Scientist conveyed his concern that no one could find their home with Google Earth, because "our house looks just like all the others!"

Their house did not look like any house in our neighborhood, but when looking at rooftops Brunette-Self had to concede that they did appear somewhat similar.

"Eureka!" exclaimed Blonde-Spouse-Documentary-Scientist as he ran out of the room.

Simply glad to have the computer time, Brunette-Self took his place and started internet surfing. The wind was gusting well that day, bringing fresh air in through the window and tickling the air with delightful wind chime symphonies. Occasionally, a thunking sound could be heard on the roof, but Brunette-Self shrugged it off as a tree branch tapping on the roof shingles.

Before Brunette-Self knew it, it was time to go meet Blonde-Spouse-Diminutive-Duplicate's school bus. As she walked to the car, a shadow of Blonde-Spouse-Documentary-Scientist fell across her path. Looking up, Brunette-Self was greeted heartily by a proud Blonde-Spouse-Documentary-Scientist standing on the roof, sporting blue painter tape rolls up and down both of his forearms.

"What are you doing?" she asked.

"I am marking our roof for Google Earth!" he gleefully responded.

Brunette-Self climbed the ladder to better see what Blonde-Spouse-Documentary-Scientist had been up to, and found he had written YOU ARE HERE in VERY LARGE LETTERS.

Brunette-Self was just happy Blonde-Spouse-Documentary-Scientist didn't think to paint it on the roof!

2-14: Plumbing Plunders

Not to be outdone by the success of Brunette-Self in constructing their front steps using the internet for research, Blonde-Spouse-Prepared-Plumber began his own knowledge quest online. The Blonde-Spouse-Prepared-Plumber visited two sites, logged off the computer and declared himself a "plumbing expert." So, Brunette-Self reacted to this proclamation by clearing a path to the water main shut off valve and by looking up her plumber friend's telephone number.

First, Blonde-Spouse-Prepared-Plumber had decided to handle their slower moving drains (the drains were moving slowly as a result of 2-41: Potting Soil and Bathtubs Do Not Equal Rivers and Soil Deposits). Although not noted in the Chronicles, Blonde-Spouse had also done something similar with food in the kitchen sink with similar outcome. The Blonde-Spouse-Prepared-Plumber poured a full bottle of drain declogger into each drain. Brunette-Self reminded Blonde-Spouse-Prepared-Plumber to set a timer so the drain declogger did't sit in the pipes any longer that the product stated it should. Blonde-Spouse-Prepared-Plumber gave Brunette-Self a snippy "Yes, Dear" reply.

Blonde-Spouse-Prepared-Plumber had then decided it was time to 'fix that leaky faucet' in the kitchen by shooting caulking up inside the faucet handles. Content he'd fixed the issue, he moved on to fixing the master bathroom toilet. Blonde-Spouse-Prepared-Plumber spied the bathtub upon entering the bathroom and remembered to rinse the drain. Unfortunately, Blonde-Spouse-Prepared-Plumber did not come to that realization minutes before while caulking the kitchen sink faucet.

The little bladder of Brunette-Self dictated a visit to the master bathroom, where Blonde-Spouse-Prepared-Plumber had just finished "fixing the toilet." The flushing handle lever that lifted the flap inside the tank to flush the toilet was made of plastic and had snapped off of the bowl. Brunette-Self had purchased a replacement part, which was still sitting in the packaging on the counter next to the toilet.

Blonde-Spouse-Prepared-Plumber confessed that he could not figure out how to remove the old one from the tank so he modified the flusher. Brunette-Self did not have the heart to tell him that all he needed to do was unscrew the old one and screw the new one on. Dangling in front of the tank was a Chinese coin, tied to yarn that led up the front of the tank and disappeared under the tank lid. Blonde-Spouse-Prepared-Plumber had tied the other end of the yarn to the flapper chain. Blonde-Spouse-Prepared-Plumber had also discarded the new float bulb replacement Brunette-Self had purchased in favor of screwing on a rather large hollow doll head from one of the dolls in the Blonde-Spouse-Diminutive-Duplicate Favorite Doll Collection because it "floated better."

"Don't think she'll be missing that?" Brunette-Self asked.

"Nah, I'm going to draw a face on the float bulb and glue it on the doll. I've already cut some yarn hair from the leftover yarn of the toilet flush and glued it on the top of the float bulb. She'll never know the difference" he replied.

Since the toilet flushed, Brunette-Self decided it wasn't worth the argument, abandoned folding the laundry and decided to assist Blonde-Spouse-Prepared-Plumber for his own safety and that of the household plumbing.

Blonde-Spouse-Prepared-Plumber resolved to be more daring and undertook creating and installing his own plumbing pipe heat tape. Brunette-Self banned Blonde-Spouse-Prepared-Plumber from power tools and anything electrical very early on in their marriage, so Blonde-Spouse-Prepared-Plumber had elected to make a portable energy source for the 'tape.'

He began to chew as much gum as he could get into his mouth at one time, then spit the gum onto the pipe and pushed it around the outside of the pipe. He repeated the process several more times, until he had about a foot of pipe covered in lightly chewed gum. He decided he would have to work on the rest of the insulative 'tape' another time because his jaw was tired from chewing. Blonde-Spouse-Prepared-Plumber unfolded a paper clip, pulled a vial of Super Glue and a AA battery out of his pocket and glued one end of the unfolded paper clip wire to the top of the battery. Once the glue set, he then wrapped the wire around the pipe and pressed it down into the gum. When he was happy it was secure, Blonde-Spouse-Prepared-Plumber then glued the other end of the unfolded paper clip wire to the bottom of the battery.

Brunette-Self decided she'd remove it later in the evening when he was distracted and then tell him when he found it missing that raccoons must have eaten the gum to steal the shiny paper clip and battery.

Brunette-Self tagged along behind Blonde-Spouse-Prepared-Plumber as he went back into the kitchen to test the caulking inside the kitchen faucet handles. Mr. Blonde-Spouse-Prepared-Plumber was very disappointed to discover his caulking fix did not work. He had also forgotten to rinse the drain declogger down the drain and it had been sitting in the drain for nearly three hours. Blonde-Spouse-Prepared-Plumber also quickly realized the drain declogger had eaten through the U-shape drain pipe--the water coming out of the faucet and leaking through the wet caulking in the handles was now gushing onto the kitchen floor through the hole in the pipe beneath the sink.

Blonde-Spouse-Prepared-Plumber then cussed under his breath and sponged up the water and wrung it out into the mop bucket, a technique that took quite some time considering he had chosen to use a small dish sponge. Finally satisfied with his cleanup efforts, Blonde-Spouse-Prepared-Plumber stood up, picked up the mop bucket full of drain declogger and food debris-laced drain water…and marched right over to the kitchen sink where he rapidly poured it down the drain.

"Son of a--!" he cried, smacking his forehead.

Blonde-Spouse-Prepared-Plumber had to again tackle cleanup, but this time Brunette-Self handed him the sponge mop and took the bucket away when he wrung the last bit into it.

2-15: The Butcher

Blonde-Spouse-Chicken-Chopper had been delegated the duty of slicing up the chicken breasts for stir fry, while Brunette-Self took care of preparing the vegetables and side dishes for the family dinner.

Blonde-Spouse-Chicken-Chopper had gotten a brilliant idea to prepare the chicken faster, so while Brunette-Self was busy slicing carrots he threw a few of the thawed chicken breasts into the blender. Mr. Blonde-Spouse-Chicken-Chopper turned on the food processor but forgot to put the lid on first. Brunette-Self turned at the sound of the food processor just in time to be assaulted in the face with spewing chicken breast parts.

Panicked, Blonde-Spouse-Chicken-Chopper started to push buttons on the food processor at random in an attempt to turn it off. He sent it from STIR to CHOP: chicken parts cleared the kitchen table and started landing on the pantry shelves.

"Ahhhhh!" he yelled as he punched another button and took the whirring blades from CHOP to PUREE', which launched the remaining chicken parts into the living room and all over the kitchen ceiling.

"AAAAAAAAAAAHHHH!" he yelled louder and punched another button. This one, thankfully, turned off the food processor.

They stood briefly in the kitchen looking at each other covered in raw chicken parts before mutilated chicken meat began to rain from above as the morsels stuck to the ceiling lost their battles to gravity. The Scottie dogs went into a feeding frenzy, licking and lapping up every piece of chicken their little snuffling noses could find.

"YOU are cleaning this up!" demanded Brunette-Self, "I'm going to go outside and turn the hose on myself. You'd best do the same, there is NO WAY I'm letting you get into the shower like that...remember the potting soil incident?" (author directs reader to Chronicle 2-11: Potting Soil and Bathtubs Do Not Equal Rivers and Soil Deposits regarding details of the incident).

Brunette-Self had the Brunette-Teenage-Son-And-Self-Designated-Peanut-Gallery-Of-Sarcastic-Commentary hose her off in the backyard until he was really sure he got all the bits, and then took a much wanted shower to an internal chorus of "ew, ew, ew.".

Coming out of the bathroom from the shower, she was confronted with Blonde-Spouse-Chicken-Chopper, who had strapped the younger of the Scottie dogs to his chest using belts and bungee cords, the poor dog's feet sticking straight out in front of them both like little flailing chicken part dowsing rods.

"Why?" was all Brunette-Self could muster.

"Oh, the dog sniffs out the chicken parts and tries to get to them. That tells me where they are so I can clean them up."

Brunette-Self left the kitchen concerned about what it would smell like in a few days, especially with the warm weather trend the area was currently enjoying. To his credit, Blonde-Spouse-Chicken-Chopper and his Canine-

Chicken-Chugging-Companion did a thorough job, the kitchen never developed the smell of rotting chicken flesh.

Brunette'Self decided it was best to hide the family food processor for awhile.

2-16: Bane Baking

Blonde-Spouse-Bane-Baker had taken it upon himself to bake Brunette-Self a birthday cake. Brunette-Self was ushered quickly out of the home that morning and whisked away by friends for a day of visiting. Brunette-Self had little concern leaving Blonde-Spouse-Bane-Baker home alone, as she was unaware of what he was about to do to her kitchen. Had she known, she would have put the local fire department on standby.

Leos were supposed to be a fire sign, and Blonde-Spouse-Bane-Baker seemed to be in great conflict with his sign. Put simply, the man couldn't start a fire to save his life when he wanted (i.e. 1-7: The Jenga Fire); and he couldn't put out a fire he was trying to avoid (1-28: Toasting Marshmallows). Chronicle 2-15 was directly in line with this 'fire conflict.'

What follows was what the insurance adjustor and fire marshal were able to piece together from their reports, well at least what they were willing to put down into public record:

Report of Fire at Blonde Residence

*The victim (Blonde-Spouse-Bane-Baker) pulled out the favorite cake recipe of of his wife (Brunette-Self), and assembled his ingredients. He measured his items to prepare the cake batter, but did not understand the difference between **tsp** and **TBSP** or what the **C** abbreviations meant on the recipe, so he 'used his best judgment.' The Firefighters on scene determined the cake had risen nearly a foot inside the oven, and concluded the victim had used significant amounts of baking powder, which caused the cake to rise into the oven elements and start the fire. The fire was further inflamed when the victim (Blonde-Spouse-Bane-Baker) attempted to put out the flames using baking soda but had grabbed the powdered coffee creamer by mistake. As the coffee creamer caused the flames to leap to the adjoining cupboards, the victim (Blonde-Spouse-Bane-Baker) was overcome with smoke and opened the window, which caused the back draft that would engulf the rest of the kitchen.*

Brunette-Self celebrated her birthday in a restaurant with a store bought cake. Even the waitstaff singing "Happy Birthday" could not cheer her up.

2-16: Grease Fire Guru

Shortly after the kitchen was restored, Blonde-Spouse-Grease-Fire-Guru was at it again, this time he got up before the house to surprise them by making bacon, eggs and waffles for breakfast. Mr. Blonde-Spouse-Grease-Fire-Guru only had one decent cooking skillet because that was all the insurance company would pay for in the birthday cake fire claim the month before, so he figured he would cook the bacon in the oven on a cookie sheet.

Brunette-Self could not understand later why Blonde-Spouse-Grease-Fire-Guru had elected this cookie sheet as the kitchen had three cookie sheets--the one he'd selected was completely flat with one edge upraised and the remaining two had edges built up all the way around them and that all three cookie sheets were clean at the time and stacked together in the oven drawer. His selection of cookie sheet caused by the fatal error in his Blonde-Spouse-Grease-Fire-Guru judgment was to have explosive results.

The smell of a delicious breakfast cooking woke Brunette-Self from her slumber. Sleepy eyed, Brunette-Self wandered out to the kitchen to retrieve a morning cup of coffee. Blonde-Spouse-Grease-Fire-Guru was busy running from the waffle maker to the skillet of scrambled eggs and stopping midsay to peek in on the bacon in the oven on his way back to the waffle maker. Everything seemed well in hand, so Brunette-Self excused herself to the living room couch to enjoy her first cup of Joe.

Soon the smell of cooking bacon in the oven turned from delightful to burnt. Blonde-Spouse-Grease-Fire-Guru reacted to the change in odor by urgently grabbing the potholders and opening the oven door. Smoke billowed out, set off the fire alarms and the howling Scottie dogs and woke up the kids and half the neighborhood.

Blonde-Spouse-Grease-Fire-Guru grabbed the cookie sheet and jerked it quickly out of the oven, causing all of the pooled and dripping bacon grease to roll off the cookie sheet and onto the oven element below, where it erupted in a grease fueled Molotov cocktail plume of flame. When the plume nearly took his eyebrows, Mr. Blonde-Spouse-Grease-Fire-Guru instinctively dropped the bacon and grease filled cookie sheet and covered his face. The cookie sheet hit the open oven door and bounced back into the oven upside down, knocking bacon and grease all over the elements inside and created a second Molotov cocktail plume of flame larger than the last.

Brunette-Self jumped sluggishly into action and pushed the fire extinguisher-holding Blonde-Spouse-Grease-Fire-Guru aside and grabbed the baking soda. Ripping open the box, Brunette-Self threw the entire thing into the oven and slammed the oven door and turned off the oven. Once the smoke cleared and the oven cooled off, she informed Blonde-Spouse-Grease-Fire-Guru that she would be drowning the entire inside with oven cleaner and that he would be responsible for cleaning up the mess. Seeing his crestfallen reaction to her biting words, Brunette-Self gave him a hug and thanked him for trying to cook breakfast for everybody. While hugging him, she whispered in his ear that he was now banned from cooking in the kitchen and from here on out would only be allowed near the BBQ as it was outside and away from the house and that one more claim would render them uninsurable.

Several months later an envelope arrived in their mailbox. Opening the envelope, Brunette-Self was dismayed to discover a bill from the local fire department. The bill had the following handwritten note upon it:

> *Due to the sheer number of visits to your residence over the course of the last year, the city has decided the taxpayers should not foot the bill for these emergency calls. Please call our office to make payment or payment arrangements. Thank you for your prompt attention to this matter and thank you for the fruit basket.*
>
> *Regards,*
> *Fire Marshall*

2-17: Butcher, Baker, Candlestick Maker

After the grease fire and subsequent warning of cancellation letter from the insurance company, Blonde-Spouse was now banned from using the kitchen to cook for life and had to resort to cooking meals on the BBQ. The ban included boiling water, which left Blonde-Spouse-Butcher-Baker-Candlestick-Maker no other recourse than to make his candles** outside with the BBQ side burner.

**For readers unfamiliar with candle making, the wax must be melted in a double boiler in a pan of boiling water. If one were to attempt to melt the wax without the boiling water buffer the wax would smoke and could catch fire. Because of this risk of flammability, especially if water and wax mix (similar to putting water into hot oil), it is imperative to melt the wax with a double boiler if melting it on a stove or other device that does not melt wax at consistent temperature that can be set (i.e. a wax vat).*

One such afternoon, Blonde-Spouse-Butcher-Baker-Candlestick-Maker put a water bath of wax on the BBQ side burner and went into the house to go the bathroom. Blonde-Spouse-Butcher-Baker-Candlestick-Maker decided it was a great day to make candles, since there was a nice breeze that would help to chill the molds faster. Blonde-Spouse-Butcher-Baker-Candlestick-Maker SHOULD HAVE given the water bath CONSTANT SUPERVISION, but figured he would be just fine because "it was only for a minute."

What the esteemed Blonde-Spouse-Butcher-Baker-Candlestick-Maker did not take into account is that a gentle breeze, when combined with a fickle flame of propane, can not only blow the flame out (causing propane gas to build up in the air around the BBQ) but it can also force the flame down into the propane tube, sending it burning through the tube directly toward the propane tank with explosive consequences. Since Blonde-Spouse-Butcher-Baker-Candlestick-Maker conflicted with his fire sign, the latter of the two happened. Blonde-Spouse-Butcher-Baker-Candlestick-Maker managed to put out the fire in the propane tube only three inches away from the top of the tank.

Brunette-Self chided herself for wishing for just a moment that he had not caught fire before it got to the tank. It did not help to remember that she had wisely taken out a large accidental death and dismemberment policy on Blonde-Spouse, and she fought with herself for quite a few minutes regarding this before coming to terms and accepting the inevitable draining of their Vacation Fund jar.

It would be another two years before Brunette-Self would allow another propane BBQ into the family, forcing Blonde-Spouse-Butcher-Baker-Candlestick-Maker to use only self igniting charcoal in a charcoal grill when cooking.

Brunette-Self controlled any candle wax water baths that occured in the household while the claim waiting period for both the house and health insurance expired.

2-18: Why Instructions Should Be Destructions

Over the years instructions have become more simplified--from multiple manuals in eight separate languages to blown apart Universal diagrams with step by step visual instructions. Yet even in marketers efforts to simplify instructions there were those who still struggle with them, and Blonde-Spouse-Directive-Destructo is one of them.

They purchased several bookshelves that were supposed to be very easy to put together; a matter of attaching the wood pieces together in the right order and screwing them together to complete the unit. Blonde-Spouse-Directive-Destructo pulled all of the parts out of the first box, spread them all over the living room carpet and proceeded to "study the instructions." Brunette-Self knew they were in for a rough afternoon when she realized the "instructions" he was so intently holding and studying were upside down in his hands and Blonde-Spouse-Directive-Destructo didn't realize the difference. Granted, most of the instructions are illustrations, but there are parts labeled next to the pictures and the print was upside down.

"What's a wersc?" Blonde-Spouse-Directive-Destructo said out loud "And what's revirdwercs? Did the manufacturer put in instructions from another country by mistake?"

Knowing Blonde-Spouse-Directive-Destructo would get angry if his error was pointed out to him, Brunette-Self offered "Well, are there any pictures of tools on there?"

"Yes!" he exclaimed, "Let me go get them!"

Blonde-Spouse-Directive-Destructo returned with a screwdriver, and then noticed two more tools listed on the instructions, with circles and lines through them: a hammer and a drill. Not realizing the circle with a diagonal line through it was the Universal symbol for "don't need these" he ran off to retrieve them.

Blonde-Spouse-Directive-Destructo scrutinized the 'supply' list again "Where am I supposed to get a little kid to climb up the front of the shelves to test them? Really, don't these people think?

He then handed off the instructions to Brunette-Self, "Ok, I know what I'm doing now, I don't need those anymore."

Blonde-Spouse-Directive-Destructo spent the next hour connecting one piece of board to another, often having to take them apart again when he attempted to stand the bookshelf up and then realized he'd made one of the long side pieces a shelf and a short shelf piece the support side, leaving a 5 foot discrepancy in length. Once he got all the long support pieces supporting the bookshelf together he screwed the screws in halfway and hammered them the rest, splintering the 'wood' on either side of the screw and destroying the tops of the screws.

The bookshelf in question was pressed particle board with a false wood laminate pasted on its surface. The manufacturer did not cover the particle board in the back of the bookshelf with the wood laminate or the underside of the shelves, most likely to cut costs because these parts of the bookshelves could not be 'seen' when properly placed against a wall. However, Blonde-Spouse-Directive-Destructo did not take this into account when adding the shelves, with some ends showing laminated wood and others raw particle board, resulting in two of the five shelves being installed upside down and backwards. While atrocious to look at, the bookshelf now stood on it's own accord, albeit a heavily leaning one.

Blonde-Spouse-Directive-Destructo began to

work earnestly on the one drawer in the bookshelf. He got the four sides of the drawer screwed and hammered together and then discovered those "grooves" in the wood were probably what held the bottom of the drawer in--which he'd forgotten to add.

He stripped two screws trying to take them out, gave up, hammered them back in and disappeared and returned with the staple gun. Turning the drawer over, he staple gunned the bottom of the drawer on. Blonde-Spouse-Directive-Destructo stepped back to admire his newly constructed drawer, and saw that he had nailed the front of the drawer on backwards, the handle to pull the drawer in and out was now located on the inside of the drawer.

Undaunted, he cut the handle off with a hacksaw, glued it on to the front and used a half a roll of duct tape to help hold the handle. He placed the drawer onto one of the shelves, and tried to pull it out to test it. The back of the drawer slid off of the shelf and landed on his foot. During the fall, the weight of the drawer was too much for the duct taped handle to bear and it came off in his hands. Blonde-Spouse-Directive-Destructo hopped up and down on his remaining good foot and nursed his bad foot with his hands "#$(*%&)(*&@#$&*()@!"

Blonde-Spouse-Directive-Destructo turned to Brunette-Self for guidance, "You have to install the drawer runners first," she said, and pointed to the two long pieces of metal next to him on the floor, "the drawer slides in and out on those runners, the runners hold the drawer in place."

Brunette-Self was about to offer to install the runners for Blonde-Spouse-Directive-Destructo, but before she could get up he picked up the first one and began drilling through it into the sides of the drawer and screwing and hammering it in place. Brunette-Self stopped him before he picked up the other one, and explained, "Half of the runner is installed on these inside walls of the bookshelf, " pointing out the larger of the two pieces, "and the smaller part is attached to the drawer."

"Now you tell me!" he laughed and used the screwdriver to wedge out the screws and remove the runner. Blonde-Spouse-Directive-Destructo placed the smaller one back on the drawer, backwards, and reattached it. He attached the larger runner, also backwards, to the bookshelf and repeated the process for the other runner. He then attempted to slide the drawer onto the runners, only to be stopped short by two metal plates protruding down into the tracks that prevent the drawer from coming off of the runner when pulled out. Frustrated, he threw down the drawer and started cussing out the bookshelf.

"I think those tabs on the shelf go in the front, and the ones on the drawer go in the back, Dear," Brunette-Self offered gently.

"Oh" he said.

Brunette-Self removed the screws from both runner halves, flipped the runners around and reattached them. "Try it now."

Blonde-Spouse-Directive-Destructo slid the drawer into place, "Thanks. So what's this big piece of wood for?"

"I believe that is the back support for the bookshelf."

"That must be what all those little screws are for."

"More than likely." Brunette-Self excused herself to the bathroom.

" $#$*&^%!!%$)(*! blast it all!" waffled on the air down the hallway.

Brunette-Self returned to the living room and observed that Mr. Blonde-Spouse-Directive-Destructo had attached the back of the bookshelf to the side containing the drawer front, thereby sealing off the drawer and holding it prisoner inside the bookshelf. Blonde-Spouse-Directive-Destructo realized his mistake when he attempted to open the drawer again.

"These #$(%&*(#(#*$& bookshelves are going back to the store! They're defective!" howled Blonde-Spouse-Directive-Destructo.

"Well, what if I put the rest of them together?" Brunette-Self said and spent the rest of the afternoon putting the bookshelves together and de-constructing other shelf as best she could for return to the store. When asked why the product was being returned, Brunette-Self gave "not Blonde-Spouse buildable" as the reason for return. The-Brunette-Salesperson was exceptionally helpful and offered to exchange Blonde-Spouse-Directive-Destructo built shelf for the extra store display shelf, already constructed.

2-19: Origami Bird Doppelganger

The family parakeet, Charlie, died suddenly at the age of 14. She was a beautiful little yellow and blue bird, and a favorite of Blonde-Spouse-Diminutive-Duplicate. Yet Brunette-Self and Blonde-Spouse were at odds with each other in how they should handle notification to Blonde-Spouse-Diminutive-Duplicate of the death of Charlie Bird.

"I think we should just buy a replacement bird that looks just like her," Began Blonde-Spouse "That way she won't even know or be upset."

"And I think we should be honest with her, left her grieve and use it as an opportunity to teach her about the frailty and beauty of life," Brunette-Self shot back, "Besides, it was getting difficult for me to feed Charlie with her cage 10 feet off of the ground. I know we placed her high to protect her from the cat, but without a stepladder it was a bit much."

"Well, what about a bird we don't have to feed?" he offered.

"What?" she asked, baffled.

"You'll see," he responded and wandered off.

Brunette-Self picked up Blonde-Spouse-Diminutive-Duplicate from the school bus and took the two of them home. As they walked into the living room, they startled Blonde-Spouse and he jumped down from the chair he was standing on underneath Charlie's cage. There, swinging to and fro on the perch swing was a yellow Origami bird marked with blue ball point pen similar to the feather markings of the late Charlie Bird.

Pulling Brunette-Self aside, Blonde-Spouse looked very pleased with himself and whispered, "This should make everyone happy, Blonde-Spouse-Diminutive-Duplicate will never know the difference and now you don't have to feed it."

2-20: The Icemaker Incident

All of her adult life, Brunette-Self wanted to have an automatic ice cube maker in her freezer. She despised the fact that no one in the family seemed to understand how to refill the empty tray. Because of the family inability to understand water was a required ingredient to make ice cubes, she had always suffered warm beverages.

When the time came for a new refrigerator/freezer, Brunette-Self and Blonde-Spouse found themselves comparison shopping for the best deal. After several weeks of this, the two selected a mid-range refrigerator with the freezer on top from a hardware store chain who also provided free delivery and pickup of their old appliance.

The next day and almost $700 later, the delivery man brought the new refrigerator and wheeled the old one out. The delivery man did not plug in the new appliance, instead he muttered a vague excuse about liability because he was not certified and abandoned the new refrigerator in the middle of the kitchen floor and made a hasty exit with their old one.

Blonde-Spouse confidently plugged in the unit and wiggle walked it back into the cubby vacated by the previous refrigerator. Blonde-Spouse picked up the manual, briefly thumbed through it, and then announced to Brunette-Self that the "ice would be ready by tomorrow morning!"

Brunette-Self arose the next morning to discover the automatic ice maker groaning and hissing but had not producing ice. Disappointed, she began to read through the manual:

> *"Automatic Ice Maker must be hooked up to the nearest cold water line available, with the copper wire water line installation kit #87-981971, available separately for $19.99. DO NOT OPERATE your unit without first installing this kit. Your Manufacturer Warranty is voided if the unit is operated without first installing this kit."*

Since appliances often break in synchronous annoyance, the dishwasher failed on queue with the evening dinner dishes by shooting out sparks and causing all the lights in the house to flicker.

This spectacle prompted response from the Brunette-Teenage-Son-And-Self-Designated Peanut-Gallery-Of-Sarcastic-Commentary, "Wow, Ma! You have really outdone yourself-- dinner and a show!"

Brunette-Self and Blonde-Spouse were back at the hardware chain store the next morning, selecting a new dishwasher to match their new refrigerator. On their way over to the appliance section, they picked up the copper wire water line installation kit #87-981971.

Brunette-Self, still found humor at this point and joked with the same salesperson who had sold them the refrigerator, "Yes, we're back again! My daughter just got a brand new kitchen play set and so I had to have one, too!"

The salesperson took pity on them as he accepted their $446.29, and arranged to have their dishwasher delivered same day. The dishwasher delivery man was not the same man who delivered the refrigerator, but they went to the same school.

After he pulled the old dishwasher out and discovered that whomever had run the electrical to the previous dishwasher had staple-gunned the electric cord to the floor, his response was the same vague excuse about not being certified as he also abandoned their new appliance in the middle of the kitchen floor and bade a hasty exit with their old dishwasher.

Before the front door shut he shot through it, "You'll need a contracted electrician to install the dishwasher, sorry." Brunette-Self wished to herself that the 'extremely helpful salesperson' had mentioned this at sale time. She discovered at dinner time that Blonde-Spouse had never emptied the old dishwasher.

"Well, I guess we can get to that water line installation now," Brunette-Self sighed as she started to search the Yellow Pages, "I wonder if there is anyone who does both plumbing and electrical? Oh, and I guess we'll need to go buy new dishes, glasses and silverware."

Two days later the Licensed-Plumbing-And-Electrical-Contractor-Guy arrived and surveyed the previous installation. Brunette-Self quietly assured him it had been installed by someone else and not Blonde-Spouse. Shaking his head, he rewired the feed properly and had a coffee break offered up by a thankful Brunette-Self. Brunette-Self told the kindly Licensed-Plumbing-And-Electrical-Contractor-Guy about their mishaps thus far, which caused the contractor to take pity on her and offer to do the water line installation for trade instead of fee.

The two settled on 5-pounds of smoked Salmon in exchange for the line installation.

The nice Licensed-Plumbing-And-Electrical-Contractor-Guy soon left with a wave, his 5-pounds of smoked Salmon and $300 tucked neatly under his arm.

Within two weeks, the dryer followed the old refrigerator and dishwasher to the refurbishment center in the sky. The $389 dryer arrived while the parents of Brunette-Self were visiting. Brunette-Self begged her Brunette-Handyman-Father to help Blonde-Spouse install it by showing him how her beloved Blonde-Spouse had used all 45 feet of the dryer ducting that came in the box to cover a distance of less than a foot from the back of the dryer to the outside vent.

Blonde-Spouse had woven the ducting back and forth along the length of the underside of the house in an attempt to "help keep the floors warm." Brunette-Handyman-Father agreed to install the dryer and shorten the ducting.

2-21: Television Programming Guide Confusion

For the first and only time to date, Blonde-Spouse succeeded in recording a television show he wanted to watch on the DVR. He asked Brunette-Self to pop some popcorn and come and watch it with him.

They snuggled in on the couch, and Blonde-Spouse hit the play button. The title, "Dancing with the Stars" came across the screen.

"Oh, boy! Oh, boy!" he exclaimed.

Brunette-Self was confused because Blonde-Spouse did not like to dance nor could he dance, had no interest in dancing and yet the only show he'd recorded was about dancing.

Blonde-Spouse delight quickly gave way to pouting and anger, "What? Why are all these celebrities dancing on this show? Where are the Stars?"

Brunette-Self commented that the Stars were the celebrities. Blonde-Spouse was dejected, "I thought it was a show about Astronomy!"

After his prolonged outburst, they decided to watch a DVD instead.

2-22: Internet Issues

"Oh, no!" uttered Blonde-Spouse, placing his face in his hands.

"What's wrong?" asked Brunette-Self.

"Oh, I just sent an email and I forgot to add something…" he began, "Wait! I'll just hit the back arrow and be back at the email before I sent it!"

"Um…"

"Hey! Where did my email go? Did it get sent to the lost email office?" he pondered "Honey, what is the address of the lost email office?"

"Lost email office?" replied Brunette-Self, dumbfounded.

"Yeah, like the lost letter office with the Post Office. Do they keep the lost emails?"

"No."

"Fine, don't be helpful then. I'll just look them up on Google Earth by myself," snapped Blonde-Spouse.

2-23: Electrical Wiring Gone Wrong

Brunette-Self and Blonde-Spouse-Diminutive-Duplicate decided to get some gardening done while they enjoyed some sunshine. Blonde-Spouse was already in the backyard, busily digging a trench from the back door outlet across the middle of the yard to the shed, already halfway to his goal.

"Hon, what are you doing?" Brunette-Self started, concerned at how deeply he was digging this trench. Last year, they had the utility company mark the electrical wires so she knew that the buried lines running from the meter and main line next to the shed to the backdoor were precariously just below his shovel tip.

"I'm getting ready to run some electricity out to the shed, so we can work in there at night." he remarked proudly "I've figured out a way we can do it with stuff we already have here at the house, no additional cost!"

"Do tell?" bemused Brunette-Self.

"Well," he beamed "First I'm going to finish this trench from the outlet there at the back door all the way over to the shed. Then I'm going to take the 50 foot heavy duty extension cord and I'm going to bury it in the trench. Then I'm going to run PVC pipe onto each end of the cord sticking out of the ground to protect the cord and plug one end into the outlet by the door, and then plug 6 plug adapter into the other end by the shed. Then we can have light and run other things at the same time! It's brilliant!"

Blonde-Spouse's face fell when he saw Brunette-Self did not share his enthusiasm. He began to look at her--the trench--then back at her in confusion.

"Snickerdoodle," she said, "I thought we'd agreed we were going to run the electricity right off of the main line since it is next to the shed."

"Well there's no outlet there!" he declared angrily and continued working on his trench.

2-24: Ladybug Barrage

Brunette-Self had purchased an indoor greenhouse and light so she could grow tomatoes, peppers and lemons year round. The growing season in the Pacific Northwest was longer than most, but it wasn't long enough for Brunette-Self, who always started craving fresh summer vegetables and fruit in the dead of winter. Due to space constraints, the only place in their home where the greenhouse could fit and not be in the way was in the master bedroom, right next to her side of the bed.

As fall and the first frost of the year fast approached, Brunette-Self and Blonde-Spouse moved the potted plants inside and placed them in the new greenhouse. Brunette-Self had started them from seed in late Spring and they had flourished as they enjoyed the summer on the patio, now halfway on their growth journey to harvest time.

Several days after moving the plants in, Brunette-Self noticed a legion of spider mites had hitched a ride on them to escape the cold nights of outdoors. The mites were enthusiastically munching up all of her hard work. Not really wanting to resort to Neem Oil because of the smell, she began to research alternate ideas. Blonde-Spouse was also very interested in organic controls as neither of them wanted to put pesticides on the food. Brunette-Self continued researching, while Blonde-Spouse took it upon himself to visit the local garden store and ask the experts.

Blonde-Spouse returned from the garden store carrying a large paper bag, which he would not let Brunette-Self investigate. He took the bag into the bedroom, locked the door behind him and was gone for several minutes.

When he returned, he informed Brunette-Self, "Smite the mites! I've unleashed Nature's perfect weapon against mite infestation!"

"Well, what is it?" she curiously asked.

"It's Top Secret!" he replied.

Blonde-Spouse and Brunette-Self went to bed that night and the nightmare began. Sometime around 3 AM, Brunette-Self dreamed she was at a banquet. The long tables were decked out in fine silver and linens and holding dozens of large covered platters. The wait staff came out from the kitchen and lifted the lids on the platters to expose--Brunette-Self.

She tore herself out of her dream and sat up in bed screaming. Her screams magnified when she realized that something really was biting her all over her body at once! The dream was real! Blonde-Spouse rushed to turn on the light to reveal the entire bed, along with Brunette-Self, covered in a swarm of angry, hungry ladybugs.

Hundreds and hundreds and hundreds of ladybugs...EVERYWHERE.

"THIS IS YOUR TOP SECRET ARSENAL?!?" screamed Brunette-Self and she bolted out of bed, swatting at herself and her hair.

No response.

"WELL?!?!?" she demanded.

"Yes, dear," was all he said, quietly avoiding her glare.

Apparently Blonde-Spouse had been advised by the local garden store staff, completely unaware that the plants were inside, that ladybugs would be a great solution to the mite problem. Blonde-Spouse confessed that the local garden store staff had told him to only release a few at a time, and to keep the rest hibernating in the refrigerator until they were needed. Because Blonde-Spouse is a firm believer in if-less-is-great-then-more-is-better, he'd decided to buy 10 packages of 100 ladybugs each and release them all at once.

"Now what are going to do?" she asked.

"Hey," he offered "We should find out what eats ladybugs, and then get some of those to eat the ladybugs!"

"NO! Absolutely not!" she ordered, "Then what would we do with the ladybug predators?

"Get bigger predators?" his eyes lit up.

"NO! Nada! Aucun! Nicht! Never Never Never!"

"Well you don't have to get huffy about it," he snapped "Fine. You figure it out then!"

Once each of them had been "debugged" and arrangements made with Blonde-Mother-In-Law to spend the next few days at her house, Brunette-Self sprang into action. She knew that attempts to bait out the colony of ladybugs in winter would be futile, organic warfare was the only way.

Brunette-Self steeled herself and went into battle, covering everything with towels and detonating the bug bombs. The ladybugs fought back. Brunette-Self knew that bug bomb would kill the ladybugs, but that a long couple of days were in store while she cleaned every nook and cranny in the house.

2-25: Multi-tasking: Do Dishes & Dust House

Blonde-Spouse had always been an avid fan of creative and unique multi-tasking; however, one such experiment in multi-tasking household chores went horribly awry. Blonde-Spouse had decided to work on the kitchen and the living room at the same time, and being incredibly "efficient," decided to combine doing the dishes with dusting.

His first few loads were relatively uneventful and rather productive, as he washed the glass knickknacks along with the coffee mugs and the plates with the vases.

The process broke down when he ran out of nonpermeable knickknacks and switched to picture frames. Blonde-Spouse had elected to not disassemble the frames and remove the pictures first, falsely assuming the glass and metal frames were water tight. He pulled out his first batch of frames sporting water colored family portraits that could have only been duplicated by Salvador Dali.

"Wow, I guess these didn't turn out so well, " he commented as he started to reach for the DVD cases.

Brunette-Self threw her body in front of the dishwasher and waved a cup of coffee in front of him, eliciting an early rest break. Once he was fully distracted, she popped the dishwasher fuse in the fuse box and then told him later that the photo ink must have clogged up the motor and that she'd have to have their Plumbing-And-Electrical-Contractor-Guy (2-20: The Icemaker Incident) come out to fix it again.

Blonde-Spouse bought her story completely, and Brunette-Self tucked the extra kindly Plumbing-And-Electrical-Contractor-Guy money into the Vacation Fund jar and waited to flip the fuse back on until Blonde-Spouse could forget all about his multi-tasking experiment.

2-26: Blonde Kibble Automation System

They had adopted an older Scottie dog rescue who had been starved as a puppy. The dog had a long standing problem with compulsively eating every bite of her kibble when it was put into the bowl at one time.

Brunette-Self and Blonde-Spouse were at odds at how to best handle the dog eating disorder. Brunette-Self felt it was best to feed the dog only twice a day, splitting up her food so she did not feel she was deprived. Brunette-Self further believed it best to fill in the day with lots of extra loves and tummy scratches. Blonde-Spouse felt it was better to give her small amounts of food throughout the day and night. He reckoned that a constant supply of kibble would keep her from feeling hungry. Brunette-Self considered this idea akin to water torture, but Blonde-Spouse was steadfast in this solution, and determined to prove it.

Donning his best Mad-Genius-Inventor smile, Blonde-Spouse began creating his BIGGEST AND BEST INVENTION EVER: The Kibble Automation System (KAS). He began by cutting off the bottom an old gallon sized vinegar bottle, removing the cap and turning it upside down. He attached a pair of vice grips to the handle of his new funnel, so when the funnel was upright, the vice grips were latched on to the bottle funnel sideways. He then set the vice grip handle onto the counter top, duct taped it down and set two 5-pound weights on top of the handle.

Blonde-Spouse disappeared to the room of Brunette-Teenage-Son-And-Self-Designated-Peanut-Gallery-Of-Sarcastic-Commentary and returned a moment later with his metronome. Walking by the piano in the living room, he reached out and grabbed the other metronome. He put both metronomes on the counter on either side of the funnel and tied string to each pendulum. Blonde-Spouse put the vinegar bottle lid on the cutting board and used the ice pick and a hammer to puncture two holes on either side of the top of the lid.

Blonde-Spouse placed the lid between the two metronomes and attached the strings to the lid through the holes and double knotted them. Content the knots were secure, he slid the lid (top side up) into position under the funnel tip and took care to slide the metronomes equally away from the funnel to bring the lid up just beneath the opening.

"Check this out!" declared Blonde-Spouse as he poured kibble into the funnel.

Blonde-Spouse slid the empty dog dish on the floor directly beneath the funnel with his foot. He set both metronomes for the same speed and then gave the one on the left a push. As the pendulum swung to the left, it pulled the lid to the left and a piece of kibble fell out of the funnel and down into the dog dish. The lid and string pulled the right metronome pendulum to the left, and in unison the pendulums swung back to the right pulling along the lid to allow another piece of kibble to fall out of the funnel and into the bowl below. Pleased with himself, he stopped the pendulums and turned triumphantly to Brunette-Self.

"So, what do you think?" he asked.

"I think it's more important what the dog thinks," replied a smirking Brunette-Self.

The old Scottie pushed the dog dish out of the way with her nose and sat down underneath the funnel, looking up at it and waiting for the kibble to fall.

The KAS worked fairly well until Blonde-Spouse-Diminutive-Duplicate discovered it, set the metronomes to different speeds and poured her milk in the funnel. After dumping the soggy dogfood into the sink, Blonde-Spouse-Diminutive-Duplicate wore the funnel as a hat and went to play at the park.

2-27: House Painting

Blonde-Spouse and Brunette-Self had spent months arguing and agonizing to select a color for their home that made them both happy. They taped dozens of paint samples to their home and held them up against their neighbors homes. Brunette-Self tended more toward earth tones and grays while Blonde-Spouse insisted they be non-discriminatory and include all the colors of the rainbow.

The two finally resorted to polling the neighbors, and the consensus was green with grey trim and white accents. Blonde-Spouse and Brunette-Self spent another two excruciating months selecting the best shade of green, finally settling on a darker grassy color over the emerald because the former would contrast better with the grey and white. Brunette-Self was relieved to finally have come to a decision everyone could live with and circled the color on the paint sample card. Blonde-Spouse let Brunette-Self pick the shade of grey and she quickly circled the charcoal sample.

She sent Blonde-Spouse and his Brunette-Best-Friend to the local hardware superstore to pick up the 5-gallon buckets of paint. When they returned, they shooed Brunette-Self and Blonde-Spouse-Diminutive-Duplicate into the house and set to work. When the first coat of paint and trim were on the house, Blonde-Spouse came in and announced the first coat was complete.

Brunette-Self came out and was nearly blinded by the brilliant shade of green on the house. The grey and white trim was exactly as she'd envisioned them to look, but the green paint took her alarmingly by surprise.

"Wow…that is VERY green," she said as she turned to Blonde-Spouse, "What happened to the color we'd agreed on?"

"Well, when we got to the store the lights were so dim in there I thought the green we picked would be way too dark, so I had them mix it a few shades lighter."

"A few shades lighter? Try the lightest green on the chart, it looks like a frog exploded on the side of the house!" she seethed, annoyed at how much time they'd wasted picking the right shade, "WHEN is ANYONE ever going to see the outside of our house under fluorescent lights?"

Brunette-Self stormed into the house, leaving the men to put on a second coat. She knew they couldn't afford to repaint the house a darker color and she would just have to live with frog color. She felt bad her neighbors across the street now had to look at a glaring green house next to a bright lemon yellow one, but appeased herself by remembering it would be easy to spot by the ambulance crew the next time Blonde-Spouse got a hold of power tools.

A few months later, Brunette-Self was trimming back the flowers along the house. As she cut, she exposed round spots of the original blue trim on the foundation and realized Blonde-Spouse had painted the grey trim around the shrubs and flowers and not all the way to the ground.

A sick feeling grew in her stomach and she went inside to look at the rooms Blonde-Spouse had painted. As she explored, she discovered he used the same painting technique inside, the original paint color exposed behind stove and refrigerator, toilet and bookshelf alike.

Brunette-Self smacked her head against the wall briefly when it dawned on her that they would have to repaint each and every room, as Blonde-Spouse had put so many coats of paint on the walls in order to cover up his previously drawn fire escape routes (1-29: Fire Safety) he'd used all of the paint. Until then, she realized, they couldn't rearrange the furniture.

2-28: The Shiny

In the Blonde-Spouse core personality, there was a raccoonish need to covet shiny things. Blonde-Spouse was very aware of his raccoon nature and would blame it whenever he defended his Brunette-Self found hordes of cigarette lighters or paperclips or whatever he had been currently collecting.

His wedding ring was his favorite shiny thing, and he would lovingly pet it repeatedly with his thumb. Blonde-Spouse became more and more possessive of his "shiny" after he had misplaced it. He'd destroyed the house looking for it, lifting furniture cushions, emptying drawers and cabinets until he finally located it wedged in the bar of soap he'd put it in to keep it safe while he was in the shower.

"My Shiny...My Shiny," he muttered as he hunched over it to rinse it off and put it back on his finger.

His protection of his "favorite shiny" led Brunette-Self into a false sense of security on their first camping trip of the season. They were camped in a beautiful clearing and had set up their kitchen in a large area of bare earth.

Blonde-Spouse had just finished washing his hands and flicked his finger tips to dry them off, when he screamed, "MY SHINY!" and dropped to his knees, frantically looking here and there on the ground.

The rest of the group immediately left the fireside to aide in the search. The search lasted the remainder of the weekend, and on Sunday "The Shiny" was declared lost forever. To soothe her sobbing sweetheart, Brunette-Self fashioned a "New Shiny" for Blonde-Spouse of aluminum foil.

2-29: Puppy Prewash

"I have found an environmentally friendly way to deal with our food wastes on our dishes," announced Blonde-Spouse.

"Really? How?" asked Brunette-Self.

"Come and see!" replied Blonde-Spouse, turning and walking into the kitchen. He began his presentation, "We don't have a garbage disposal in our sink and we can't put dairy or meat into our composter, so I've come up with a solution to clean off the plates before their rinsed and put in the dishwasher. I give you, The Puppy Prewash!"

Blonde-Spouse picked up a plate and held it in front the Scottie dog. He turned the plate like a steering wheel as the dog licked it and then gave it a rinse in the sink and placed it in the dishwasher.

Looking at Brunette-Self for a reaction and finding none, he ventured "I came up with the idea when I was barbequing the hamburgers. I had grease all over my glasses and I noticed that the dog seemed really interested in them. So I took them off my head and held them in front of her nose and she licked off all the grease. We'll even save a ton of money on dish soap because the dog takes grease out of our way!"

2-30: Coloring Easter Eggs

Brunette-Self returned from the store to discover Blonde-Spouse-Easter-Bunny and Blonde-Spouse-Diminutive-Duplicate sitting quietly on the couch with their hands clasped on their laps. The two were covered in multiple-colored splatters. Both of them stoicly refused to look at Brunette-Self, instead focusing intently on their hands.

Brunette-Self took in their sorry sight and proceeded to the kitchen to set down the dozen eggs, when she noticed the laundry room was covered in the same rainbow spectrum of splatters.

Returning to the living room, Brunette-Self confronted the two blondes sitting on the couch "Elaborate."

Blonde-Spouse-Diminutive-Duplicate started to cry and would not speak. Blonde-Spouse-Easter-Bunny bear hugged Blonde-Spouse-Diminutive-Duplicate, took a deep breath and confessed.

Apparently Blonde-Spouse-Easter-Bunny was more excited to do the "fun part" of decorating the Easter Eggs with Blonde-Spouse-Diminutive-Duplicate, so he got a clever idea to accelerate the monotonous task of dying the Easter Eggs.

Spouse-Easter-Bunny and Blonde-Spouse-Diminutive-Duplicate put in the yellow, orange and red dyes with the presoak cycle and then added the blue, green and purple colors during the spin cycle. Blonde-Spouse-Easter-Bunny and Blonde-Spouse-Diminutive-Duplicate kept lifting up the washer lid to "see how the eggs were looking" and that was "how the splatters got out of the washer."

They ran the eggs through the washer cycle a second time to rinse them and added a third spin cycle to make sure they were "really really dry." When they started to pull out the eggs from the washer, they found bits of shell a putrid purplish black color and bits of hardboiled egg.

"So great timing coming in with some more eggs, Dear," offered Blonde-Spouse-Easter-Bunny, "Now we can get started on a new batch! I think this time, though, we're not using the spin cycle."

Brunette-Self decided it was time for her to take a much needed mental-break vacation before his blondeness drove her past the brink of sanity.

She excused herself and began looking online for vacation locations. After hours of searching, she decided to simply rent a hotel room for the weekend and save on the family budget. She figured once she decompressed a bit, she could then figure out how to repair the damage done by Blonde-Spouse-Easter-Bunny's most recent escapade and also have a little left over for the laundromat the family would be forced to use for the next several months.

Without another word, Brunette-Self packed a bag and left for the hotel after Blonde-Spouse-Dimunitive-Duplicate had gone to bed.

She had no sooner checked in and got into the tub for a long soak when there was a knock at the door.

Grumbling to herself and putting on her bathrobe, Brunette-Self went to the door. Standing in front of the door were Blonde-Spouse-Dimunitive-Duplicate and Brunette-Teenage-Son-And-Self-Designated-Peanut-Gallery-Of-Sarcastic-Commentary.

"How did you find me? What are you doing here?" she demanded, annoyed.

"I overheard your call, Mom" replied Brunette-Teenage-Son-And-Self-Designated-Peanut-Gallery-Of-Sarcastic-Commentary "Can we stay the night with you? Dad decided it was faster to dry the Easter Eggs in the microwave and the fire department says we can't go home until tomorrow.

Sanity Break Doodle Page:

3 THE BEGINNING OF THE END

3-1: Blight of the Boxers

Blonde-Spouse walked through the front door limping in pain and grumbling to himself.

"Rough day at work?" queried Brunette-Self as she got up to give him a hug.

"The worst!" he whined, "I have this terrible pinching and my boxers keep riding up into my crack and I just couldn't get comfortable all day. I think the boxers you bought were the wrong size or something."

"I'm sorry," she offered, knowing full well they were the right size "Why don't you give them to me and I'll wash them and cut them up into ties to tie back vines in the garden?"

Blonde-Spouse unbuckled his jeans and let them drop to his feet. Brunette-Self glanced down and observed that Blonde-Spouse had put his boxers on backward that morning. She pointed to direct his gaze to his boxers and Blonde-Spouses face colored deep red.

"Well, now I see why I couldn't pee standing up today," he stated, embarrassed, "I just thought they didn't cut the opening in the front so I had to sit down to pee all day."

"Why didn't you just pull the boxers down with your jeans?"

"Oh, I never thought of that!" he responded, and smacked his forehead.

Brunette-Self thus quickly joined him in the smacking of her forehead, when she'd realized she'd married him and they had a child together.

3-2: Drunk Blonding

Blonde-Spouse decided to go out on the town with his Brunette Best Friend. Brunette-Self thought this was a great idea and even offered to drive them to the bar and drop them off. Brunette-Self entrusted Brunette-Best-Friend to keep Blonde-Spouse out of trouble, handing the wallet to him and telling him to not relinquish it to Blonde-Spouse under any circumstances and to instead pull and return money by proxy when it was Blonde-Spouse's turn to buy the round.

Because Brunette-Best-Friend was painfully aware of Blonde-Spouse's "Blondness," he heartily agreed to be in charge of both the wallet and its wayward owner.

Brunette-Self dropped the boys off at the bar and the kids at the grandparents and went home to enjoy a quiet night. About 2 am, the phone rang.

"Hiiiiiiiiiiiiiiiiii Hooooooooooooneeeeeeeeey!" slurred Mr. Blonde-Spouse-Bountifully-Sloshed, "Um…um…sooooo, you remember that bar you dropped us off at? Yeah, we're not there anymore, so could you please come pick us up………k?"

Brunette-Self heard muffled swishing sounds as Blonde-Spouse-Bountifully-Sloshed fumbled with the phone and dropped it on the floor, followed by Blonde-Spouse-Bountifully-Sloshed sounding as if he was yelling from far away, "We'll be waiting, bye."

Brunette-Self hung up the phone and went back to her book. A few minutes later, the phone rang again. His Brunette-Best-Friend garbled, "We're at Freddy's" and hung up.

Brunette-Self marked her place in her book, took a pit stop in the bathroom and slipped out the door to the car. She pulled up in front of Freddy's, where she immediately saw weaving precariously to and fro her Blonde-Spouse-Bountifully-Sloshed and Brunette-Best-Friend clinging to each other in a drunken attempt to remain upright and on their feet.

Once they saw her, the two meandered their way toward the car. Brunette-Self then noticed that Blonde-Spouse-Bountifully-Sloshed was sporting his rose-colored glasses nearly sideways on his face and that he was missing a lens. Brunette-Self got out of the car, opened the front and back passenger doors and poured the two boys in, buckled each one up and rolled down their windows "just in case."

After buckling her own seat belt, Brunette-Self turned to Blonde-Spouse-Bountifully-Sloshed and asked, "Does the world look a little different to you?" as she flipped down the sun visor to show Blonde-Spouse-Bountifully-Sloshed his lopsided reflection.

"Yeah!" slurred Blonde-Spouse-Bountifully-Sloshed, as he peered at himself, "Sometimes it's rosy and then sometimes it's blurry and not rosy and maybe I'm just being moody."

Brunette-Self realized she would have to repeat this conversation again in the morning and until then, it wasn't going anywhere. She started the car and turned the wheel in the direction of home. Halfway up the hill, Blonde-Spouse-Bountifully-Sloshed managed to light a cigarette (and his hair) on fire. Brunette-Self barely got them to the shoulder when Blonde-Spouse-Bountifully-Sloshed panicked and swatted his head and dropped the lit cigarette directly onto his crotch. Blonde-Spouse-Bountifully-Sloshed then noticed the lit cigarette in his crotch and reacted by opening the car door and attempting to jump out while still in his seat belt. Brunette-Self spied the lit cigarette about to roll down the seat and swept it out of the open door just as Blonde-Spouse-Bountifully-Sloshed landed back into the seat and onto her hand.

Retrieving her hand from underneath Blonde-Spouse-Bountifully-Sloshed, Brunette-Self reached over him and pulled the door shut. Annoyed, she signaled and pulled back in to traffic. When they arrived home, they discovered that a young couple on a date had parked next to their parking spot intending to "get to know each other a little better." Noting just how well that "getting to know each other" was going, Brunette-Self vehemently hoped Blonde-Spouse-Bountifully-Sloshed and Boozed Brunette-Best-Friend would not notice and decide commentary was in order.

Brunette-Self unbuckled her drunk passengers and cut them loose to open their own doors and remove themselves from the vehicle. The two extricated themselves and kept that forward motion going straight into the "getting to know you" car. Being plastered to the windows, the two boys could not help but notice what was going on inside.

Blonde-Spouse-Bountifully-Sloshed, thinking himself as more experienced than the young boy, felt compelled to get his attention and give him some tips.

"Hey! Hey you!" he yelled, as he knocked on the window repeatedly, "Try little circles, they like little circles."

Brunette-Self slid up behind Blonde-Spouse-Bountifully-Sloshed and whispered in his ear, "Why don't you follow me, Big Boy, and show me little circles?" she cooed.

Her ploy worked, Blonde-Spouse-Bountifully-Sloshed tore his attention away from the stage show in the car and started to follow her toward the front door. She mouthed a quick apology to the couple in the car and lifted up an imaginary beer to her face several times to imply he was very drunk.

Brunette-Self walked backwards and motioned toward the house, and once Boozed-Brunette-Best-Friend realized he was being abandoned he reluctantly followed suit.

Mr. Blonde-Spouse-Bountifully-Sloshed had partially untied his boots in the car and walked out of first one, then the other. He paused to lean against Boozed Brunette-Best-Friend and pulled off his socks.

Leaving the footwear in the roadway, he continued weaving toward the door as he removed his coat, shirt, and belt and dropped them in a trail leading to the house. By the time Blonde-Spouse-Bountifully-Sloshed reached the front door he had dropped his jeans to his ankles, which caused him to destroy everything in his path from the front door to the bedroom as he stumbled and careened to passing out diagonally on the bed.

Brunette-Self steered Boozed-Brunette-Best-Friend toward the couch, pushed him down, threw a blanket on him and put a puke bowl on the floor by his head.

"Night," he got out before the snore.

Brunette-Self returned to the bedroom to heave Blonde-Spouse-Bountifully-Sloshed onto his side of the bed and placed a bowl on the floor next to his head.

Brunette-Self spent the next two hours cleaning up the swath of destruction left in the wake of Mr. Blonde-Spouse-Bountifully-Sloshed and put herself to bed in the son's room.

Neither of the boys remembered the incident the next morning, and it was nearly afternoon before said Blonde-Spouse-Bountifully-Sloshed realized he'd lost a lens to his rose-colored glasses.

He spent the next week creating paths of destruction throughout the house while his new glasses were being made. The two never saw the young couple again, but Brunette-Self likes to think her Blonde-Spouse-Bountifully-Sloshed played a small but important role in teenage birth control. She would not discover until years later the two had been 86'd from Freddy's forever. Despite her bests efforts to determine why, all Freddy's staff would state was "Under the advice of our attorney, we are not to discuss this matter."

3-3: Sasquatch Sighting

Blonde-Spouse-City-Slicker offered to go into town to pick up some more ice for the ice chests. A mere 14 miles from the campsite, the "town" consisted of a bar, an espresso and gift shop, a restaurant, a resort and about six residences.

Brunette-Self was more than happy to agree, not wanting to face the pothole-riddled forest road again so soon. Brunette-Self also knew that even though Blonde-Spouse-City-Slicker would NEVER admit it, he deplored using the porta-potty and really missed toilets with running water.

Blonde-Spouse-City-Slicker was gone for about an hour and returned at a rapid rate of speed given the condition of the road, sliding the car to a stop in a cloud of dust.

Blonde-Spouse-City-Slicker barreled out of the car screaming, "I've found Sasquatch! I've found him! COME QUICK! COME SEE!"

Excited, the kids abandoned their tents and sprinted for the car followed slowly by a skeptical Brunette-Self.

Blonde-Spouse-City-Slicker sped down the road--the car jolting up and down so violently Brunette-Self feared she'd end up in traction--until they blissfully reached the highway. Blonde-Spouse-City-Slicker drove aggressively, passing slower cars and RVs in his race to show his family his discovery.

When they came in to town, Blonde-Spouse-City-Slicker pulled in to the espresso and gift shop and hurriedly pushed them all out of the car. He ran up the steps and into the building and held the door for the rest of them to come inside.

"This way!" he exclaimed, taking Brunette-Self by the hand and led her toward the back room of the gift shop. There, propped in the corner, was a standing stuffed black bear that wore a Sasquatch mask the shop owner had jokingly placed on it.

"Lame," the kids declared in unison and then distracted themselves with shopping.

Blonde-Spouse-City-Slicker looked crushed, "It's not Sasquatch, is it?"

"No, honey," soothed Brunette-Self and patted his shoulder, "it's a stuffed bear with a Sasquatch mask on it's head."

"Well, that wasn't very nice of that bear! Now I'm not going to give him any berries!" retorted Blonde-Spouse City Slicker.

Brunette-Self sighed and led Blonde-Spouse-City-Slicker over to the espresso counter for a conciliatory mocha beverage.

3-4: Shoo Cats!

Like most neighborhoods in America, their neighborhood had its fair share of dueling tomcats. Blonde-Spouse had decided to stop their fighting by spraying them with the hose. His method was immensely effective in the short term, but did nothing to deter the cats from fighting again in another location. Eventually, the tomcats started to wise up and began hosting a daily fight club in the crawl space underneath the house.

Before Brunette-Self could get to the faucet to turn it off, Blonde-Spouse declared war and pointed the hose through the open crawl space door, spraying back and forth underneath the house at full stream. Brunette-Self stooped to look at the damage through the door and came face to face with two fleeing, drenched and terrified tomcats.

They clawed by her and ran out into the yard, where the Scottie dogs gave chase. Both toms cleared the fence, but not before the younger Scottie had nipped one in the tail. Hissing their disapproval, they jumped down to the other side and disappeared from view.

Brunette-Self went into the house and poured hydrogen peroxide over the scratches left by the duo of fleeing tomcats. She picked up two headlamps and returned to the yard, where she and Blonde-Spouse again peered under the house. It was instantly obvious that Blonde-Spouse had drenched everything equally, most alarming of which was the floor insulation. Crying inside, Brunette-Self went back into the house to the Vacation Fund Jar and emptied it yet again to fund the damages caused by Blonde-Spouse.

3-5: "The Canine Kibble Claw"

All inventors must be a little crazy in order to dream up their creations, but Blonde-Spouse-Insane-Inventor took this to a new level. Thus began Chronicle 3-5: "The Canine Kibble Claw."

Blonde-Spouse-Insane-Inventor yelled from the other room for Brunette-Self to "come check out what I made!"

Brunette-Self, wondering how much this was going to end up costing them, dutifully wandered into the kitchen so she could, indeed, "check it out."

Blonde-Spouse-Insane-Inventor turned from the counter and held up his right hand, which was covered in an ace bandage up to the fingertips. He had wrapped 5 plastic measuring spoons to the ends of each of his fingers.

"I call it, 'The Canine Kibble Claw,'" he said, proudly, "It's for grabbing and serving kibble faster."

Blonde-Spouse-Insane-Inventor proceeded to demonstrate "The Canine Kibble Claw" and scooped up a handful of kibble and attempted to feed it to the dog. The dog, apparently, found "The Canine Kibble Claw" a bit threatening and reacted by viciously and repeatedly attacking it.

"The Canine Kibble Claw" was scrapped by the Emergency Room Doctor, who then took Brunette-Self aside and suggested she consider admitting Blonde-Spouse-Insane-Inventor for 48 hours of observation for his own safety.

Brunette-Self declined and took Blonde-Spouse-Insane-Inventor home, where he immediately began development on his next invention, the "The Groom and Grasp."

3-6: "The Groom and Grasp"

"The Groom and Grasp" was the next "Top Secret" invention of Blonde-Spouse-Insane-Inventor; the idea birthed from "The Canine Kibble Claw" incident (3-5: "The Canine Kibble

Claw.) "The Groom and Grasp" was composed of a rubber cleaning glove and five toothbrush heads cut from their handles and super glued to the fingertips of the glove.

Blonde-Spouse-Insane-Inventor had finished construction of "The Groom and Grasp" and promptly attempted to demonstrate it in action upon the unsuspecting Scottie dog sleeping in his lap. Blonde-Spouse-Insane-Inventor should have waited, at least, for the glue to dry. The first stroking pass along the dogs back was relatively uneventful, however the second pass stopped short midway down the dogs back.

"It's stuck!" declared Blonde-Spouse-Insane-Inventor, as he tried to pry his hand off the now waking dog. The dog, upon finding herself fused together with Blonde-Spouse-Insane-Inventor, attempted to roll over for a tummy rub, wrapping Blonde-Spouse-Insane-Inventor arm around her as she rolled over.

Blonde-Spouse-Insane-Inventor was leaning over the Scottie dog on her back, who then became threatened and started to flail her feet wildly and nip randomly in an attempt to turn back over and get away, scratching his face and chest in her panic.

Brunette-Self aided the terrified Scottie dog by rolling her back over onto her stomach and then appeased her with a dog treat. Brunette-Self directed her Brunette-Teenage-Son-And-Self-Designated-Peanut-Gallery-Of-Sarcastic-

Commentary to retrieve a towel and to apply pressure to the cuts on Blonde-Spouse-Insane-Inventor's body to help stop the bleeding.

"Why don't you take your hand out of the glove?" snapped Brunette-Self.

"Um, it's stuck, too," confessed Blonde-Spouse-Insane-Inventor "I guess I should have washed the glue off of my hands first."

Armed with this knowledge, Brunette-Self was unsure of how to proceed: should she take the two to the vet or to the emergency room for further assistance? After a call to both, they ended up at the vet first, where the dog was painstakingly extricated from "The Groom and Grasp" and from Blonde-Spouse-Insane-Inventor with a small pair of scissors by the bemused vet, who could hardly contain her laughter during the procedure.

Once the Scottie Dog was freed from the entanglement, Brunette-Self sent Brunette-Teenage-Son-And-Self-Designated-Peanut-Gallery-Of-Sarcastic-Commentary home with Blonde-Spouse-Diminutive-Duplicate and her now half bald and heavily traumatized dog.

Blonde-Spouse-Insane-Inventor sadly tossed his new invention into the same garbage can in which his previous invention, "The Canine Kibble Claw," had been buried the night before. As he was treated by the same Emergency-Room-Doctor, the Emergency-Room-Doctor advised Brunette-Self that if they "were in here again within 24 hours that Blonde-Spouse-Insane-Inventor would be forcefully admitted for observation." Brunette-Self realized that the next time, they would have to go to a different emergency room.

The experience convinced Blonde-Spouse-Insane-Inventor to pack away his drawing board--at least for awhile. Brunette-Self contemplated on how she could dispose of the drawing board forever.

3-6: Budget Booster Seat

Brunette-Self hopped into the car where the rest of her family was already waiting to depart for the store. As she glanced over her shoulder, she saw Blonde-Spouse-Diminutive-Duplicate seatbelted securely on top of a stack of phone books.

"Honey, why didn't you just move the booster seat from the van into the car?" Brunette-Self began, "I don't think that will comply with the state Child Restraint law."

"Well, it was good enough for me when I was a kid," Blonde-Spouse replied, referring to his childhood with the Blonde-Mother-In-Law, "Besides, if we are on a trip, we'll be able to look up gas stations and restaurants in the area!"

Brunette-Self, undaunted, "But honey, I think you are thinking of those times when your mom had you sit on phone books at the dinner table so you were up higher in the chair."

"No," he replied, "I had a stack in the kitchen chair and one in the car."

While at the store, Brunette-Self and Blonde-Spouse-Diminutive-Duplicate quickly excused themselves from the boys and went over to the children's section, where Brunette-Self picked out a second booster seat for the car.

3-7: DIY Home Security Theft Deterrent

Brunette-Self stood in the back yard, watering the flowers. Blonde-Spouse disappeared for about an hour and returned with a triumphant look upon his face, "I have developed some additional security for the house."

"What did you come up with?" asked Brunette-Self, not sure she wanted to know the answer to her question.

"Come with me and see," he said, as he walked out of the yard and toward the front door of the house. Brunette-Self dropped the hose and followed him. Blonde-Spouse pointed to the living room window directly next to the front door, where he had blown up a life size color photocopy of a Doberman Pincher head and upper body, cut it out and scotch taped it to the window. On the front door was a sign that said, "Ring the Doorbell." Brunette-Self, very apprehensive, refused.

"Here, let me do it for you then," said Blonde-Spouse, irritated, and he pushed the doorbell. Instead of ringing, there was a moment of silence followed by a muffled recording of Blonde-Spouse yelling, "Bark! Bark! Go Away! Bark! Bark!"

"Are you kidding me?" was all Brunette-Self could get out before her brain was seized with a horrific migraine that threatened to put her down on the couch for the rest of the day.

3-8: Computer Confusion

Brunette-Self was on the computer and remembered that her favorite music CD was still in the drive. She attempted to eject the CD, but heard a whirr and then an error message appeared on the screen to advise that the "CD could not be ejected."

She crawled under the table and noticed that someone had wrapped a bike chain (Chronicle 2-12: Bike Chain Security) around the computer tower.

"Honey!" called out Brunette-Self "Get in here, please!"

"What's up?"asked Blonde-Spouse as he rounded the corner and came into the room.

"Did you put this here? Or was it our daughter playing?"

"Oh, I put that there," he said, satisfied with himself "The computer told me to 'lock it,' so I did. I used the lock I made since you already got another one for munchkin."

Brunette-Self decided that trying to explain that 'lock it' meant 'lock your profile using control-alt-delete' was too complicated and could open the door to another entry into the Chronicles, and instead asked, "Do you remember the combination?"

Blonde-Spouse began to hedge "Well, um, I…" as he backed out of the room, then turned and fled down the hallway.

Brunette-Self smacked her forehead and then wandered over to the neighbor's house to borrow his wire cutters to crack 'the lock.'

3-9: Lawn Care

Brunette-Self should never have allowed Blonde-Spouse to have a hardware superstore credit card. The result of this poor decision making had resulted in hundreds of dollars in emergency room copays (along with an ever growing Christmas fruit basket gift list for all of the nurses, doctors, police and EMTs), high blood pressure in Brunette-Self, and the creation of several Chronicles, for which Brunette-Self was now paying the hardware superstore a high percentage rate of interest.

Blonde-Spouse-More-Is-Better had also taken to watching landscaping shows on TV with

Brunette-Self, which would later prove to be a fatal error in judgment when combined with said Blonde-Spouses hardware superstore credit card: Chronicle 3-9: Lawn Care.

Blonde-Spouse-More-Is-Better had decided to surprise Brunette-Self by taking it upon himself to green up their backyard lawn, which had started to show signs of stress. Blonde-Spouse-More-Is-Better ventured to the hardware-superstore-with-the-super-helpful-salesforce-and-the-super-high-percentage-rate-of-interest and consulted with The-Lawn-Care-Expert at the store regarding the issues facing their lawn. The-Lawn-Care-Expert, according to Blonde-Spouse-More-Is-Better, was also a highly knowledgeable very cute redhead.

The-Lawn-Care-Expert had advised Blonde-Spouse-More-Is-Better that a good fertilizer was in order, and had asked Blonde-Spouse-More-Is-Better how big the lawn was. Blonde-Spouse-More-Is-Better, talking to the cute redhead, then exaggerated its size. The-Lawn-Care-Expert then sold the lying Blonde-Spouse-More-Is-Better multiple bags of lawn fertilizer and a spreader.

Brunette-Self would like to call attention to the fact that the dimensions of the backyard lawn measure approximately 16 feet long by 20 feet wide, or about 320 square feet. Blonde-Spouse-More-Is-Better had purchased enough fertilizer to cover up to 10,000 square feet.

Blonde-Spouse-More-Is-Better had decided to spread all of the bags of fertilizer on the lawn so it would "green up faster." Instead of waiting to sprinkle the fertilizer on the lawn just prior to rain, Blonde-Spouse-More-Is-Better opted to turn on the hose at full stream and leave it sitting in the middle of the yard. Distracted by something shiny, he promptly forgot about the lawn.

Several hours later, Brunette-Self answered a pounding knock at the door to an upset neighbor, who was yelling that their home was hemorrhaging water and had flooded his driveway and the road. Brunette-Self came out to the back door and found her yard had become a lake. Almost as if adding insult to injury, Blonde-Spouse-Diminutive-Duplicate's pool toys (rubber ducks) were bobbing about in the 3-inch deep lake that had formerly been the back yard. She rushed out and turned off the water.

"HONEY, GET OUT HERE!" she screamed.

Blonde-Spouse-More-Is-Better sauntered out the back door, his eyes becoming large and his face pale as he took in the lake, "Ah, whoops. I knew I'd forgotten to do something."

Blonde-Spouse-More-Is-Better then proceeded to confess his ill deeds to Brunette-Self. Brunette-Self decided to send Blonde-Spouse-More-Is-Better on an errand for his own protection from the rage she felt threatening to overflow out of her, and told him to take their insurance card over to the neighbor to copy if he needed to make a claim and to apologize to the neighbor for flooding him out.

It took nearly a full week for all of the water to be absorbed into the lawn, which quickly turned it into a field of mud that would ensnare the feet of Scottie dog and child alike, who would--of course--then diligently transport the mud throughout the house.

It would take another three months to resolve the payment plan Brunette-Self had to take out with the utility company in addition to paying the damage deposit on her homeowners insurance, during which time the backyard became a fungus wonderland of mushrooms and moss.

A full four months after the lake had dried up, Brunette-Self was finally able to pay down the bill from hardware-superstore-with-the-super-helpful-salesforce-and-the-super-high-percentage-rate-of-interest card enough to run it back up again with the purchase of new sod to replace the back lawn.

3-10: Pouring the Patio

Blonde-Spouse had avoided assisting with any outdoor tasks involving the backyard until Brunette-Self had had time to calm down over the fertilizer incident (3-9: Lawn Care); but felt relatively safe that she had gotten over it by the time the new sod had been established in their backyard five months later.

Blonde-Spouse decided to complete the patio under their covered gazebo before winter set in and they would have to wait another year. Learning a lesson from the lawn care incident, Blonde-Spouse had asked their next door neighbor to assist him in determining how much material he would need to construct the patio.

Next-Door-Neighbor cheerfully complied and provided Blonde-Spouse with a hardware-superstore-with-the-super-helpful-salesforce-and-the-super-high-percentage-rate-of-interest shopping list.

Blonde-Spouse couldn't understand what the sand and damper were to be used for, so he decided to leave them off the list completely. He returned home with his concrete and a 5-gallon bucket of latex house paint he had mistakenly believed was the concrete color tint Next-Door-Neighbor had put on the list.

Blonde-Spouse, determined he didn't need to read the instructions (2-18: Why Instructions Should Really Be Called Destructions) because he was just mixing everything together anyway. He cut open each bag of concrete and poured the powder on the ground in the gazebo, raking it around to make sure the area was covered evenly. He opened the 5-gallon bucket of latex house paint, poured it into the lawn fertilizer spreader and "spread" the paint over the top of the concrete mix. Brunette-Self ambled out into the backyard just in time to see Blonde-Spouse turning the hose on his patio mixture.

The next weekend, Next-Door-Neighbor assisted Brunette-Self and Brunette-Teenage-Son-And-Self-Designated-Peanut-Gallery-Of-Sarcastic-Commentary with the rental of a jack hammer and the removal of the Blonde-Spouse patio. Feeling rather bad about his part in this fiasco, Next-Door-Neighbor kindly offered to pay the costs of taking the rubble to the local refuse transfer station. Thanking him and taking him up on the offer--her wallet still stinging--Brunette-Self sighed and resigned herself to another winter of a muddy gazebo floor.

3-11: Homemade Hot Tub

Because Brunette-Self had a birthday coming up, he wanted to surprise her with a shared romantic bubbly bath by candlelight. Blonde-Spouse realized there was a strain on their marriage after his bungled attempts in their backyard that summer. He knew that because of his home improvement mistakes, the two could not afford the hot tub purchase for another year and set about creating one for her in their master bathroom tub on a budget.

Blonde-Spouse went down to the local tropical fish and pet store and purchased a few dozen different types of fish aquarium bubblers. He put his favorite bubbler (the one shaped like a pirate ship) in the middle of the tub. He then placed them around the base of the tub and ran the cords to an extension cord with multiple outlets. Happy with his arrangement, he poured in an entire bottle of bubble bath, turned on the water and went to retrieve Brunette-Self.

Blonde-Spouse did not take into account that one dozen assorted bubblers + one bottle of bubble bath + running tap water = bubble expansion to the tenth power. Leading Brunette-Self into the master bathroom bathed in candlelight, Blonde-Spouse pulled back the shower curtain to expose a wall of bubbles nearly three feet high. The bubble wall--with a rising water foundation--lost its shower curtain support and immediately frothed out and over the top of the tub and onto the floor and the stunned couples feet. Brunette-Self realized the two were standing dangerously close to an extension cord with multiple outlets, all full, that was plugged into the nearby outlet on the wall. She tore off her robe and threw it between the advancing flood of water and bubbles and their sure death in the overloaded extension cord.

"Now that's what I'm talking about!" declared Blonde-Spouse.

Brunette-Self reached out and turned off the water and started to throw towels off the shelf and on to the floor.

"Yeah! Right here on the floor right now, Baby!" yelled Blonde-Spouse.

Brunette-Self then heard the bubblers in the tub, and turned to see them agitating and beginning to froth up the soap saturated water remaining in the bathtub. Risking electrocution, Brunette-Self plunged her hand into the tub to pull the drain.

Turning her back on her confused and now naked Blonde-Spouse, Brunette-Self left the bathroom and through the house to the other bathroom. There she completely dried herself off and returned to the hallway to pop the outlet fuses in the fuse box.

Blonde-Spouse had retired to their bedroom, pouting. He stayed there and refused to talk to her the rest of the night. Brunette-Self stayed up late after a failed attempt at reconciliation with Pouting-Blonde-Spouse: drying the bathroom floor, removing the bubblers and washing and drying all of their bath towels.

3-12: Linoleum Angels

There was a knock on their door. Brunette-Self opened it to a policeman standing with his hands on the shoulders of Blonde-Spouse and Blonde-Spouse-Diminutive-Duplicate, both looking at their feet.

"These two belong to you?" the policeman asked, a smirk upon his face.

"I don't know, Officer," Brunette-Self replied, "I think it depends on what they've done."

"Well," began the officer, "I responded to a call from security at the local grocery store about disturbing the peace. When I got there, I discovered these two lying in the middle of the frozen food aisle doing linoleum angels. They'd managed to convince kids of other customers to join them. This angered the parents of the kids who complained to the store manager."

"Whose idea was it?" accused Brunette-Self toward her blonde family members. The two continued looking at their feet and simultaneously pointed a finger and indicated the guilt of the other.

Clearing his throat, the Officer continued, "I don't know if you remember me, but we met during the suppository situation (Chronicle 2-5: A Question of Suppositories.) Since I'm aware of your...history," he paused with a nod of the head toward Blonde-Spouse, "I managed to talk the store manager out of pressing charges; however, he wants your assurance these two will never return to the store unsupervised again."

"Thank you, Sir," she said gratefully, "I promise to make sure they are properly escorted in the future. Would you please leave me your card? I'd like to send along a thank you fruit basket for you to share with your esteemed colleagues and office support staff."

"Oh, that won't be necessary," he replied, again giving a nod of the head toward Blonde-Spouse, "I'm sure we'll meet again in the future. You have a nice day now."

Brunette-Self waited for the officer to pull away from their house and ordered the two to their rooms until dinner.

3-13: Over Inflated Protective Measures

After pumping gas, Blonde-Spouse pulled over to the air hose to check the air in the tires.

"What's the right pressure again, Babe?" inquired Blonde-Spouse as he opened the door to get out.

"32 psi, pounds per square inch. Just make sure it reads at 32 on the gauge and you'll be fine." said Brunette-Self, still engrossed in putting her wallet back into her purse after paying for the gas.

Blonde-Spouse disappeared from view as he bent down to check the pressure of the drivers side front tire "Crap!"

"Now what?" snapped Brunette-Self through the drivers window.

"I let out too much air and now the tire is flat" Blonde-Spouse declared.

Sighing, Brunette-Self pulled her wallet out of her purse, leaned over the steering wheel and held a few quarters out of window.

Blonde-Spouse-If-Some-Is-Good-More-Is-Better plugged all of the quarters into the air hose and pulled the end over to the front wheel on the passenger side of the car, where he proceeded to let all of the air out of that tire trying to get it onto the valve.

Undiscouraged, he continued to grapple with it until he got the compressor nozzle on the valve and started to refill the tire. Once he'd filled the tire to 'his' desired pressure, he moved on to the back passenger tire and filled it as well. Standing, he ran around the back of the car to do the back tire on the drivers side, but ran out of hose and was knocked off of his feet. Brunette-Self, witnessing this event in the rear view mirror, shook her head and continued reading her book.

Blonde-Spouse regained his footing and retraced his steps and around the front of the car, passing by the flat tire in the front to fill the one in the back. The time ran out on the compressor as he walked midway from the back tire to the front, so he stooped into the window and asked Brunette-Self for another quarter.

Brunette-Self put her book down, dug out her wallet again and gave him two dimes and a nickel. Blonde-Spouse turned and sprinted for the convenience store to exchange them for a quarter, but got distracted at the door by the shiny vending machines and bought a gumball instead. Brunette-Self could see Blonde-Spouse smack his forehead before he came back through the door and out to the car to ask for yet more change. He was successful on this trip, returning with a quarter which he fed the machine and stooped to fill the last tire.

Happy all of the tires were now inflated to 'his' pressure, Blonde-Spouse stood up and let go of the air hose, the nozzle hitting and denting the hood of the car as it retracted to the compressor at lightening speed "Whoops."

Blonde-Spouse returned to the car and they left the parking lot, turning right and heading for home. It became immediately apparent to the passengers that the car ride was now very bumpy. There were no potholes in the road to explain it, so Brunette-Self asked Blonde-Spouse to pull over at the first available parking lot. Muttering under his breath, Blonde-Spouse complied and pulled over a half a block further down the road.

Getting out of the car, Brunette-Self could quickly see the problem: Blonde-Spouse had significantly over inflated the tires.

"What pressure did you get these up to?" she asked, already knowing it was much higher than 32 psi.

"I don't remember, but 32 psi just didn't seem like enough so I added a bunch more," he said hotly "But I think they are all the same pressure. I figured we'd save more gas."

Brunette-Self grabbed the tire gauge out of the glove box and spent the next several minutes deflating the tires back to 32 psi. She made a mental note to budget for new tires as soon as possible.

3-14: The Craigslist Creation

It wasn't long before Blonde-Spouse-Insane-Inventor (3-5: The Canine Kibble Claw and 3-6: The Groom and Grasp) pulled out his drawing board and began another invention that would "change the world forever."

His inspiration came from a local Craigslist ad, giving away a water wheel with its axle. The wheel itself was heavy and about 6 feet in diameter, so Blonde-Spouse-Insane-Inventor had talked Neighbor-Down-The-Street-With-Flatbed-Trailer into helping him out.

The two picked up the water wheel and brought it back to the house, where Neighbor-Down-The-Street-With-Flatbed-Trailer took out the axle so they could roll the wheel through the gate to the backyard. They then carried the axle into the backyard, setting it on end and sliding it down into the deep hole Blonde-Spouse-Insane-Inventor had managed to dig with posthole diggers without severing any utility lines. They filled in the hole around the axle with concrete mix and poured the water down into the hole to set overnight. Neighbor-Down-The-Street-With-Flatbed-Trailer then took leave with a shake of his head.

The next morning, Blonde-Spouse-Insane-Inventor and Brunette-Teenage-Son-And-Self-Designated-Peanut-Gallery–Of-Sarcastic-Commentary lifted the wheel into position on the axle. Blonde-Spouse then staple-gunned the handles of several pet leashes around the edge of the wheel, spacing them about two feet apart.

It was when the two came hunting for the household pets to test run the new invention, that Brunette-Self became aware of what the water wheel, sticking up sideways out of the ground, was doing in the middle of the backyard.

"I made a Pet Walking Wheel!" Blonde-Spouse declared, attaching the cat to the leash directly next to and in front of the dog, already connected to the wheel. The two animals, normally the best of friends, became enemies in their terror of this "contraption."

The dog howled and leapt at the cat, who jumped up on to the wheel and pulled back on the leash, trying to escape. This reaction prompted the dog to give chase, causing the wheel to spin rapidly and flinging the cat around in the air, still attached to the leash.

The cat slammed into the wheel, sliding outward as the dog ran faster, the cat desperately clawing at the wood trying to hang on to the wheel.

They stood frozen in horror as the cat lost its grip and landed on top of the running dog, and the dog reacted by changing course in an attempt to run away from the wheel--only to be jerked off of its feet as the wheel continued to spin, sending both animals airborne.

Brunette-Teenage-Son-And-Self-Designated-Peanut–Gallery-Of-Sarcastic-Commentary was the first to find his feet, and he sprung into action and splintered his hands as he stopped the wheel from spinning. The cat and the dog collapsed on the ground, panting for air. Brunette-Self immediately freed the animals, who bolted away from the wheel and hid.

"Nice" was all Sarcastic-Brunette-Self could muster.

The cat and the dog did not come out of hiding until Brunette-Self and Neighbor-Down-the-Street-With-Flatbed-Trailer disassembled the water wheel and dug out the axle. Brunette-Self quickly found a home for the wheel by posting it again on Craigslist:

Free Water Wheel And Pet Leashes

> *Free Water Wheel with axle available for immediate pickup. Blonde-Spouse attached leashes to the wheel, but leashes can easily be removed. Please do not ask why, it's too soon. Email for directions. For liability purposes, the wheel will only be given to Brunettes or Redheads. Thank You.*

3-15: Christmas Decoration Disaster

Blonde-Spouse and Brunette-Self purchased dozens of strands of Christmas Lights in varying sizes and colors, to decorate their front yard and home for the holiday. Blonde-Spouse had been studying electricity, so he was careful to select the right amperage rating for each extension cord to comfortably hold up to six strands of lights.

Brunette-Self spent all day meticulously stringing the lights around light posts and shrubs in their front yard, while Blonde-Spouse installed larger bulb lights along the rooftop of the house. Plugged into her I-Pod, Brunette-Self was not aware Blonde-Spouse was attaching the cord to the house with the staple gun, as the two had purchased hooks to install for just this purpose. Nor was she aware how key this mistake would be in the failure that was about to occur, or how much additional damage it would cause.

Brunette-Self went to meet the bus of Blonde-Spouse-Diminutive-Duplicate coming home from school, while Blonde-Spouse spent the rest of the daylight painstakingly connecting six strands each to each of the newly purchased extension cords.

After dinner when it was dark enough, Blonde-Spouse ushered his family out into the street to look at the house. He went around the back to turn on the show.

He seemed to be gone for an incredibly long amount of time. The boy declared a search party should be formed before Blonde-Spouse wandered off.

Almost on queue, Blonde-Spouse hollered that he had to go and find a flashlight so he could see what he was doing in the dark.

Brunette-Self stopped the boy from opening his mouth again and stated, "Yes, we all know there is a light switch by the backdoor."

What follows is the version told and retold to others by Blonde-Spouse-Diminutive-Duplicate:

> *"Well, we were all standing in the street to watch the show and it was all dark outside and I was scared but Momma said to not be scared because it's just the dark but it's still our house and so I wasn't. Then Daddy went in the back to plug in the lights and then the lights all lit up and they were so pretty and we all said "Awwww" and then the lights flickered and then there was a big ZAP and then smoke and then the lights didn't light anymore and it made me sad and so I cried but then it got brighter and brighter and the all along the roof it was like a candle and then the fire department came and they said 'Shame on you for plugging all those lights into one extension cord and then into one outlet, no wonder you had a fire' and we had to stay the night at Grandmas. Then Mommy wouldn't let Daddy have the staple gun anymore."*

3-16: Shoveling Snow

The family had traveled across the state this year to spend Christmas with the family of Brunette-Self.

Young Blonde-Spouse-Diminutive-Duplicate was incredibly excited, as it would be her first Christmas with snow. Blonde-Spouse promised her the two would build a snowman together Christmas Day.

Blonde-Spouse got up just before dawn on Christmas morning, donned his headlamp (2-6: DIY Headlamp) and went out to remove the Christmas Eve snow from the walk and driveway so that everyone would be spared having to plow through it on their own.

He chose the snow shovel instead of the blower in order to keep his surprise quiet, and proceeded to the walk toting a wheelbarrow and the snow shovel. Blonde-Spouse started to work on the walkway, stopping only to cart his snow loads down to the end of the driveway where he dumped each load next to the last. He continued shoveling the walkway and started on the driveway.

He changed his method for the driveway, and simply pushed the snow down the hill to the end of the driveway, where he left it in front of his wheelbarrow loads. He was nearly finished when the sun came up, and snuck in to the house to brew coffee and wake the household.

While everyone enjoyed a morning cup of coffee and the kids explored under the tree in anticipation of what Santa brought, the temperature outside rose and the falling snow turned to rain. The family sat down to breakfast when a pounding at the door interrupted them. It was Brunette-Cousin-From-College who apologized for being late for breakfast but explained she could not get in to the driveway and had to park down the block instead. She then informed everyone that there was a wall of ice blocking the end of the driveway. Blonde-Spouse reacted to this news by whistling nervously.

Brunette-Self excused the two of them and they walked down to assess the damage. Blonde-Spouse admitted he'd shoveled the walk and driveway, as the two took in the now 2-foot tall 3-feet thick wall of ice blocking them all in. The rain, running down the driveway, had begun to pool up against the ice wall.

"I'll take care of it," assured Blonde-Spouse, shooing Brunette-Self back up the driveway, "You go eat breakfast with the kids."

As she sauntered back up the driveway, Brunette-Self realized the drizzle had turned back to snow. She hoped that whatever Blonde-Spouse came up with, he'd come up with it rather quickly.

Blonde-Spouse returned to the dinner table just in time to eat a quick bite and help tidy up the kitchen. The family retired to the living room, to sort and exchange gifts. A short while later their holiday was interrupted by the sound of squealing tires and crunching metal.

Leaping to the windows, the family discovered that Blonde-Spouse had removed a large section of the ice wall. There appeared to be the shape of a lake that originated from the missing ice wall section, flowing away from the section in a stream to pool in the form of the now frozen lake coating the street. On the sidewalk shore of the other side of the lake sat the neighbors car crunched into their mailbox.

Blonde-Spouse, his mouth just above her right ear as he peered out the window over her shoulder, whispered, "I guess I shouldn't have melted the wall with your dad's welding torch. Let's just keep this between us, ok?"

Brunette-Self cried a little inside and shook her head in agreement.

3-17: The "Gee-I-didn't-know-I-needed-one-of-those-I-thought-I-already-had-one-of-those-already" Christmas Gift

After the family helped the neighbor detach his car from the mailbox and get it back on to the frozen lake, they went back to opening gifts. Blonde-Spouse set a rather large box in front of her, kissed her cheek and said, "Merry X-mas."

Brunette-Self opened the gift to reveal a microwave box. Confused, she opened the box thinking there was something else inside it. When she discovered it really was a microwave, she looked quizzically at Blonde-Spouse, "But we already have a microwave?"

"Oh, I thought you'd really like this model," he said, "and it's bigger than our old one and more powerful, we can cook more with less time! Soooooooo, I got rid of the old one and got you this better one."

Brunette-Teenage-Son-And-Self-Designated-Peanut-Gallery-Of-Sarcastic-Commentary lived up to his name, cough-talking into his hand, "Bullshit."

"You know something about this?" Brunette-Self turned and asked her son.

"Oh, yeah," he said, "Dad bought a pie at the store even though you asked we don't buy pie at the store and make it from scratch instead. Dad didn't want to bake it in the oven because he knew you would be home soon and that we would be leaving to come over here, so he took it out of the box and threw it in the microwave on high for 20 minutes.

Blonde-Spouse looked like he was going to kill the young Brunette-Teenage-Son-And-Self-Designated-Peanut-Gallery-Of-Sarcastic-Commentary, who stuck his tongue out at him and continued, "Then Dad left the room. I go off to my room to play video games for awhile. Blonde-Spouse-Diminutive-Duplicate comes banging on my bedroom door yelling for help. We go running in the kitchen and see the microwave is shooting lightning bolts because dad put the metal pie tin in the there, too. So, I turned off the microwave and tracked Dad down in the bathroom who gave me $200 to go buy you a new one, wrap it up and sneak it into the trunk of the car while he kept you busy trying to pack stuff we didn't need to bring."***

*** *The remaining chronicle has been edited for content due to a motion granted the defense attorney for Blonde-Spouse.*

3-18: Weatherizing the Water Meter

Local meteorologists had warned everyone an unprecedented cold snap was on its way, so Blonde-Spouse set off to the hardware-superstore-with-the-super-helpful-salesforce-and-the-super-high-percentage-rate-of-interest to buy supplies to insulate the new water meter.

He returned and went immediately back into the back yard without stopping in the house, so Brunette-Self went about making dinner. Blonde-Spouse came in briefly to pick up a hammer and a box of nails. When considering the general nature surrounding the winter weatherization of plumbing his choice of tools got the attention of Brunette-Self, who dropped making dinner and began getting dressed for the cold so she could go check in on Blonde-Spouse.

Coming out the back door, Brunette-Self saw what appeared to be a gigantic pile of pink cotton candy over the top of what was the water meter coming out of the ground.

"What's all this?" she asked, making her way over to where Blonde-Spouse was busily hammering over a large pine box.

"Insulation for the pipes," he replied as he drove the last nail into his lopsided box. Brunette-Self turned her attention to the box, which was leaning precariously to one side and was large enough to be a coffin for an elephant.

"What's that going to be used for?" she asked, pointing to the elephant coffin.

"Oh, that's to cover up the insulation" he said and gave her a wilted look.

Brunette-Self went back into the house, shaking her head and wondering why the hardware-superstore-with-the-super-helpful-salesforce-and-the-super-high-percentage-rate-of-interest had not offered heat tape as a solution.

3-19: Low Budget Light Timer

Most of the Blonde-Spouse-Insane-Inventor's creations ended in extended hospital stays, however, the "Low-Budget Light Timer" was a blessed exception.

The "Low-Budget Light Timer" consisted of two old turntables he'd acquired at Goodwill, both missing the arm and needle. Each turntable had a plastic spatula handle turned sideways onto the turntable and duct-taped onto it, with the spatula part sticking well past the edges of the turn table.

Blonde-Spouse-Insane-Inventor modified the end of the light switches by super gluing to the end of each switch in the row a thick wire 2-feet along the length of them. He set a small but taller table directly under the light switch and used books to raise it up to the proper height.

He set one turntable on its side on the edge of the table, making sure that the spatula could get all the way around without hitting the table top and mirrored its placement on the other side of the table, also facing outward, the other turntable. Blonde-Spouse-Insane-Inventor then lined up the spatulas and gently pushed the entire unit until the spatulas both touched the wire he'd glued along the ends of the light switches.

Blonde-Spouse-Insane-Inventor set the right turntable to play in reverse and left the other to play forward. Upon plugging in the invention, he set both to the same speed and started the first turntable. The spatula came around, struck the wire and pushed the switches down, turning the lights off. Focusing intently as if he was timing when to enter a game of double dutch jump rope, he turned on the second turntable.

The second turntable began to spin and turned the lights back on as the spatula passed the wire and continued its journey around. Now both turntables were going and the lights were turning on and off, the duct-tape giving just enough to get the spatulas by the wire each time they passed and pushed it to its stopping point.

Encouraged, Blonde-Spouse-Insane-Inventor turned the RPM from 33 to 78, the lights responding with increasing speed until they were nearly strobe lights. The duct-tape started to slip on the turntable that was turning the lights back on, finally giving way after passing the wire and flew across the living room nearly taking out little Blonde-Spouse-Diminutive-Duplicate. Mr. Blonde-Spouse-Insane-Inventor turned off the turntables and sat down, thinking and scratching his head while he cocked it toward his invention.

Exasperated, Brunette-Self started pricing new light switches online and deciding which bill would get paid late that month.

3-20: Car Cracking Walnuts

Brunette-Self had been gifted a great reference book on how to preserve food. The book also came with great ways to prepare large amounts of food for preservation by canning or storing. Blonde-Spouse was very interested on the How To section relating to cracking large amounts of Walnuts at one time.

The book illustrated a wood trough that could be built with one end open to allow for a clean car tire to roll through the length of the trough. The car tire then crushed all of the walnut shells at once, and then they would be collected and sorted from the trough.

Blonde-Spouse-More-Is-Better decided the trough wasn't really necessary and laid out a tarp on the driveway. After hosing off all of the tires and letting them dry, Blonde-Spouse-More-Is-Better parked the car on top of the tarp.

He laid walnuts under all four tires and

revved the engine, hollering at Blonde-Spouse-Diminutive-Duplicate to "Stand back!"

Brunette-Self became aware of his actions when the first Walnut launched through the living room window, shattering it. Brunette-Self hit the floor, thinking that someone was shooting at the house. She could hear "bullets" striking the side of the house followed immediately by crying, screaming children.

She rushed outside to find Blonde-Spouse-Diminutive-Duplicate, completely unharmed, in hysterics. She grabbed the child and had just enough time to dive around the other side of the van as Blonde-Spouse-More-Is-Better again drove over the walnuts.

They shot out in every direction, shredding shrubs, dinging the oil pan and striking and cracking the windshield of the car across the street. Motor Oil began to ooze into the walnuts, which by now had been pulverized into walnut flour, turning it into a tar-like goo.

Blonde-Spouse-More-Is-Better got out to check his work, and disappointed, folded up the tarp and threw it in the garbage can.

He then mumbled something about going to get the oil pan fixed and got in the car and drove away, leaving Brunette-Self to calm the hysterical Blonde-Spouse-Diminutive-Duplicate and to locate the owner of the parked car to exchange insurance information.

3-21: Frost Failure

Blonde-Spouse decided to clean out the inside of the deep freezer because a juice concentrate had burst its container while freezing and had bled orange mango guava all over the inside. Brunette-Self had asked him not to worry about it, that she would clean it up the next day. Brunette-Self then went to run errands.

Blonde-Spouse knew it was a frost-free freezer so he figured he did not have to unplug it to defrost it. He knew Brunette-Self had to go to the post office because she had to mail a package and then stop at the grocery store, so she would be gone long enough for him to clean it up quickly and return the food before she got home.

Blonde-Spouse removed the food and washed out the inside of the freezer. He was rinsing it with buckets of water when Brunette-Self got home, hollering hello to the household as she walked through the door. Panicked, because Brunette-Self was home before he could sponge out the water that had accumulated in the bottom of the freezer, Blonde-Spouse threw the food back in and slammed the door of the freezer just before Brunette-Self rounded the corner.

"What are you doing?" she quickly asked, suspiciously eying the hand he had clinched on the lid of the deep freezer.

"Oh, I was looking for some ice cream, but we're out. You didn't get any at the store did you? Here, let me help you put those groceries away," he responded as he gently directed her back to the kitchen and away from the freezer.

As the two unpacked the groceries, Blonde-Spouse offered to "run the freezer stuff back there for you, your back must be killing you." He then went outside, carrying a bucket with him. Brunette-Self raised an eyebrow at the bucket, but promptly dismissed the nagging feeling and started working on dinner. The rest of the evening passed without incident and the two got a good nights sleep.

The next morning, Brunette-Self decided to make a roast for dinner by throwing a frozen one in the crockpot for the day. Blonde-Spouse instantly sprang up and offered to get it for her, his eyes shifting and hands wringing.

"What's going on with the deep freezer, Honey?" Brunette-Self accused.

"Nothing, Dear. Nothing at all, I just want to help!" feigned Blonde-Spouse.

"Huh. Right. Well, thanks anyway but I've got it."

Blonde-Spouse tried to distract Brunette-Self with another cup of coffee, blocking the doorway back to the deep freezer. Brunette-Self smiled, and then excused herself to the bathroom. She wandered back around through the house, entered the master bathroom through the bedroom and came out the other door into the hallway to arrive in front of the freezer and behind pacing Blonde-Spouse blocking the hallway entrance. Grinning to herself at outwitting him, she lifted the freezer lid and peered inside.

The first thing that caught her eye was their 20-pound turkey, partially embedded in 3 inches of solid ice on the bottom of the freezer. As her eye traveled along the carnage, she realized nearly all of their meat, frozen vegetables, jams and juices were also trapped in the ice sheet. Her sharp intake of breath caused Blonde-Spouse to wheel around, splashing coffee all over the two of them.

"I can explain," he began "I was trying to help! It was frost free so I didn't have to unplug it to defrost and I just was rinsing it when you got home and I didn't want to make you mad so I hid everything...and then I forgot to fix it when you went to bed," he blurted quickly.

"Well, we're going to have to defrost it now," she replied angrily "and throw all of this food out. If we're lucky, you didn't damage the freezer, too."

"Well, why can't we just have a big BBQ?" he offered.

"Because all of the meat was soaking in soapy water, you idiot," she snapped, "We'd give everyone diarrhea." For a brief moment, her evil side considered feeding him the meat anyway.

It took six hours to melt out the ice, and another four loads of laundry to wash all the towels Brunette-Self had to use to mop up the lake at the bottom of the freezer.

It took another three weeks and nearly $400 to replace all of the food. Brunette-Self installed a latch on the lid, which she now locks whenever she is out of the house. Not only has it protected the contents from Blonde-Spouse, she discovered the lock also kept the Brunette-Teenage-Son-And-Self-Designated-Peanut-Gallery-Of-Sarcastic-Commentary out of the ice cream, too.

3-22: Sealing the Driveway

Many of the Chronicles were witnessed through the eyes of the children, who then reported dutifully back to Brunette-Self and "ratted Daddy out." Because Blonde-Spouse still had not caught on to the fact that they were little double agents, Brunette-Self had managed to glean quite a bit of information on what Blonde-Spouse thought he did without Brunette-Self finding out about it. Such was the case of Chronicle 3-22: Sealing the Driveway.

Brunette-Self and Brunette-Teenage-Son-And-Self-Designated-Peanut-Gallery-Of-Sarcastic-Commentary (BTSADSPGOSC) had patched the holes in the asphalt of the family driveway. The two made plans to re-tar the surface later on in the summer, when there were fewer rain storms. Unbekownst to them, Blonde-Spouse-Construction-King overheard their conversation concluded that he should take care of sealing the driveway. He, after all, was the one who had worked for the Department of Transportation (DOT) as a highway roadway construction flagger.*** The next morning, Brunette-Self was nudged from sleep by Blonde-Spouse-Diminutive-Duplicate, Double Agent. She gleefully informed Brunette-Self, in her best tattletale voice, of what had happened while Brunette-Self had been asleep.

Blonde-Spouse-Construction-King had been watching television and came across a commercial advising people to seal their asphalt with their product. Moreover, Blonde-Spouse despised the smell of tar.

*** *He occasionally still put on his gear, pulled his stop sign out of the closet and attempted to direct the traffic of pets and children about their house. Once, Brunette-Self even caught him singing "Stop, in the Name of Love" in front of the mirror in his DOT flagger outfit. She teased him about being really late for the Village People concert and he got a bit upset.*

Blonde-Spouse decided the advertised product was not sufficient to seal the asphalt composing the driveway, so he chose to go with an industrial wax polish and sealant and reasoned that this would cause the rain to bead up and run off. Blonde-Spouse did not mentally connect that the wax product was for linoleum floors, not asphalt.

Because the asphalt was textured, Blonde-Spouse-Construction-King determined that he would need to work it in the lowered surface parts by using a floor wax buffer.

He asked his friend, Redhead-Janitor, if he could borrow the wax buffer and some wax from Redhead-Janitor's work. Redhead-Janitor-Friend asked Blonde-Spouse what he wanted it for and when Blonde-Spouse told him his plan, Fiendish-Redhead-Janitor-Friend agreed to loan Blonde-Spouse-Construction-King the items and asked if he could come and "help."

Blonde-Spouse misunderstood the true nature of Fiendish-Redhead-Janitor-Friend's offer of 'help,' thanked him for offering and took him up on his 'offer.'

Fiendish-Redhead-Janitor-Friend arrived early the next morning with a wax buffer and a tub of floor wax. The Blonde-Spouse-Construction-King had already pulled both cars out of the driveway and had blocked the end of the driveway by parking the van in front of its entrance to the street.

The surface of the asphalt was still clean from the preparation of yesterday's patching jobs that Brunette-Self and the BTSADSPGOSC had completed, which left the Blonde-Spouse-Construction-King and the Fiendish-Redhead-Janitor-Friend an opportunity to get started without delay.

The Blonde-Spouse-Construction-King and Fiendish-Redhead-Janitor-Friend spread the wax over the surface of the driveway. Fiendish-Redhead-Janitor-Friend encountered the first patched pothole, still very warm, and began to have twinges of guilt.

"Are you sure you want to do this right now?" asked Fiendish-Redhead-Janitor-Friend "These pothole patches are still warm, they aren't strong yet."

"Oh, no, they're tougher than they look," replied Blonde-Spouse-Construction-King, "and besides, I am the DOT road construction expert here, remember?"

Fiendish-Redhead-Janitor-Friend smirked and bit his tongue "Ok," he finally managed.

Fiendish-Redhead-Janitor-Friend then showed Blonde-Spouse-Construction-King how to safely operate the wax buffer. Still feeling a bit guilty, Fiendish-Redhead-Janitor-Friend decided to warn Blonde-Spouse the buffer was powerful and would require a lot of arm strength to control it when it ran.

Blonde-Spouse-Construction-King switched

the unit on and was swiftly ripped off of his feet, the buffer taking off like a bullet down the driveway. Blonde-Spouse regained his footing after a few feet, and started to make swaths back and forth across the driveway.

The first porthole patch appeared to explode when the buffer went over it, sending shards of tar and gravel jetting outward in all directions. Fiendish-Redhead-Janitor-Friend was hit by the debris, screaming and falling to his knees.

The movement distracted Blonde-Spouse-Construction-King, who turned his focus from the buffer to his injured friend. The buffer took advantage of his loose grip and responded by launching out of his hands and down the driveway, spewing more pothole patch in its wake as it mowed them down brutally.

The launching debris slowed down Blonde-Spouse's chase of the buffer, and he fell to the ground to "duck and cover." The buffer continued its path of destruction down the driveway and smashed into the side of the van.

The first collision knocked the buffer away from the van, but the brushes moved it forward to collide with the van again, denting in the door in a new place with each strike. Fiendish-Redhead-Janitor-Friend limped quickly down the driveway to put an end to the buffers assault on the van, but not before it had scratched and dented nearly half of the vehicle.

The Blonde-Spouse-Construction-King and Fiendish-Redhead-Janitor-Friend took in the sight of the van in dismay, until Blonde-Spouse suggested they could "use the buffer on it's side to buff out those scratches." Fiendish-Redhead-Janitor-Friend, realizing his friendship with Brunette-Self may have just ended, vetoed the idea and suggested they just "keep this between themselves."

Satisfied with her report, Blonde-Spouse-Dimunitive-Duplicate-Double-Agent skipped out of the room.

Blonde-Spouse then came through the door with a cup of coffee and rushed to give Brunette-Self a peck on the cheek. He muttered something about taking the van to get serviced and quickly took his leave.

Brunette-Self rose out of bed and went over to the Family Vacation Fund Jar, still so sadly empty despite years of her hard effort to fill it. She sighed in the realization that Blonde-Spouse incidents took the money out faster than she could put it in.

3-23: The Umbrella Tree

When they purchased their home, it came with only a lawn and a few ferns for landscaping. In order to landscape on a budget, Brunette-Self concluded they needed to plant trees in the first year because they would take the longest to grow.

She purchased and planted two dwarf maples, an ornamental maple, a lilac bush and a weeping Cherry tree. She had placed the two dwarf maples next to each other in the backyard.

Over the next three years, Blonde-Spouse and Brunette-Self had almost finished the yard, and it was as it neared completion that Brunette-Self discovered her twin dwarf maples were not twins. The summers had been fairly cool up until that year, when the mercury rose and one of the maples began to die. The trees, now old enough to be distinct, were in fact two different varieties of red maple. Their only distinguishing characteristic was a slight change in the shade of the red leaves. A little research led Brunette-Self to the conclusion that the nursery had mislabeled one of the seedlings all those years ago, and that the maple that was dying was of the type that required quite a bit more shade.

Somewhat discouraged, Brunette-Self was determined to correct her planting area by transplanting the suffering maple to a more shade-enriched part of the yard. The maple, unfortunately, had grown quite a bit over four years and now stood at a height of nearly 6 feet. Because of the size of the tree, Brunette-Self brought up the dilemma to Blonde-Spouse. The two stood in front of the tree, frowning at it as they debated on how to best move the tree to its new location. Blond Spouse was struck with an idea, "Eureka!"

He went over to the umbrella table and started to slide it (with the umbrella still open in the middle of the table) across the yard and over to the tree. He positioned and tipped the umbrella so it would fit over the top of the maple tree.

Turning to Brunette-Self, he exclaimed "There! Now we won't have to move it all!"

Brunette-Self, tickled at his solution, could not bear at that moment to burst his bubble by informing him that the dwarf maple tree would still grow to be 20 feet tall. Brunette-Self was also concerned this would give him the idea to construct a "Mega Umbrella," and could envision what would happen to it in the next wind storm. She figured he would find out soon enough as the tree continued to grow, but made plans with Brunette-Teenage-Son-And-Self-Designated-Peanut-Gallery-Of-Sarcastic-Commentary to move the tree the next day Blonde-Spouse was at work and she hoped he would have forgotten the umbrella tree by the following evening.

3-24: Outdoor Lighting

Blonde-Spouse decided the driveway needed more lighting at night than the front porch light currently provided. He had to get creative because Brunette-Self had long since banned him from power tools (1-5: Banned from Power tools), so he snuck off to the hardware-superstore-with-the-super-helpful-salesforce-and-the-super-high-percentage-rate-of-interest for supplies.

Brunette-Self was guarding the pressure cooker and canning carrots in the kitchen, so Blonde-Spouse had free reign to implement his solution. He completed it just prior to the pressure cooker cooling-off time, so he and Brunette-Self played a few hands of Gin Rummy while they waited. Once the pressure cooker had cooled enough to be left safely unattended, Blonde-Spouse took her by the hand and led her outside.

He had purchased several small candlestick table lamps, which he had wired onto picture hooks he'd attached to the siding of the house. He had removed the lampshades, so the lamps would be "flush up against the house and not stick out in the walkway."

To connect his string of "outdoor lights," he had purchased several 10 foot extension cords, which he had connected end to end and had so cleverly spaced each lamp above each cord connection so they could "easily be plugged right in."

He had run the extension cord closest to the front door under the Welcome mat and over the threshold just beneath the hinges of the front door. Inside, he had slipped the extension cord underneath the living room carpet to the nearest outlet, where it popped above the blue carpet like the Loch Ness Monster (it's head reaching up from the lake for a treat), seeking to be fed from the outlet on the wall above it.

"See I even plugged it into the outlet that can be turned off and on with the switch, so it's just like real outdoor lighting!" he announced.

Brunette-Self declined to educate Blonde-Spouse that the lamps and extension cords he'd purchased were indoor use only, and that they would most likely short out and start a fire with the very first raindrop.

She elected to instead invite over Brunette-Best-Friend (Chronicle 3-2: Drunk Blonding) while Blonde-Spouse was at work to help her remove the lamps, seal the hook holes and touch up the paint. Brunette-Self told Blonde-Spouse when he got home from work that night that the lamps had been stolen by metal thieves and she had already filed a police report. She then distracted him with an offer to go into the kitchen and microwave AOL CDs together.

3-25: Bike Bumpers

Blonde-Spouse-Diminutive-Duplicate slammed the front door as she came running in from outside, sporting a bike helmet, her shoes on backwards and a tear and dirt streaked face.

"What's the matter, Pumpkintater?" consoled Brunette-Self.

"Daddy ruined my bike!" she wailed.

"What?!?" hollered Brunette-Self.

"I'll show you what he did, Momma, he ruined it!" shouted Blonde-Spouse-Diminutive-Duplicate as she led Brunette-Self outside.

Blonde-Spouse was hovering uncertainly near her bike. The bike was covered in large odd-shaped chunks of upholstery foam he had cut into pieces and then glued on all over the frame with spray contact cement.

"What the Hell?" demanded Brunette-Self.

"Bumpers!" shot back Blonde-Spouse, puffing up "So if she crashes her bike she will bounce back up!"

Blonde-Spouse-Diminutive-Duplicate got a new bike and Brunette-Self got a new Chronicle.

3-26: The Club

The local police department had a fundraising drive each year in which they sell a home security item of some type by telemarketing the local citizenry. Brunette-Self had been lucky each year to be the individual in the family to take these calls, purchasing an item to support the officers and keeping Blonde-Spouse in the dark on the matter.

Luck was not with Brunette-Self this year when the phone rang. Blonde-Spouse was on the computer when the call came in and stopped typing to pick up the phone.

"Hello?" he said into the receiver. He paused for a few minutes, presumably listening to the caller, and then answered "Yes."

He fell to silence and raised his hand and began pointing at each room in the house, circling his head as he pointed. Brunette-Self found his body language disconcerting.

"Yes, we'll take eight. Here's our card number," which he then gave over the phone.

Brunette-Self, now very alarmed, focused intently on the back of his head as he hung up the phone.

"Eight of what?" she queried.

"Oh, that was the police. They were selling security stuff so I bought a lock for each window of the house."

Relieved, Brunette-Self let the matter drop. Two days later a package came and was left on the front doorstep. Brunette-Self saw the police department return address label and swooped up the package and brought it inside. She set the package down on the kitchen counter and cut the tape on the top of the box. There, nestled safely in their bubble wrap packaging, was eight count of the security product the department was selling that year, The Club. For the reader unfamiliar with The Club, The Club is an anti-theft device made up of a steel rod that adjusts in length, with two rubber coated U shaped ends. In the middle of The Club, is a keyed lock to lock the steel rod at a certain length. The Club is placed over the steering wheel of an automobile, where each U shaped end rests on the inside of the wheel and the user then locks The Club onto the steering wheel, making it impossible to drive the automobile.

Brunette-Self picked up the phone and dialed. "Police Department" answered the dispatcher.

"Yes, hi. I just received the package you sent for your fundraiser and my husband bought eight of The Clubs from you. We only have two automobiles, and he mistakingly believed he could use these on the windows of our house. I don't suppose it would be possible to return six of them to you? It's such a wonderful product I'm sure they would resell again very quickly."

"Sorry, Ma'am, the officer who called would not have known you wanted these for windows, many people buy several at a time in order to give them as gifts. I'm sorry your husband misunderstood what the product was for, but at least your that much closer to finishing your holiday shopping! Thank you again for supporting your local police department, we appreciate it" finished the dispatcher as she hung up.

Everyone in the immediate family received The Club that year, regardless of whether or not they owned a car.

3-27: Sealing the Wood Slats

Brunette-Self took the kids to visit family for the weekend. Blonde-Spouse stayed home with the dogs because he had to work. Concerned he would be left unattended for two entire days, Brunette-Self asked Redhead-Neighbor-Friend to "keep an eye on the house and call the fire department as needed."

The trip across the state was uneventful, Brunette-Self checking in with Redhead-Neighbor-Friend to make sure the house still stood before they turned off the freeway and left cell phone reception behind. Redhead-Neighbor-Friend assured Brunette-Self just before the call dropped that the house was still in one piece and uncharred and that she should relax and enjoy her weekend. Brunette-Self heeded her advice and they had a pleasant overdue visit with family.

On Sunday, a very relieved Brunette-Self pulled into the driveway to a house that appeared just as they had left it on Friday. Blonde-Spouse was at work, so when Brunette-Self opened the front door she was greeted by two very happy Scottie dogs with very full bladders. She gave them each a tummy rub and walked to the backdoor to let them out to use the bathroom.

She froze when she opened the door, completely unaware that both dogs bolted through her legs and out into the yard. Her eyes took in their newly constructed wooden step landing, now striped in what appeared to be expandable yellow Styrofoam insulation. She stooped down, touching the nearest yellow stripe wedged between the slats of wood that comprised the landing, hoping the insulation was still wet. Alas, the foam was rock solid.

She picked up her cell phone and angrily left a message for Blonde-Spouse to call her on his break.

An hour later, Blonde-Spouse called back, "Hey, Honey! How was your trip?"

"Fine," she retorted "until we got home and discovered yellow foam on the landing. Why did you spray foam in the slats?"

"Oh, that! I had noticed little Blonde-Spouse-Diminutive-Duplicate was sticking her fingers between the slats the other day and decided to fill them in so her fingers didn't get stuck."

Brunette-Self was able to remove most of the foam with a putty knife and a hammer, but scarred the wood heavily in the process. Bits of foam still clung rebelliously above the landing floor, creating a tripping hazard. The landing was replaced with a set of temporary wooden steps.

3-28: Musical Spot Bot

The moment Blonde-Spouse-Insane-Inventor saw one advertised on television he began nagging Brunette-Self to pick one up for the household, even dragging her out to the mall to see one in action. Brunette-Self had resisted because she could foresee his creative usage of the machine leading to multiple disasters. The Spot Bot is a machine with two large rotating brushes that is set on top of a carpet stain and left to scrub and remove the stain. Not to be dissuaded by Brunette-Self, Blonde-Spouse-Insane-Inventor thought up a way to improve upon the Spot Bot invention. He led the family to the living room couch, seated them then returned to stand in front of a large boxy objected covered with a sheet on the carpet.

"The Spot Bot is a great invention that lacks something," started Blonde-Spouse-Insane-Inventor's presentation "It doesn't move so it's boring. The Spot Bot has to sit and work on a stain for hours, making this loud and annoying sound. Well, what if that annoying sound was replaced with music?"

Blonde-Spouse stepped to the side, turned and grabbed the corner of the sheet and flicked his wrist upward, fluffing air under the sheet and lifting it off to reveal the large boxy object underneath it.

Blonde-Spouse-Insane-Inventor had modified his reel-to-reel.* It lay upside down on four bricks laid on the carpet in a square with the reel to reel suspended between them. He had wired scrub brushes to the reels, the brushes just touching the carpet.

---

*For readers born after 1963, reel-to-reels were the primary form for recording and playing back music until the 1960s, when cassettes** took over as the dominant form. Reel-to-reels were two large wheel shaped reels with recording tape wound on them, that were fed through a tape head assembly that translated the tape into music. The wheels were mounted on spindles to a large box shape base that contained the electronics and speakers. **For readers born after 1990, cassettes became the primary form for recording and playing back music and replaced the reel-to-reel. Cassettes were small plastic containers that held a miniature version of reel-to-reel tape. The cassettes where placed into the player, and the tape fed through in the same way as the reel-to-reel tape. Cassettes were replaced in the mid 1990s with compact discs. Compact discs were then replaced by MP3 players*** at the turn of the century ***For readers born after 2000, go outside and play. You are only kids and have no business reading this book. You parents are trying to turn you into a geek, rebel and go be a kid. This book is not rated for children under the age of 17 anyway. Nana Nana Boo Boo.

"Ooooo" declared the kids in unison.

"Uh oh," muttered Brunette-Self under her breath.

Blonde-Spouse-Insane-Inventor dumped a bottle of carpet stain remover onto the stain centered beneath the reel-to-reel and turned on the machine. A muffled and distorted sound of Sly and the Family Stone could be heard in conjunction with the brushes on the carpet.

"It works! It works!" he squealed as he jumped up and down.

Sly and the Family Stone appeared to be slowing down in speed, which directed everyone's attention back to the "Musical Spot Bot." The entire bottle of carpet stain remover had really saturated the carpet, and the brushes were kicking splatters of the liquid up and into the reel to reel, slowing it down and causing it to start smoking.

Alarmed, Brunette-Self sprung from the couch as the first curl of flame melted the tape, killing Sly and the Family Stone and replacing it with zaps and pops. Seconds later, the flame appeared into view along the edge of the "Musical Spot Bot." Blonde-Spouse-Insane-Inventor ran to the front door and began opening and closing it rapidly in an attempt to dissipate the smoke, and instead fueled the fire with oxygen so it erupted and engulfed the entire machine. The fire alarms went off, sending the dogs into a howling frenzy.

Brunette-Self ran to the kitchen and grabbed the fire extinguisher from under the kitchen sink, sprayed the Musical Spot Bot down and doused the flames. Parts of the melted reel-to-reel plastic began to drip down on to the carpet below.

Brunette-Self sent the Brunette-Teenage-Son-And-Self-Designated-Peanut-Gallery-Of-Sarcastic-Commentary down the hall to trip the main fuse box. Upon hearing the all clear, she pushed a very stunned Blonde-Spouse-Insane-Inventor out of the way of the door and opened the door wide. She grabbed the pot holders from the kitchen and heaved the "Musical Spot Bot" out the front door, nearly hitting Investigating-Concerned-Neighbor.

"Well, I see you have the situation well in hand, then," quietly hedged the Investigating-Concerned-Neighbor as he backed slowly down the driveway, "I'll talk to you later then."

3-29: Home Sprinkler System

The misadventure of the "Musical Spot Bot" got Blonde-Spouse to thinking again about Fire Safety (1-29: Fire Safety.) He decided that just adjusting the alarms for better smoke detection had been an excellent idea, as he felt the "Musical Spot Bot" misadventure had illustrated this success in early smoke detection. Blonde-Spouse had to concede that smoke alarms were now "not enough" protection, and that only the addition of a Home Sprinkler System would ultimately guarantee complete fire protection.

Brunette-Self agreed a home sprinkler system was a good idea and started pricing them online. Blonde-Spouse told her "not to waste the money," that "he could do it for a fraction of the cost."

Brunette-Self tried to convince Blonde-Spouse that the system would have to be installed by professionals in order to be considered a homeowner insurance discount. Blonde-Spouse decided to verify this with the insurance agency, who helpfully advised him that as long as it was inspected and passed the system could be installed by the homeowner and still qualify for the discount.

Blonde-Spouse departed on a pilgrimage for supplies, leaving Brunette-Self silently seething that her insurance company would take such a risk in giving said Blonde-Spouse this advice given his history of homeowner claims. A point, she decided, she would take up should another claim raise their premium.

Upon Mr. Blonde-Spouse's homecoming, Brunette-Self excused herself to go count the money in their Vacation Fund Jar and to estimate the potential damages. She knew any argument from her would only result in the damages being larger and more costly.

She left the bedroom door open behind her as she snuggled onto the bed with the jar, pausing to look up only once to see Blonde-Spouse walk by with a garden hose. Sighing, she returned to her budgeting.

"Ok, Dear, it's all done!" declared Blonde-Spouse from the bedroom door.

Startled, Brunette-Self realized she had fallen asleep. Rubbing her stiff neck, she got up and followed him out into the living room.

"I've got them installed in all the rooms but the bedrooms," he began, pointing up to the ceiling, "I've got to get another faucet splitter before I can finish the bedrooms."

Brunette-Self looked up to the ceiling to see a rotating sprinkler wired upside down and hanging from a chandelier hook. Her eyes followed the garden hose down to the wall, where Blonde-Spouse and looped it over the candle sconce to keep it out of the walkway to the open kitchen. The garden hose then returned to the ceiling slowly as it crossed just under the ceiling fan above the kitchen table and over to the top of the cupboard on the other side of the room, where it was held in place by the closed cupboard door along with a second garden hose that traced to another rotating sprinkler wired upside down from a hook in the kitchen ceiling.

Brunette-Self began to follow the garden hoses toward the backdoor, to find a third sprinkler on the laundry room ceiling. Here Blonde-Spouse had taken a detour into the master bathroom and for a fourth sprinkler had routed all of the hoses out of the bathroom window directly behind the toilet. The two followed the hoses outside by walking out the backdoor to the only outside faucet, each hose attached to a splitter which was then attached to the faucet.

Blonde-Spouse had purchased a splitter that had individual on/off levers for each hose, thereby making it easier to control the direction of the water flow and allowing for outside watering without turning on the Home Sprinkler System.

However, Brunette-Self had noticed the hoses had been jumbled and twisted together along the back of the house, so now it was very unclear which hose went to which splitter. She decided to mention this to Blonde-Spouse, given the possibility he would water outside before the inspector came to inspect his installation.

Blonde-Spouse corrected the twisted garden hoses and even labeled each one by writing which room it led to on the hose with magic marker. Satisfied Blonde-Spouse would not water the house until the inspector arrived, Brunette-Self opted to let the rest of the matter drop and leave it to the inspector to be the Big Bad Guy.

The inspector came a few days later. Blonde-Spouse met him at the door and led him in to show him the system. The inspector took one look, burst out laughing and said he'd "seen enough to issue his report to the insurance company." A very confused and disappointed, Blonde-Spouse saw him back to the door.

A letter soon arrived from the insurance company indicating a policy coverage change that would exclude any water damage claims unless the homeowner could show proof the home sprinkler system had been fully removed.

Begrudgingly, Blonde-Spouse disassembled his sprinkler system and Brunette-Self emailed the pictures to their agent, who then removed the water damage restriction from their policy.

3-30: DIY Dental Disclosing Rinse

"See how clean my teeth are?" said Blonde-Spouse as he emerged from the bathroom and flashed Brunette-Self a brilliant red smile.

"They are red, Honey," Brunette-Self replied.

"What? Oh no!" yelled Blonde-Spouse "I used too much! Hey, kid, stop your brushing!"

Brunette-Self cringed as Blonde-Spouse-Diminutive-Duplicate appeared with the same red mouth and teeth to ask why.

"What did you do?" demanded Brunette-Self.

"Well, you know those red dental disclosing mouth rinses? You know, those little rinses that stain your teeth red so you can brush back the plaque? And then when you check when you're done, if you see any red, you know you still need to brush there."

Smirking, Brunette-Self asked "So, did you check for red?"

"Oh, of course we did!" lied both the Blonde-Spouse and the Blonde-Spouse-Diminutive-Duplicate in unison, neither wanting to get into trouble.

"Then why are your mouths still red?" Silence.

"Well, why didn't the rinse work?" she directed at Blonde-Spouse

"Oh, well I wanted to help munchkin get better at brushing her teeth, so we looked for the mouth rinse. They were pretty expensive so we decided to make our own. We bought a bottle of red food coloring and used it right out of the bottle as the rinse. I guess the rinse is watered down or something."

It was blissfully silent for several days as they hid their mouths and teeth from view while they returned to normal color, and Brunette-Self chided herself for entertaining the wish that they had used permanent dye.

4 AN ENDING

4-1: No Peeking

Blonde-Spouse-Diminutive-Duplicate had been caught many times trying to sneak a peek at her fourth birthday presents, so Blonde-Spouse decided he would better secure the packages for her fifth birthday to assure surpise.

Blonde-Spouse vanished to the bedroom to wrap the birthday gifts. Brunette-Self kept Blonde-Spouse-Diminutive-Duplicate very busy decorating her birthday cake. Slowly, guests trickled in for her party. Blonde-Spouse reappeared from the bedroom carrying a sealed black garbage bag of presents and set them down next to the others brought by guests.

The cake was a hit, of course, which hyped up all the kids on sugar just in time to sit them all down for Blonde-Spouse-Diminutive-Duplicate to open her birthday gifts. She started with the sealed black garbage bag, struggling to open the knot in the top. In tears, she sat back down and crossed her arms. Brunette-Self suggested she move on to other gifts while Blonde-Spouse opened the bag.

Blonde-Spouse-Diminutive-Duplicate opened one gift after another, while Blonde-Spouse struggled with and swore at the black bag in the kitchen. When she'd opened the last gift, the party turned its attention to Blonde-Spouse, who was now standing on the black bag while gripping the knot and pulling upward as hard as he could. The bag stretched but refused to give way. Sighing, Brunette-Self offered to take over. Blonde-Spouse handed over the bag, which Brunette-Self promptly cut open with a pair of kitchen shears.

"Son of a--" started Blonde-Spouse and stopped abruptly when he realized the room of children staring at him.

Brunette-Self set the bag down in front of the Birthday girl, who reached in and pulled out the first gift. Blonde-Spouse had used an entire roll of scotch tape, wrapping and wrapping it around the gift in all directions. Blonde-Spouse-Diminutive-Duplicate began to cry.

"Shhh, it's ok, Pumpkintater," soothed Brunette-Self, "Maybe Daddy wanted it to be like a piñata?" The comment brought a smile to her face, and the kids went out to the park to play.

"Nice going, Hon," snarled Brunette-Self at Blonde-Spouse.

"What?" he shot back "She peeked last year and you said then you didn't want her to be able to get into her gifts next year!"

"I meant not peek at them," she retorted, "which meant we hid them better! NOT to wrap them so they couldn't be opened."

Brunette-Teenage-Son-And-Self-Designated-Peanut-Gallery-Of-Sarcastic-Commentary grabbed the hacksaw and "sawed his way in."

4-2: Dog Walking by Remote Control

They went to the local city park to have a picnic and enjoy the sunshine. Brunette-Self sat on the blanket and lazily watched the kids play Frisbee. Unbeknownst to her, Blonde-Spouse had stepped away from the blanket while she watched the kids frolick and play.

The sound of a remote control monster truck toy drew her attention away from the kids. On the pathway down the hill from them, her Scottie dog puppy tugged back in protest while she was drug along by the monster truck, driven remotely by Blonde-Spouse (whose hysterical giggling gave away that he had climbed up into the tree behind where she sat on the blanket).

"Look Honey, no hands!" he laughed, jostling the remote in the process.

The monster truck toy whirred ahead at an accelerated speed, leading the puppy ever faster directly into the parking lot, where it's full grown cousin weaved to avoid a collision. The larger truck smacked into the fence.

Blonde-Spouse reacted by tossing the remote down onto the blanket next to Brunette-Self and climbing higher in the tree.

Brunette-Self ran over to scoop up the terrified puppy, now trapped with the monster truck toy spinning its wheels in the air next to the curb on the other side of the parking lot. She then ran over to its full size cousin, now backed away from the fence.

The kindly brunette in the truck decided not to take their insurance information after she pointed to the tree. The two could see Blonde-Spouse attempting to hide from view with a tiny branch, oblivious to the fact it only hid about 7 inches of his body and the lower part of his face. The kindly brunette then introduced Brunette-Self to his blonde wife, uttered under his breath that he "knew the feeling" and made her promise to take the toy away from Blonde-Spouse permanently.

4-3: Angel Hair Pasta

Blonde-Spouse was incredibly gifted in the Chef realms, and usually his creations were a delight to the eye and palette. That evening's dinner, however, was not among them.

Brunette-Self wandered into the kitchen to observe her Blonde-Spouse-Supper-Superstar rolling a ball of dough into a ball the size of his fist.

"Hon, is that my cinnamon roll dough?" she asked, eyeing the dough in his hands.

"Yeah, I need some," Blonde-Spouse-Supper-Superstar replied as he finished rolling the ball in his hands, "I'll make you some more so you can still bake them tonight."

"Ok," replied Brunette-Self, seating herself at the kitchen table to see what Blonde-Spouse-Supper-Superstar was going to do with the dough.

Blonde-Spouse-Supper-Superstar pulled the medium sized cheese grater out of the drawer, set it across a bowl and began to run the ball of dough back and forth across the grater.

Brunette-Self watched as little dough snakes fell into the bowl and her curiosity got the better of her, "Hon, what are you doing?"

"Oh!" declared Blonde-Spouse-Supper-Superstar, "I went to grab the angel hair pasta out of the cupboard, but we were out. So I'm making pasta!"

"So, are you going to deep fry the dough or something?" she asked.

"No, that would not be good for us. I'm going to boil it!" snapped Blonde-Spouse-Supper-Superstar, dumping the bowl of dough snakes into the boiling water pan on the stove.

The pasta did hold together long enough to cook most of the way through, but what Blonde-Spouse-Supper-Superstar forgot was that Brunette-Self always added spices to her dough and that cinnamon dough had rising yeast in it. The family ate in silence while their puffed pieces of pasta enriched in Cinnamon, Nutmeg and Clove-taste clashed with the Oregano, Garlic, Onion, Rosemary and Thyme in the tomato sauce.

4-4: Traffic Trauma

Blonde-Spouse and Brunette-Self found themselves on the freeway heading into the city to run an errand. Because neither had been to the location they were headed to before, they opted to plug the address into the GPS for guidance. Blonde-Spouse, until that point, had avoided driving with the GPS in the presence of Brunette-Self due to the chiding he got from her after the Gas Station Incident (Chronicle 1-30: Gas Station Goofs.)

The GPS directed them off of the freeway and into the downtown corridor. As they pulled up to the stop light at the end of the ramp, Brunette-Self noticed the GPS and reality did not match. The GPS was directing Blonde-Spouse to turn left onto a right turn only one way street. Apparently, the GPS also 'realized the error' because it immediately began 'recalculating.' Blonde-Spouse, distracted by the GPS, did not see the light turn green and jumped in his seat as the cars behind them honked their horns.

In a panic, Blonde-Spouse followed the directions last given by the GPS and attempted to turn left (and the wrong way) in the intersection. He looked up from the GPS just in time to slam on the brakes before hitting the fire engine waiting at the light. The shocked firefighter honked his disapproval of Blonde-Spouse's navigational choice. This near collision caused Blonde-Spouse to panic even more, and he attempted to correct the car to go forward through the intersection.

That was when the two terrified occupants of the vehicle saw the police car sitting at the light on the other side of the intersection facing them, and discerned the street was yet another one way street that Blonde-Spouse was also attempting to drive up the wrong way. Blonde-Spouse corrected and turned the car again back toward the fire engine, then saw his error and finally stopped the car in the middle of the intersection.

"Would you tell me where to go already!" he screamed, picking up the GPS and throwing it on the dashboard in disgust.

The light changed and the cars on the street with the fire engine began to honk at Blonde-Spouse, causing him to throw his arms up in exasperation. Brunette-Self turned the wheel to the right and told him to drive. As Blonde-Spouse finally turned the car in the correct direction, Brunette-Self risked a glance at the officers, who were both laughing hysterically. She saw the officer driving the patrol car point to his head and mouth the word "Blonde" to his partner. The two officers decided to take pity on Blonde-Spouse and Brunette-Self and did not pull them over, instead pulling up next to them at the next light and breaking into laughter again at the sight of them. The officer driving the patrol car was still wiping tears from his eyes as the light changed and the two vehicles continued down the one way street. Brunette-Self took possession of the GPS, forced Blonde-Spouse to keep his eyes on the road, and started yelling at him.

Blonde-Spouse, stinging from her insults, retorted, "Well, I don't know why you are so mad at me, the GPS gave the wrong directions!"

The two did not speak again until they arrived at their location, when Brunette-Self snatched the keys out of his hand, "Look," she said, "the officers may have let you off the hook but being blonde is not a valid defense to a ticket. I want to get home alive."

4-5: Doorknob Defense

Brunette-Self sat blissfully and enjoyed her very first Blonde-Spouse-Diminutive-Duplicate unattended body waste-removal event since the child could walk. Part way through, Brunette-Self had an eerie feeling of being watched.

She glanced at the door and saw for the first time that someone had removed the doorknob. She also noticed an eyeball, peering through the door at her through the previously vacated doorknob hole.

"Oh, hi, Momma," came the guilty little voice of the Blonde-Spouse-Diminutive-Duplicate through the hole in the door.

Disappointed that this was not to be her first unattended bathroom visit since the birth of

Blonde-Spouse-Diminutive-Duplicate, Brunette-Self finished up and went in search of Blonde-Spouse.

As she made her way from one room to the next, Brunette-Self noted that all of the doorknobs had been removed, each door sporting a hole and a small preview of the room on the other side of it.

She discovered Blonde-Spouse in the other bathroom relieving himself, having seized an opportunity to pee without the Blonde-Spouse-Diminutive-Duplicate audience, and cornered him, "What happened to all of the doorknobs?"

"Well," hedged Blonde-Spouse, "I wasn't going to tell you, but…"

"TELL ME WHAT?!?"

"Yesterday when you were at the doctor's office, the munchkin locked herself in the bathroom by accident. She couldn't figure out how to unlock the door so I had to kick it in," he paused and flushed for effect, "So I took all of the door knobs off, except the ones to the outside doors, so she couldn't lock herself in the bathroom again."

He washed his hands and awaited her praise. Not hearing it forthcoming, he turned to look back at her in confusion.

"Hon, for the billionth time, there is a nail resting on the threshold of every door--on both sides of every door--in this house to push into the lock to open it for this very reason. Don't you remember the time you locked yourself in the closet? That is why the nails are there."

[Blonde-Spouse was still in therapy dealing with the trauma of his weekend long locked stay in the closet, so it was removed from the chronicles at the suggestion of his therapist, although it was never understood why he didn't just open the door by turning the knob from the inside.]

"Yes," sobbed Blonde-Spouse, "which is why it was so important to me to make sure it didn't happen again, especially since it was so traumatic and it also happened to our daughter."

"Well, what if we bought doorknobs without locks, then?" soothed Brunette-Self, and seriously regretted bringing up the closet trauma and decided to not point out that Blonde-Spouse could have just removed the door hinges and pulled the door off and out of the lock.

"Only if you let me put arrows on the knobs so our child knows which way they turn."

Brunette-Self agreed. She installed the new doorknobs the next day and convinced Blonde-Spouse-Diminutive-Duplicate that the Massive-Eyeball-Poking-Finger-Of-The-Super-Snoopiness-Through-The-Empty-Door-Knob-Hole-Monster would get her should she peer through in the meantime.

4-6: Car Prowler Protection

Blonde-Spouse, upon hearing a neighbor down the street had been the victim of a car prowl, had come to the conclusion that the vehicle theft deterrent systems were not enough to protect them from a prowler. Blonde-Spouse turned to a marketing campaign from his childhood for the solution.

"Hey, where is that box of kid proofing stuff we had when our daughter was a baby?" he asked of Brunette-Self.

"In the hall closet," she absently replied, focused intently on her drawing.

Blonde-Spouse retrieved the box and returned outside with it. Brunette-Self, once his question sank in and tore her away from the artwork, went outside after him. Blonde-Spouse was adding something to the windshield and did not hear her approach.

She glanced under his arm to see him affixing a Mr. Yuk sticker to the glass. He glanced over at her and volunteered an explanation, "I heard about the car prowler. The ignition kill switch won't stop them from getting in and taking the stereo and neither will The Club (3-26: The Club.) But everyone knows who Mr. Yuk is! Mr. Yuk says 'do not touch!'"

4-7: Home Improvement Challenge

An excerpt from the diary of Brunette-Self:

June 3rd
Home Improvement Challenge

Purpose: To install shower surrounds in both bathrooms so we can bathe. Should be fairly straight forward enough, the kit says it takes one day to install it.

Primary Goal: All pieces fit correctly, successful installation. No Emergency Room trips from passing out from the glue or because power tools will need to be involved.

**Note: Employed the help of his friend who kind of knows construction but has never installed shower surrounds before so he doesn't kill himself or blow up the house. A woman can dream.
Current Status: Both helpers still sleeping, having stayed up all night playing video games. It's nearly afternoon, I hope they wake up soon.

Anticipated Potential Future Status: Fully caffeinated trip to Home Depot to purchase the said surround, followed by the successful installation and much needed shower after the appropriate drying times have concluded.

Inner Battle With Sarcastic Little Narrator Voice:
Please stay with us, after the Commercial Break will be much fun and humor and several swear words while 3 non-Construction people attempt to work to install said kit in one very tiny bathroom.

June 4th
Saga of Home Improvement Challenge, continued

Frustration Creeps In...had to go to the home improvement store on my own because the deadbeats didn't wake up until nearly 2 P.M...as a result having difficulty moving today, left the two to begin installation and resorted to bed rest...One EMT visit for treatment of inhalation of fumes while flashing for his "construction oriented" friend prone to exaggerating his skills.

#$%*#@...still...no...working...bathroom.

Almost 9 PM....one panel of surround is installed and held onto the wall with enough wood brace supports to have leveled a forest. They had to reinstall all of the supports again when hubby attempted to climb on them like he would a tree, had to perform minor surgery on his left buttocks to remove the splinter. Drowned myself in perfume because my own stench is making my eyes water. Debating if I can get away with washing up in the local fast food bathroom without getting myself arrested. Must ponder this. Might be worth the risks involved.

June 5th
Saga of Home Improvement Challenge, still
continued

Panels in one bathroom now braced against the walls with even more wood. I noticed the panel they installed yesterday is one half inch higher up the wall than the three they put in today. Still on bed rest, so I didn't see their mistake until the glue had hardened too much to move the panels. Decided we could hide both ends of the surround with trim, need to shower strong now and affecting my decision making skills. Quality is suffering as a result but I smell so bad now I don't care. I tried to use diaper wipes to clean up but now I smell like stale perfume, armpit and baby powder. Surround will still need to have the plumbing fixtures reinstalled and will have to be trimmed and caulked, which should take another few days. No medical interventions required, today was a good day.

June 6th
Saga of Home Improvement Challenge, AGAIN

The two made progress today, getting all of the surround installed and braced in the Master Bathroom. Think I'm hallucinating on the glue fumes, but I didn't even mind my husband had cut the hole for the tub faucet too low and had to enlarge the hole nearly a foot to accommodate it. I figure I can just put a tile mosaic art piece around the faucet and along the top and bottom of the surround, because the blind morons got every single panel at a different height on the wall and none of them match up. Got creative tonight and bathed in the sink while I did the dishes. Wish I could wash better, though, I can still smell armpit. Of course, that might be my two "helpers." I installed the trim and caulked the other surround today, should be ready to use in another day.

June7th
Saga of Home Improvement Challenge, will it ever $#@^&*$ end?

The goofball nearly burned his face off today, trying to light a match in the bathroom after his bowel movement and igniting the remaining glue fumes in a small flash fire. His mishaps would really be funny if they didn't involve so much property damage.

We couldn't work on the Master Bathroom today, the smoke drove us out of the house for too long to get anything done. Well, at least I got to eat out for dinner! Tipped the waitress extra because she had the fortitude to stand above our stench and still serve us with a smile. It rained all day, so the caulking isn't dry yet. Stopped off at in-laws after dinner and we all finally got to take a shower, my nose is most completely r-e-l-i-e-v-e-d.

June 8th
Saga of Home Improvement Challenge HELL

The caulking finally dried enough to use one bathroom. Two of the panels slid down the wall a bit but they actually line up now, with only two panels in the back not lining up. It looks like the corner piece is crooked because the left side of the panel top lines up with the surround on the adjacent wall but not the right side, it's about an inch above the panel next it on the wall. *sigh* I tiled the top and bottom of the Master Bath surround using bigger tiles to cover up the crooked corner panel top, but the mosaic is going to take some time. In the meantime we all have to share a bathroom, so I made a schedule for everyone.

The kids joked today about suffocating Dad with a pillow, but I'm not sure they were kidding...will keep an eye on them, just in case. Besides, I think the little one might be suffering brain damage from the fumes that still stink up the house. Have all the windows open and fans going, but it is still unbearable.

June 11th
cry

Mosaic is complete and drying overnight, tomorrow I'll be ready to caulk the surround. Picked up new drapes for the bathroom window since he torched the other ones in the flash fire incident. Just glad only one wall will have to be repainted, the others should come clean with a good scrubbing. House still reeks of smoke and glue fumes. I'll probably have to clean all the curtains and walls in *the house to get rid of the smell, maybe shampoo the carpets and furniture, too. I'd make him do it but I just know that will lead to more clean up, and possibly an electrical fire. The idiot admitted he'd used twice as much glue as required. No wonder the house reeks so much.*

July 3rd
FINALLY

We are FINALLY DONE with installing both shower surrounds and cleaning up the smoke damage! I celebrated today by taking a bubble bath! I have also decided any major installations from here on out would be worth paying a contractor to complete and could potentially save lives.

4-8: Star Spangled Screw Up

Blonde-Spouse took the kids over to the reservation to buy fireworks and support our local tribe. Brunette-Self had sent him with $80, enough to pick up a few fireworks but to price him out of most of the more dangerous ones. She figured the fireworks stands were temporary so they'd be cash only, especially since the stands had no electricity. Little did she know the tribe used generator power, not only giving them lighting but also giving them power to run debit card machines.

The trio returned nearly two hours later, $350 poorer and with a trunk full of fireworks ranging from sparklers to finale packages that would rival a professional pyrotechnics show.

"They took debit cards!" declared Blonde-Spouse as they unloaded the boxes, "so I took the kids to lunch with the $80 you gave me."

Mentally switching that nights BBQ menu from steak and chicken kabobs to hotdogs, Brunette-Self started preparing the yard for that night's fireworks show. She hosed down the house, fence and everything in the yard. She filled 5-gallon buckets full of water and spaced them throughout the yard. She concluded her preparations by removing the extra propane tanks and carefully winding the hose on the ground so it could be unwound quickly if the need arose. She attempted to help Blonde-Spouse get the launching pad ready for the mortars, but he refused her help and continued to work in secret.

Family and friends enjoyed the holiday and filled up on traditional BBQ foods and settled in to lawn chairs with throw blankets wrapped around them as the sky grew dark. Blonde-Spouse gathered the kids around him and pulled out the first box of sparklers. He removed all of them from the package and held them as a bundle in his hand, grasping the wrong end of the sparkler. He tried for several minutes to light the metal handles, until a helpful child suggested he turn them around. Distracted, his hand moved and the sparklers ignited in blinding ferocity, scattering screaming children.

Blonde-Spouse hurled the sparklers, launching them outward and into the back of the house where they dropped to the ferns below and scorched them.

Children began to cry as parents rushed in to check fingers, toes, nose and other body parts for burn or injury. Blonde-Spouse did a quick visual double check of the munchkin and their son to make sure both were still whole and unmarred.

Brunette-Teenage-Son-And-Self-Designated-Peanut-Gallery-Of-Sarcastic-Commentary jumped into action and doused the flames with the first 5-gallon bucket of water. Blonde-Spouse was hopping up and down, holding his hand and yelling. He'd managed to burn several of his fingertips, though not too severly.

After a heated debate in the kitchen with Brunette-Self, the two returned to their confused guests in the yard. Blonde-Spouse was now sporting a gallon sized Ziploc bag full of ice on his right hand, duct taped around the wrist to help hold it on.

Apologizing for the delay and shooing away his persistent wife, Blonde-Spouse started the next round of fireworks--the spinning flowers, fountains and roman candles. Upon seeing these, most of their guests excused themselves quickly and thanked them for the day, nearly stumbling over themselves in their haste to escape. A few brave souls remained, and the second round of fireworks were uneventful and enjoyable, lulling them into a false sense of security and wellbeing.

Blonde-Spouse brought out round three of the fireworks--bottle rockets and mortars. He stuck the bottle rockets into the ground, and these fired off as expected. It was really dark by this time, so no one noticed when he brought out the mortar launching pad that he'd attached the launching tubes to the plywood with duct tape instead of nails. Earlier in the day, he had wound the fuses of groups of mortars together to light several off at once. The force of the mortars projecting from the tubs pried loose the duct tape but the tubes held upright, so the launchers now merely sat upon the board. Blonde-Spouse dropped in the second group of mortars and then lit them with his free hand. The first launcher dropped before the mortar launched, bringing the others over with it. All of the launchers were now pointed directly at the remaining few guests and their lawn chairs. People again scattered, as the mortars launched into the back of the house and shattered in an explosion of multi-colored fire and pretty sparks showers.

Blonde-Spouse grabbed the hose and flipped on the faucet, running for the back of the house as it started to catch fire. Blonde-Spouse caught the hose on the corner of the gazebo where it stopped short and knocked him off of his feet and out of breath. Brunette-Self grabbed the hose and started spraying down the back of the house, while stunned guests regained their composure and picked up the buckets strewn about the yard to attack the fire. Once everyone was sure the fire was out and that no one was injured, they intervened upon Blonde-Spouse and forcefully set him in a chair for the rest of the evening to nurse his burnt fingers.

Brunette-Teenage-Son-And-Self-Designated-Peanut-Gallery-Of-Sarcastic-Commentary quietly burst into song with his own version of the Star Spangled Banner "…and the rockets red glare, the bombs bursting in hair. Gave proof, through the night, that the Blonde was still there…" but dwindled off under the glare of Brunette-Self. She then tasked him with completing the grand finale. The grand finale was impressive enough to keep their friends and family from suing them but not enough for them to want to celebrate another 4th of July with Blonde-Spouse in charge of the fireworks show. Brunette-Self couldn't blame them and was content to attend someone else's party next year to save money for the Vacation Fund Jar.

4-9: Digging a Hole to China

Brunette-Self was enjoying a nice hot shower on Saturday afternoon. She had just lathered her hair and was standing with her head tipped back rinsing in the warm rain of the showerhead when the sun came out. Brunette-Self opened her eyes to gaze upon the dry showerhead. Feeling apprehensive, she turned around and started toying with the faucets, neither responding to her requests for water. Brunette-Self dried off and wrapped a towel around her soapy hair, slipped on her bathrobe and headed for the water main in the backyard.

There, in the yard stood Mr. Blonde-Spouse and Miss Blonde-Spouse-Diminutive-Duplicate waist deep in what appeared to be a large sinkhole full of muddy water. On second glance, Brunette-Self thought the sinkhole actually looked more like a bubbling fountain, as a geyser of water shot up out of the middle and the pond water crested quickly out of the sinkhole and onto the lawn.

Blonde-Spouse and Brunette-Self both made a beeline for the water main switch on the other side of the yard, while Blonde-Spouse-Diminutive-Duplicate tried in vain to extracate herself from the growing sinkhole. Her cries redirected Brunette-Self to her rescue, while Blonde-Spouse lifted off the pine elephant coffin cover and began unwinding the cotton candy insulation mountain buried in it (3-18: Weatherizing the Water Meter.) Brunette-Self saved Blonde-Spouse-Diminutive-Duplicate and carried her to safety. Without thinking, Brunette-Self removed her bathrobe and wrapped it around the child.

Brunette-Self ran to help Blonde-Spouse, now struggling with the coiled snake shaped cotton candy insulation mountain as it clung to his wet body. The two finally uncovered the water meter shut off switch and turned off the geyser.

A split second passed before Brunette-Self realized she now stood naked in the backyard covered in insulation with a lopsided towel on her head of soapy wet hair. The realization was followed immediately by panic and horror at the sound of a voice on the other side of the gate.

"Everything okay back there?" asked the Nervous-Neighbor, having seen Old Faithful's appearance in their backyard.

Brunette-Self glanced to the gate in time to see his hand reach over to unlatch it, "Just a second!" she yelled and ran for the backdoor.

Blonde-Spouse waited for her to get in the door before he let Nervous-Neighbor in through the gate, Brunette-Self saw a glimpse of the Nervous-Neighbor dropping his jaw before the backdoor slammed shut. The insulation started to itch and irritate her skin, but she threw on a sundress and went immediately back outside.

Blonde-Spouse was scratching his now fuzzy pink body and talking to Nervous-Neighbor, "We were digging a hole to China. Blonde-Spouse-Diminutive-Duplicate got the idea from a kid at school and since she's always wanted to go I thought it would be cheaper and more fun than flying there."

Nervous-Neighbor and Nervous-Neighbor's-Soon-To-Be-Son-In-Law-But-Right-Now-Because-They-Are-Taking-It-Slow-Sort-Of-Boyfriend-Of-His-Daughter-And-Sometimes-Handyman-Dan helped to repair the water line, and the three very drenched and very itchy misadventurers were soon able to shower and wash away their misdeeds.

Unfortunately, their misdeeds clogged the bathtub drain again. Brunette-Self seized the opportunity to fix the drain before Blonde-Spouse could get ahold of it, and ran the snake down to retrieve the bits of pink fluff that had nestled in the drainpipe.

4-10: DIY Diatomaceous Earth

The Blonde-Spouse-Garden-Guru had been watching too many garden shows. He'd learned to compost and now wanted to try his hand at organic pest control. Brunette-Self had banned him from natural predator controls (reader referred to Chronicle 2-24: Ladybug Barrage), so he researched alternatives for slugs and settled on sprinkling diatomaceous earth (DE)* in the garden beds.

Diatomaceous earth (DE) is made of diatoms (microscopic skeletons of algae-like plants.) It is made up of magnesium, silicon, calcium, sodium, iron and other trace minerals like titanium, boron, manganese, copper and zirconium. When sprinkled on the ground, DE is used as a natural barrier for insets and slugs, having small razor sharp edges that cut into the body of the creature attempting to crawl over it. The creature succumbs to the cuts and the plants inside the DE ring are thus protected from these predators.

Brunette-Self assumed the DE he was sprinkling on the beds came from the nursery she'd just sent him to, so she sent him out to coat the garden beds using the hand held fertilizer spreader.

Blonde-Spouse-Garden-Guru followed his DE spreading by laying two inches of mulch on top of it. Brunette-Self knew this immediately negated any affect the DE would have on combating slugs but decided to allow the Blonde-Spouse-Garden-Guru the opportunity to learn this lesson on his own in time. She reasoned the DE was harmless, anyway, although it was a wasted expense now covered by mulch.

The Pacific Northwest rains lightly watered the garden over the next few days, keeping the two from the garden. The next sunny day drew them back outside, where Brunette-Self noticed several of her "newly protected" plants had become yellow and completely wilted.

She confronted Blonde-Spouse-Garden-Guru about the DE he'd spread on the beds. He immediately confessed to "making some adjustments."

After pricing diatomaceous earth, Blonde-Spouse-Garden-Guru concluded it would be more frugal to make his own. He couldn't figure out how to get diatoms, so he omitted them from the recipe and focused on mixing the minerals instead. He'd managed to get most of the minerals listed in the ingredients on the DE box covered by crushing up a bottle of childrens chewable multi-vitamins** "plus it made a pretty rainbow." He had used table salt for the sodium and substituted pennies for the copper on the list. He had smashed dishes for the "sharp edges to replace the diatoms, I looked for them but I couldn't find them."

Blonde-Spouse-Garden-Guru and Brunette-Self spent the rest of the day raking up as much of the mulch and "DE" as they could. Brunette-Self enacted a new house safety rule that evening, "No Barefoot Gardening for the next several years."

** *Children's chewable vitamins included both the gelatin and powder form vitamins. Blonde-Spouse-Garden-Guru had placed both in the food processor for several minutes. It took six runs through the dishwasher to remove the gelatin blobs from the food processor.*

4-11: Flash and Fine

The local community had installed traffic cameras in the school zone. Brunette-Self and Blonde-Spouse were watching the news when the story came on, and Brunette-Self reminded Blonde-Spouse the next morning as he left for work to remember the traffic camera was now in the school zone. Even though school was out in the Summer the news had warned the camera would still be active. Blonde-Spouse went off to and returned from work without incident or comment.

Brunette-Self assumed Blonde-Spouse had heeded the warning and had slowed down in the school zone or had found an alternate route to work. The rest of the work week went well, until Brunette-Self retrieved the mail that fateful Friday.

The mail contained an 'official' looking envelope from the local district court. Opening it, Brunette-Self revealed a $124 speeding ticket showing three photographs of Blonde-Spouse speeding through the school zone.

When she confronted him regarding the ticket, he puffed up and defended himself, "I saw the traffic camera and thought if I sped up I could get out of the frame before the picture was taken."

Blonde-Spouse had to pick up some overtime hours in order to pay the fine.

4-12: Wash and Wax Windows

Blonde-Spouse and Brunette-Self spent a large sum of money paying a local window company to build and install custom double hung vinyl windows in their home. The windows came with a lifetime guarantee and a year supply of window cleaner. A major selling point for Brunette-Self was the ability of the windows to be tipped inside, so one could wash both sides of the window from inside the home. This tipping in for easy cleaning made it easier to reach and better clean the windows, and the company window cleaner did a fantastic job of cleaning off dirt and wiping off streak free.

The first sunny day of Spring bit Brunette-Self with spring fever and she was excited to wash her new windows for the first time. When she went to retrieve the cleaner, she found the box the company had given them was empty. She confronted Blonde-Spouse, who admitted he'd used them to clean all of the metal faucets and appliances in their home so they were "especially shiny!" (Chronicle 2-28: The Shiny)

The disappointment on her face must have been obvious, as Blonde-Spouse offered to wash the windows for her. Brunette-Self agreed and used her time to prep dinner. Blonde-Spouse grabbed the bucket and sponge mop and started outside. Brunette-Self rolled her eyes, put her prep work away and wandered after him. She found him in the driveway, having already wet down the windows. He was busily mopping the windows with a Pine Sol solution and then hosing them down. When he saw his wife, he grabbed the hose and started rinsing the windows, the sounds of rushing water splashing interjected with objections of Blonde-Spouse-Diminutive-Duplicate, who had been sitting on the other side of the window in the living room, now being drenched with hose water and Pine Sol. Blonde-Spouse had forgotten to check that the windows were completely shut before he'd started his cleaning procedure.

Brunette-Self went back inside with a sigh to tend to Blonde-Spouse-Diminutive-Duplicate. She washed her hair and scrubbed the Pine Sol off in the tub. After Blonde-Spouse-Diminutive-Duplicate got dressed, the two went back outside to check on Blonde-Spouse. Blonde-Spouse was finishing the last window, this time mopping with yet another sponge mop.

Brunette-Self could smell what seemed to be linoleum floor wax, "Honey, is that Mop and Glo?"

"Yes!" he declared, proud of himself, "Now the water will bead up on the windows and make prisms in the sunlight instead of streak them!"

Brunette-Self turned on her heel and returned to the house. Going to the computer, she started researching products that could strip floor wax.

4-13: Purple Pancakes

Blonde-Spouse was determined to make it up to Brunette-Self for forgetting their anniversary. He chose to make her breakfast in bed, and got up extra early to prepare a feast. He knew blackberries were her favorite, so he made blackberry pancakes with bacon and eggs.

Brunette-Self was woken gently by a tray set down over her. She sat up and saw that Blonde-Spouse had made her breakfast in bed. Touched, she thanked him and blew him a kiss. She sat and sipped her coffee, taking in the bacon and eggs with a smile. Her smile faltered when her eyes spied two purple discs covered in syrup.

"Hon?" she inquired, "What are those?"

"Blackberry pancakes! Your favorite!" replied Blonde-Spouse.

The "pancakes" were a deep crusty looking purple, appearing 'bruised' under the maple syrup. Once she got past their appearance they were actually quite tasty.

"I think you're supposed to add the berries after you've mixed the pancake batter," she mumbled through a mouth full of food.

"But then they wouldn't be purple! That's your favorite color, isn't it? Besides, you won't let me near the food coloring since the mouthwash thing!" he retorted (Chronicle 3-30: DIY Dental Disclosing Rinse.)

"They're still delicious, though, honey, thank you!"

Blonde-Spouse bade a quick exit to "clean up" the kitchen. Brunette-Self continued to enjoy her breakfast in bed. When she finished, she returned the tray of dishes to the kitchen, where Blonde-Spouse was standing on the table wiping down the fan.

"Whatcha doin??" she asked, setting down the tray on the counter.

"Well, I guess I had the mixer on too high making the pancakes, cause there's little purple splatters all over the kitchen," What Blonde-Spouse had not realized was that blackberry juice stains about as well as Kool-Aid or the red food coloring he and Blonde-Spouse-Diminutive-Duplicate had dyed their teeth with, "I'll just repaint the kitchen."

Rather than risk another Chronicle, Brunette-Self took the painting of the kitchen into her own hands.

4-14: Beehive Blunder

The Blonde-Spouse-Diminutive-Duplicate had developed a keen interest in studying bees, butterflies and flower life cycles. Brunette-Self-Scientist was ecstatic by her interest, and the two poured over books and web pages together researching the subject. They wanted to raise honey bees, but Brunette-Self had suggested the two could build a butterfly hutch and collect caterpillars to raise into butterflies to be released before committing them to a bee farm.

It was still early Spring, and the mornings had been frosty. This morning was no exception, with a thick layer of frost still covering the windshield, Miss Blonde-Spouse-Diminutive-Duplicate and Brunette-Self set off to buy supplies early the next morning. Brunette-Self gave herself a mental pat on the back for giving the two ample time to construct the butterfly hutch before the caterpillars made their appearance.

Not to be outdone, Blonde-Spouse went out to hunt for beehives to start the bee farm. He had amassed a half a dozen hives of different types on the kitchen table by the time they had returned from the store.

Hearing them pull into the driveway, he rushed out to meet them, "I collected some hives for the bee farm! Come and check these out!"

Brunette-Self shrugged and followed the two inside, knowing Blonde-Spouse-Diminutive-Duplicate could view their construction up close.

Brunette-Self took a quick leave to use the bathroom, when a bunch of screaming and yelling from the kitchen had ushered her to hurry up and investigate. Blonde-Spouse and Blonde-Spouse-Diminutive-Duplicate were shrieking and batting at the air above the kitchen table, now swarming with half awake and very angry bees. Apparently, Blonde-Spouse had not selected empty hives but hibernating hives, now awake in the warmth of the kitchen and very cranky.

"I'm grabbing the hose!" yelled Blonde-Spouse as he ran out the door, taking part of the swarm with him. Brunette-Self grabbed the child and held her still and close to her body, the angry bees now moving further away in their confusion, and slowly withdrew to the bathroom, where she tossed the child inside clothing and all and turned on the shower. The remaining stragglers soon abandoned their assault of the little one, and wandered lazily back to their hives on the kitchen table. Leaving her huddled in the shower, Brunette-Self moved slowly throughout the house opening doors and windows as she went. She turned off the heater and began a fan in front of the door, bringing in the chilly air to cool the house as quickly as possible.

She went slowly back to the bathroom to check on Blonde-Spouse-Diminutive-Duplicate, who was still huddled and crying in the shower. A quick check showed that amazingly, she had not been stung. Blonde-Spouse, returning wet and shivering from the yard, had not been so lucky. His face and hands began to swell quickly. Brunette-Self helped to get the two dried off and dressed while waiting for the ambulance to arrive. The paramedics gave Blonde-Spouse an antihistamine injection and pulled the stingers out with tweezers, and provided Brunette-Self with a list of symptoms to watch for in case further medical care was needed. It took about an hour for the swarm to return to the warmth of the hive, and Brunette-Self was able to don gloves, place them in an empty 5-gallon bucket with a lid and relocate the hives down along the river.

Brunette-Self and Blonde-Spouse-Diminutive-Duplicate would still like to have a bee farm, but Blonde-Spouse refused to discuss it.

4-15: Creative Coat Rack

Blonde-Spouse and Brunette-Self agreed that both were tired of their bed becoming the coat rack when guests arrived, so the two began shopping for a coat rack. Neither could agree on what style to buy, so Blonde-Spouse dropped Brunette-Self off at home and (unbeknownst to her) went in search of supplies to make one.

He arrived at the local thrift store, where he located a wrought iron stand to use as a base. He took his new purchase down to the auto wrecking yard, where he began sorting through parts that would work with the new wrought iron stand. After he found what he was looking for, he paid an additional fee to have the staff person weld the part onto the wrought iron stand.

He returned home and asked Brunette-Self to go into another room while he carried in the new coat rack and put it in to action. Content in his arrangement, he brought her out in to the room and pulled off the sheet he had over the top of his new coat rack. The coat rack consisted of a truck steering wheel column welded into a wrought iron stand. Shower curtain hooks hung along the wheel, so that coats could be hung around the wheel. The steering wheel coat rack functioned well.

4-16: In an Air of Confusion, Just Sleep On It

Blonde-Spouse offered to depart before the rest of the family to procure and hold their favorite camping spot for the first trip of the season. He said he'd take the dog with him and start setting up the camp, "so you can roll into a set up campsite."

After making sure she was carrying all of the fuel and fire and shushing Brunette-Teenage-Son-And-Self-Designated-Peanut-Gallery-Of-Sarcastic-Commentary, Brunette-Self agreed. Brunette-Self added that she and the kids would be a few hours behind him as they had to do a few chores and the grocery and supply shopping for the trip. After a quick gauge and exterior check of the van by Brunette-Self, Blonde-Spouse and Scottie-Dog-Co-Pilot-And-Co-Adventurer departed for the woods.

The trio finished watering the garden and yard and soon left for the grocery store. It was nearly 3 pm when they finally drove into the clearing of the family favorite camp spot, expecting to be greeted with a full camp kitchen, two tents, a porta-potty bathroom set up, a built fire pit, a writhing-wagging Scottie dog and a smiling Blonde-Spouse already sporting a dirty face. Instead, they were greeted with the van, one tent and a sleeping Blonde-Spouse and Scottie-Dog on top of the air mattress inflated between the van and the tent door.

"I told you he'd need brunette supervision and assistance," started Brunette-Teenage-Son-And-Self-Designated-Peanut-Gallery-Of-Sarcastic-Commentary, who had earlier lived up to his name trying to escape the watering and shopping chores, "you should have let me come with him."

"Well, you can assist him now, smart mouth," shot back annoyed Brunette-Self, directing him to the set up of the porta-potty portable bathroom for the now "I gotta go pee pee" dancing Blonde-Spouse-Diminutive-Duplicate.

Brunette-Self sent the two kids off and proceeded over to the air mattress and her sleeping Blonde-Spouse. She shook him awake. He stretched and yawned and opened an eye, bolting upright and stumbled over himself in his effort to explain, "I got one tent set up and blew up our air mattress--but then I couldn't get it through the door. At first I tried to force it, but it knocked the tent halfway back down so I had to set it up again. Then I thought I could just cut the door wider with a knife, but then I knew you would be mad at me. So I sat down to think about it and must have fallen asleep," he dwindled off, looking sheepish.

"Going to get it all set up, huh? Enjoy your nap did you?" Brunette-Self snapped as she pulled the plug underneath sitting Blonde-Spouse and still sleeping Scottie-Dog, who had by now proven herself completely worthless in her guard dog duties. The air whooshed out of the mattress, quickly connecting Blonde-Spouse buttocks with the ground and startling the sleeping Scottie-Dog. He rolled off of the bed, and Brunette-Self swooped it into her arms. She carried it in to the tent, rolled it out on the floor and replaced the plug. She then walked by her confused and watching Blonde-Spouse, and grabbed the air pump, still plugged into the cigarette lighter of the van.

"Oh! Inflate it IN the tent!" he declared, smacking his forehead.

Dragging the pump nozzle and hose back through the tent door, she put it in the air mattress and yelled back at him to turn on the van and the pump.

"Uh oh," he responded.

"YOU DIDN'T TURN THE VAN OFF BEFORE YOU SAT DOWN TO THINK ABOUT IT?!?" she screamed.

"Whoops."

"Gah!" spewed a very disgruntled Brunette-Self as she came out of the tent and sent Blonde-Spouse away with the other tent in hand to begin construction. She pulled the car between the now dead van and the tent and inflated the mattress. Brunette-Self then jumped the van with the car and left it running to charge the battery while she unloaded the sleeping gear into the tent.

The kids were done with the porta-potty set up, so Brunette-Self sent the two back to town in the car to buy gas for the van and two large gas cans to carry it in. She then moved the van over to the other tent and repeated inflating the kids air mattresses, turning it off and leaving it parked next to it.

She tasked Blonde-Spouse with unloading and stacking the firewood and building the fire pit while she put together the camp kitchen. As she completed the camp kitchen, she went over to the fire pit to re-build it to a third of the size Blonde-Spouse had constructed it and sent him down to the river to collect dishwater to boil.

Brunette-Self had just gotten a good fire going when the kids returned from town with gas for the van. Too tired to cook after battling the grocery store and setting up camp, she speared hotdogs on skewers and handed them off to the kids to cook their own dinner. She then moved the Blonde-Spouse stacked fire wood 20 feet further away from the fire pit and to safety.

"I had it next to the fire pit so the wood could be dry if it rained," offered Blonde-Spouse to the by now nearly deaf ears of his bitterly angry brunette wife, watching as she drug the wood to a safe distance away and covered it with a tarp, "I didn't cover it with the tarp because the fire would melt it."

"The tarp is to keep it dry, DEAR," snapped an exasperated Brunette-Self.

Realizing there was no pleasing her that night, he fell to silence and roasted his dinner.

Exhausted, she put Brunette Teenage-Son-And-Self-Designated-Peanut-Gallery-Of-Sarcastic-Commentary in charge of the fire pit and went to bed before the sun went down.

4-17: Portable Perk Pot

Brunette-Self awoke at dawn and found her way out of the tent. She could smell brewing coffee in the air and was concerned she hadn't hidden the long handled lighters to the camp stove well enough from Blonde-Spouse, whowas missing from her side when she awoke that morning.

"Morning, Sweet Cheeks!" called Blonde-Spouse, standing by the trunk of the car holding a large silver object, "I couldn't find the long handled lighters to brew coffee on the camp stove, but lucky for us I found the 32-cup perk pot in the trunk of the car! I guess we forgot to unload it when we'd picked it up at your mom's house."

Brunette-Self noticed he'd wrapped a rope around the perk pot and had tied it to the antenna, occasionally sliding the perk pot back up slightly curved and exceptionally shiny (Chronicle 1-21: Car Maintenance Mistakes) trunk lid. The perk pot would again start to descend down the trunk lid slowly, sliding in slow motion down the curve until Blonde-Spouse would diligently push it back up the 'slide' again.

"Is the rope a safety tether to keep it from falling off of the trunk?" she inquired, as she turned her head toward a whirring noise coming from the driver's seat.

"Yes!" he responded, "It's nearly done perking, coffee soon!"

Brunette-Self continued along the length of the car to peer in the drivers window, where the car power outlet adapter plug sat on the seat, smoking.

"Uh, Hon," she started and turned toward Blonde-Spouse, "I don't think the adapter is supposed to smoke. Did you check your amperage ratings?"

Blonde-Spouse shoved her out of the way and tore open the car door, "It's starting to catch fire!" he yelled and instinctively reached down to pop open the trunk, where the fire extinguisher was located.

"NNNNNNNNNNNNN--" was all she could get out as she rushed to stop him, the lever releasing the trunk which sprung open in response.

The spring loaded opening trunk launched the still brewing perk pot into the air where it smashed into the top of the back window as it reached the end of it's "safety tether," shooting scalding coffee grounds and boiling coffee water all over the car, woods and the stunned two standing by the car door.

Their screams brought the head of Sleepy Brunette Teenage-Son-And-Self-Designated-Peanut-Gallery-Of-Sarcastic-Commentary (SBTSASDPGOSC) out of the front of the kids tent, "You guys ok?"

Brunette-Self grabbed the fire extinguisher in the trunk through the back of the fold down seats and released a little on the fire. She unplugged and disconnected the pot and adapters, when SBTSASDPGOSC appeared at her side.

She tasked Brunette Teenage-Son-And-Self-Designated-Peanut-Gallery-Of-Sarcastic-Commentary with brewing another pot of coffee--this time on the camp stove--while she and Blonde-Spouse went for a morning skinny dip in the glacial water of the nearby stream to wash off the coffee ground napalm and soothe

the developing burns on their skin. Kindly-Brunette-Teenage-Son also got a good fire going for the two to shiver next to while they drank the camp stove coffee. Brunette-Self sent him in to town with money for the car wash and a little extra for a treat for himself.

Blonde-Spouse was designated porta-potty emptying and water retrieving duties for the rest of the camping trip.

4-18: Directionally Challenged

Brunette-Self and Blonde-Spouse were trying the "back way" out of the town they were visiting, and departed down the rural highway toward the junction for the mountain pass that would ultimately lead them home. Brunette-Self drove while Blonde-Spouse "navigated." She didn't notice his misdirection until he argued the turn should be left instead of right. She risked a glance at her passenger and noticed he was holding the map upside down.

Frustrated, she reached out and turned it around in his hands and thus missed the junction turn for the mountain pass. The two continued to drive along the rural highway for what seemed to be hours. Both cell phones were dead, so they were unsure of exactly how long they had been driving. When a gas station appeared on the horizon, Brunette-Self steered them in to check their directions.

The two walked in to the store and inquired of the clerk. The-Helpful-Clerk grabbed a map off of the rack and opened it up on the counter. The three peered at the map.

"You are here," she said pointing to an area on the map about one inch south of the Canadian border, "The turn you want is back here," as her finger moved down and across the map nearly 5 inches, "You missed your turn about 3 hours ago. Would you like to buy this map? We sell them for $3.49."

Brunette-Self declined the offer explaining the map was "beyond the Blonde," and giving a nod to Blonde-Spouse. Thanking the clerk, they made a quick pay phone call to let family know they'd be even later as they'd detoured nearly to Canada. They gassed up the car and turned around.

Blonde-Spouse suggested they go to Canada anyway, since the two were so close. Brunette-Self declined stating the marshals at the checkpoint would most likely not accept "we got lost" as a valid reason to visit Canada, even with Blonde-Spouse holding the map in his lap.

Blonde-Spouse went back to "navigating," again holding the map upside down. Brunette-Self made a mental note to remember the GPS next time.

4-19: "The Portable Coffee and Cigarette Break"

After the Perk Pot incident (4-17: Portable Perk Pot) , Blonde-Spouse-Insane-Inventor was at it again. He'd decided to develop an alternative to coffee that didn't involve launching coffee ground napalm.

He had Brunette-Self roll and extra pack of cigarettes, which he promptly disappeared with. He did not return with them, so Brunette-Self quickly forgot about his odd request. A week later, the two woke up to begin their day.

"I've got something for us to try this morning" said Blonde-Spouse as he reached out to stop Brunette-Self from brewing their morning pot of coffee. Brunette-Self recognized this must be important for Blonde-Spouse to get between her and her first cup of coffee, so she reluctantly agreed to be led away.

He sat her down on the couch and reached into his pocket, pulling out the pack of cigarettes she'd rolled the week before. He removed what appeared to be a brown cigarette out of the package, and handed it to her.

"I call it the 'Portable Coffee and Cigarette Break'" he said, lighting the brown cigarette for her, "I soaked the pack in coffee for two days and then let it dry out in the sun."

Brunette-Self inhaled the cigarette and nearly choked on the still wet tobacco inside. She had to admit it 'tasted something like coffee' but it just wasn't the same as having a cup.

"I don't think this has the same caffeine content as a cup of coffee, honey," she said and stood to return to the coffee pot and brew their morning Joe.

"Nah, I've got it," he said, dejected, as he wandered in to make the pot.

He returned a few moments later with a big grin on his face and a steaming cup of coffee for Brunette-Self. Gratefully, she took the cup from his hands and took a large drink. Immediately she realized he'd put something else in the coffee and spit it out, "WTF?"

"Oh, well, you said the coffee cigarette didn't have enough caffeine, so I dumped the tobacco out of the cigarettes and into the pot, a reverse portable cigarette break, for the smoker in the non smoking area."

Brunette-Self advised Blonde-Spouse that nicotine ingested can be poisonous, Blonde-Spouse greened in response and picked up the phone to call 911. After the two left the ER with Blonde-Spouse rubbing his freshly pumped stomach, Brunette-Self made him promise to end any quest to create a portable coffee and cigarette break.

4-20: My VERY Near Death Experience, by Blonde-Spouse

When Brunette-Self began this chronicle, it was not with the support of Blonde-Spouse. He felt she was using it just to make fun of him.

What he did not realize was writing the Chronicle had kept him still married and alive all these years. As the chronicles expanded and integrated into the running joke of the family, Blonde-Spouse started to become supportive of them. At the end of his exploits, he would now turn to his Brunette Wife and state, "Now there's an entry for ya!" One afternoon, he asked if he could write his own. Shocked and delighted, Brunette-Self agreed.

Without further ado, his Chronicle:

"My Near Death Experience, By Blonde-Spouse"

I thought I'd take a turn at writing one of these thingies, since the wifey is always jotting things down in her mental notebook and recording them later...now it's my turn!

Yesterday, Brunette-Wifey was being a real fuss-n-boots about every little thing and getting all snarly. She nearly bit my head off when I washed the laundry but forgot to put in the soap. Geesh, it's not like they didn't get rinsed so I don't know why it was such a big deal, but she hit the roof and yelled at me for, like, ever about it. She stopped when I started to cry and said she was sorry, she had PMS and just was really cranky about everything. I should have just accepted her apology and left it at that, but I felt I had to be helpful and offer her some advice. This turned out to be an error on my part.

I had absolutely no idea what was in store for me, and to be honest, even if I did know the look on her on her face was totally worth the terror that came afterward. Had I but known I could get to her this way, well, let's just say I'm going to make it an occasional practice to do so. You know, live on the edge sort of thing. The kind of adventure that makes you think you are young and stupid again. The feeling of a first kiss, or a roller coaster ride, or the unknown – what will happen next? Let's find out, shall we? Soooo....

I told Brunette-Bitchy-Wifey that when she admits and apologizes for being cranky with PMS, that she should announce her bitchiness and the reason for it to everyone in her life* and offer bitchiness restitution** to those she unleashed it on, that these were part of the 12 steps to recovery for PMS.***

---

*Note to Self: Do not ever, never, ever, EVER tell PMS wifey she is being a bitch...even if she admits to it.

NEVER EVER EVER tell PMS wifey she should make it up to me by dressing up like a cheerleader and performing a pom pom routine for me in the bedroom. AND WHATEVER I DO NEVER EVER EVER EVER EVER EVER EVER tell her that I think that maybe just maybe she isn't as hot as my favorite sex symbol at that moment. **NEVER.

***And NEVER EVER EVER EVER EVER think she's incapable of launching a cast iron skillet like a Frisbee.

The next thing I know, my life is flashing before my eyes. I see my Brunette-Wifey has saved my life quite a lot, literally. As I started to come to, I also realized my Brunette-Wifey was just as capable of taking it away and making it look like an accident. I kept rubbing the spot on my noggin where the skillet hit it, and through the twinklies in my vision I could see my concerned PMS-wifey standing over me, gasping and apologizing and saying over and over that she hadn't meant to actually hit me with it. I knew I needed to make good on that hurtful comment, so I asked how I could make it up to her.

Brunette-Wifey said, "Take our daughter trick or treating tonight and collect donations for me for the PMS Candy Stash. Except when she says, 'Trick or Treat,' you say, 'Please, donations for my wife's PMS Candy Stash?'"

Munchkin and I made quite a haul in Halloween candy. Next time PMS-Brunette-Wifey gets bitchy I'm just going to pop chocolate into her open mouth…and NEVER mention how hot my favorite sex symbol of the moment is again.

4-21: Superintendent of Safety

Mr. Blonde-Spouse-Safety-Superintendent had been on patrol all day: correcting Blonde-Spouse-Diminutive-Duplicate for turning on the hot tap before the cold one; advising Brunette-Teenage-Son-And-Self-Designated-Peanut-Gallery-Of-Sarcastic-Commentary that he had too many cords plugged into one power strip; and letting Brunette-Self know she left Blonde-Spouse-Diminutive-Duplicate's shoes right in front of her bedroom door where they could be tripped over.

Blonde-Spouse-Safety-Superintendent, after alienating the family, then became Blonde-Spouse-Biggest-Sophist when he finished loading the dishwasher.

Brunette-Self wandered into the kitchen coffee pot and was nearly electrocuted by the large space heater running on the linoleum in a large puddle of soapy water.

Blonde-Spouse-Biggest-Sophist had used hand soap instead of dishwasher soap and forced the door of the dishwasher mostly shut, with a handle of a spatula resisting cleaning sticking out of the door on the left side. Blonde-Spouse-Biggest-Sophist then turned on the dishwasher and the heater and left the room, thereby missing the foaming flood that engulfed the running space heater.

When confronted with his creation of this dangerous situation, Blonde-Spouse-Biggest-Sophist justified his soap selection by educating Brunette-Self that he was washing greasy pans, and "Dawn takes grease out of your way."

Brunette-Self retired wordlessly to the fuse box in the laundry room, and returned holding the sponge mop and empty bucket and handed them to the Blonde-Spouse-Biggest-Sophist.

Blonde-Spouse-Biggest-Sophist spent the rest of the afternoon mopping the floor.

The family discovered that evening the floor was still suffering a soapy and slick residue, and after returning from the urgent care clinic to assure no one slipped a disc during their wild ski ride across the floor, the Blonde-Spouse-Biggest-Sophist washed and mopped the floor repeatedly late into the night.

4-22: Tire Rotation Trouble

Brunette-Self and Blonde-Spouse got into the car and started toward the store. Turning out into traffic, Brunette-Self accelerated and quickly became conscious of the fact that the car was "thunking" down the road. Pulling into the first parking lot, the two got out of the car to take a look.

Expecting to see a flat tire, Brunette-Self saw instead the two tires in the front were one backwards without their lug nuts tightened down, one of which was still barely on the threads of the wheel. Suspecting espionage, she proceeded around the car to look at the back tires, registering one is on correctly and the other is replaced with the tiny spare donut tire normally residing in the trunk for flat tire emergencies.

"Uh oh," floated quietly on the wind to her waiting ears.

She turned to face Blonde-Spouse, who was now looking at his feet uncomfortably, "Do you know anything about this?"

"According to the car manual, it was time to rotate the tires. I rotated all but the one," he said, pointing to the only tire on correctly, "I couldn't get that one off of the car."

As she smacked her forehead, Brunette-Self asked, "So where is the other tire?"

"Oh, I put it in the trunk where the extra tire goes."

It took an hour and a half for Brunette-Self to jack up the car three times and correct the Blonde-Spouse Tire Rotation. Blonde-Spouse assisted her by robbing her purse of all of its change to feed the bubble gum vending machine and then dutifully chewing up the gum to "build up the low spots" developing on the tire treads.

4-23: DIY Car Stereo

Brunette-Self had banned Blonde-Spouse from any exterior car maintenance after the tire rotation experience (Chronicle 4-22: Tire Rotation Trouble), so Blonde-Spouse turned to "fixing up the inside."

The van had been missing the stereo for quite some time now, ever since Brunette-Self had had to remove it in order to get the van started again (Chronicle 2-10: Milk Crate Construction.)

Brunette-Self forbade him from connecting his new "fixed up Top Secret stereo" to the van battery or electrical system in any way shape or form, as she was still reeling from the portable perk pot and air mattress episodes. Feeling confident in these restrictions, Brunette-Self gave Blonde-Spouse leave to create his "fixed up 'Top Secret' car stereo." She popped some popcorn and set down in a lawn chair along the driveway to watch.

Blonde-Spouse started by bringing out his large home speaker collection of tweeters, sub woofers and woofers and bungee cording them to the door arm rests around the van. He carefully connected the wiring of each speaker, bringing the wires to meet in the middle of the van, where he twist tied them and staple gunned them to the middle of the ceiling of the van and toward the direction of the front seats.

He went back into the house and returned carrying his home stereo components, which he lined up on the dashboard of the van and connected. Once he had them connected properly to each other and to his freshly installed speaker system, he duct taped them down to the dashboard.

After he tested each component 'slide ratio,' he wandered back into the house for several minutes. Brunette-Self had just begun to worry about his absence when he returned, unwinding the heavy duty orange electrical extension cord as he backed out of the front door and toward the van. Brunette-Self stifled a smile as he rolled down the drivers window and plugged in his "fixed up 'Top Secret'" car stereo system. "I haven't figured out how we'll play the records yet, but it's all done!" he declared.

"I like how you incorporated surround sound, Snickerdoodle," she began--and waivered, "but I can't help but wonder how we'll handle the electrical cord when we drive it away from the house?"

"Oh, no---"

4-24: Child Proof Cap Challenge

"Sweetie Cakes! HELP?!? I can't get this stupid cap off of munchkin's chewable vitamins!" Blonde-Spouse whined to Brunette-Self.

She turned around and noticed him screwing and unscrewing the cap rapidly.

"Here, Daddy," offered Blonde-Spouse-Diminutive-Duplicate, reaching out and wrenching the bottle out of his hands. She grasped the cap and opened it, handing it back to Blonde-Spouse, "Here ya go."

"I don't understand, I was following the arrows!" he said, scratching his head.

"Oh, Daddy," she said, "You only follow one arrow for OPEN and one for CLOSED."

Brunette-Self put the medicines in a locked chest and then she locked in another locked chest. She then put it on the highest shelf she could reach

4-25: "The Hamster Stroller"

The Blonde-Spouse and the Blonde-Spouse-Diminutive-Duplicate were at odds, the two arguing over what type of pet she could have.

"What about a fish?" asked Blonde-Spouse.

"I want a pet I can play with!" she pouted.

"How about a hamster?" he offered.

"Well, I could play with a hamster, but I couldn't take it for a walk like I could a puppy!" she countered, pushing for a dog.

"Well, a dog is just too much responsibility for you right now. I think a hamster would be a better choice—two so they don't get lonely."

"But I couldn't walk it!" she reminded him, ever the saleswoman, "If I had a puppy, I could walk it every day...and you always say I need to get more exercise. A puppy and I could go and get the mail each day on our walk, and you always say you hate going to go get the mail."

"That's true," Blonde-Spouse-Insane-Inventor responded, thinking, "but I still think a dog is too much responsibility. What if I made it so you could walk your hamsters?"

Knowing she'd been outwitted, Blonde-Spouse-Diminutive-Duplicate begrudgingly agreed.

"Why don't you and Momma go and pick out your hamsters while I work on your cage?" Blonde-Spouse Blonde-Spouse-Insane-Inventor said, as he grabbed pen and paper and began to scribble madly.

"Ok," she agreed. The two left for the pet store with the pet carrier, leaving Blonde-Spouse Blonde-Spouse-Insane-Inventor to his creation. After painstaking selection, Blonde-Spouse-Diminutive-Duplicate finally chose two hamsters. They returned a short while later, with hamsters, hamster food, water bowls and dishes in hand.

Blonde-Spouse-Insane-Inventor yelled over the backyard fence, "Come on back and check it out!"

The two wandered into the backyard carrying their legion of hamsters and supplies. Blonde-Spouse-Insane-Inventor stood next to a shopping cart covered in a large bow. He had wrapped the entire outer surface of the shopping cart with chicken wire. Inside, he'd constructed a maze of small chicken wire ladders and tubes for the hamsters to climb on.

"I even left room for a wheel!" he said, pointing to an area along the side of the shopping cart, "and here is the door" he included, pushing down the plastic child seat. He took the food dish and water bottle from Blonde-Spouse-Diminutive-Duplicate and wired them to the side in the child seat area, to make it easy to fill them.

"What about their poo?" asked Brunette-Self.

"Oh, we just park the cart over a litterbox for easy clean up," he replied, turning to Blonde-Spouse-Diminutive-Duplicate, "I call it the 'Hamster Stroller.' Now you can push your hamsters for a walk in their mobile cage!"

"The Hamster Stroller" was a huge hit in the neighborhood until the local grocery store caught wind of it's wayward cart and sent the local police to retrieve it. Luckily for Blonde-Spouse-Insane-Inventor, the officer who arrived was The-Friendly-Officer (Chronicles 2-5: A Question of Suppositories and 3-12: Linoleum Angels) and Blonde-Spouse-Sympathizer who kindly let him off the hook again.

4-26: More Milk Crate Construction: The Retaining Wall

Blonde-Spouse-Garden-Guru decided to make a few raised vegetable beds. Fresh out of railroad ties and not wanting to make multiple trips to the river gravel bar with a wheelbarrow, Blonde-Spouse-Garden-Guru had figured using milk crates would be the best solution to his raised vegetable bed needs. He reasoned the plastic would wear forever and the crates had lots of holes so the soil could breath and worms could get in and out to work the soil.

Blonde-Spouse-Garden-Guru knew he would still need some rocks to weigh down the crates, so he sent Brunette-Teenage-Son-And-Self-Designated-Peanut-Gallery-Of-Sarcastic-Commentary back and forth with the wheelbarrow the few blocks to the river to retrieve enough to weigh the crates down. While the boy ran back and forth, Blonde-Spouse-Garden-Guru stacked the crates four across and eight long. He filled the bottom crates full of rocks and stacked a second row on top, also filling it with rocks.

Blonde-Spouse-Garden-Guru and Brunette-Teenage-Son-And-Self-Designated-Peanut-Gallery-Of-Sarcastic-Commentary then filled the bed with soil and planted tomatoes, peppers, basil and onions. Pleased with himself, Blonde-Spouse-Garden-Guru set the sprinkler in the middle, turned it on and went out front to pull weeds.

Brunette-Self brought out a new batch of seedlings to harden off, when she noticed a muddy waterfall cascading out of what appeared to be a milk crate dam. She ran to turn off the water and yelled for Blonde-Spouse-Garden-Guru. The top of the bed, hosting the new plantings, had sunk in rapidly, upending root balls and slamming all of the plants in together in a jumbled mess.

Brunette-Self and Blonde-Spouse-Garden-Guru gently untangled and replaced the plants into their planters. They removed the top layer of crates and stacked the rocks. Slowly, the two removed the bottom crates one by one and filled each vacated hole with stacked rocks. The process was repeated until all of the remaining rocks were used. With apologies, Brunette-Self sent her young Brunette-Teenage-Son-And-Self-Designated-Peanut-Gallery-Of-Sarcastic-Commentary back for more rocks to finish the bed, now only half the height it had been built originally.

"You're not mad?" Blonde-Spouse-Garden-Guru asked hopefully.

"Nah," she replied, "Your heart was in the right place. Besides, we needed some soil down there to help fill in the low spot you created digging your hole to China (Chronicle 4-9: Digging a Hole to China.)"

Blonde-Spouse-Garden-Guru then hosed off the containers and set them in the sun to dry.

4-27: More Milk Crate Construction: The Platform Bed

Undeterred from the raised vegetable bed milk crate construction calamity, Blonde-Spouse-Insane-Inventor was at it again. He was tired of watching Brunette-Self struggle painfully out of bed each day and decided a platform bed was in order. Blonde-Spouse-Insane-Inventor pulled Brunette-Self out of bed that morning, and shooed her into the living room with a cup of coffee. He then closed off the bedroom and set to work. Brunette-Self could hear him moving things around, but had no desire to investigate because of what had happened the last time her Blonde-Spouse had moved furniture (Chronicle 2-1: Furniture Rearrangement Fiasco.)

"Okay, Honey, I'm done!" he declared and opened the door to the bedroom.

Brunette-Self got up from the couch and shuffled in to their bedroom. Their bed was now raised to her waist, making it very easy to get in and out of bed. Blonde-Spouse-Insane-Inventor had laid a row of milk crates upside down under the bed, turning the crates on the outside of his support rectangle on their sides and facing outward, where he'd stashed the couples shoes and back packs.

The Milk Crate Platform bed turned out to be a wonderful invention of Blonde-Spouse-Insane-Inventor--until it was time to attempt to vaccum under their bed. What transpired has been edited to protect Blonde-Spouse's dignity.

4-28: Floor Repair

Brunette-Teenage-Son-And-Self-Designated-Peanut-Gallery-Of -Sarcastic-Commentary had been playing Evil Knieval with his friends by rolling from his loft bed to land on his futon 5 feet below. What the numbskulls failed to consider was the force of their falling body weight exceeded the threshold of the sub flooring in the corner of the boys room.

The sneaky hooligans moved the futon over a few inches and pulled the carpet flush to hide the hole in the corner of the room. Their plan would have worked, but the brilliant future generation then decided to light a contraband note from one of their girlfriends on fire. Not thinking about how quickly paper burns, the offending pyromaniac panicked and dropped it into the orange plastic wastebasket of Brunette-Teenage-Son-And-Self-Designated-Peanut-Gallery-Of -Sarcastic-Commentary.

As the garbage can began to melt in on itself and fused with the carpet, the fickle friends of Brunette-Teenage-Son-And-Self-Designated-Peanut-Gallery-Of-Sarcastic-Commentary promptly flung open the door to his room, fanned the flames in the wastebasket and ran out of the house yelling, "This is not good!" Brunette-Teenage-Son-And-Self-Designated-Peanut-Gallery-Of -Sarcastic-Commentary came barreling after them and ran through the living room and into the kitchen, sliding to a stop in front of the cabinet housing the fire extinguisher. Smoke billowed from his open bedroom door, setting off the fire alarms and Scottie Dog howls.

"Which one of you did it?" was all Brunette-Self could muster through her clenched teeth as she surveyed the damage to the bedroom.

"I dunno," was all he could say, looking at his feet while he shuffled them back and forth.

"You know this is coming out of your allowance."

"I know."

Sighing, Brunette-Self began to scour the internet, and luckily for Brunette-Teenage-Son-And-Self-Designated-Peanut-Gallery-Of-Sarcastic-Commentary, she scored a free carpet remnant and carpet pad off of Craigslist that would work for his room. She put him immediately to work boxing up his room and moving the furniture outside to the gazebo. She then sent the two off to pick up the remnant, and started to remove the damaged carpet and pad. Ironically, she started in the corner in which the boys had just hidden the newly formed hole in the floor.*

When the two returned, she tasked Blonde-Spouse with contacting his best friend, Brunette-Construction-Oriented-Friend-Prone-To-Exaggerating-His-Skills (Chronicle 4-7: Home Improvement Challenge) for help in repairing the sub floor while she and Brunette-Teenage-Son-And-Self-Designated-Peanut-Gallery-Of-Sarcastic-Commentary went to buy supplies at the hardware-superstore-with-the-super-helpful-salesforce-and-the-super-high-percentage-rate-of-interest.

---

*Her reaction was edited for content to assure appropriate language -- Publisher.

Brunette-Construction-Oriented-Friend-Prone-To-Exaggerating-His-Skills was chatting with Blonde-Spouse over coffee when the two returned with the bags of supplies.

Brunette-Construction-Oriented-Friend-Prone-To-Exaggerating-His-Skills and Blonde-Spouse-Captain-Construction-Catastrophe set to work removing the damaged section of the sub floor. The Brunette-Construction-Oriented-Friend-Prone-To-Exaggerating-His-Skills appeared after a half an hour to give a "Status Update."

"Looks like the manufacturer installed 6 inches of linoleum flooring from the bathroom into the bedroom," Brunette-Construction-Oriented-Friend-Prone-To-Exaggerating-His-Skills began, "I'm going to need to use the jig saw to cut it off."

"It's in the laundry room in the closet," Brunette-Self directed, confused.

"Thank you much" said the Brunette-Construction-Oriented-Friend-Prone-To-Exaggerating-His-Skills disappeared back into the bedroom with jig saw in hand.

Brunette-Self got up, stretched, and went into the bathroom next to the bedroom.

"Just whack that last piece of linoleum with the hammer," offered a muffled Blonde-Spouse-Captain-Construction-Catastrophe.

A whack resonated on the other side of the wall, and Brunette-Self looked down and saw the linoleum in the bathroom splitting, "Stop!"

she yelled through the wall, "the linoleum is splitting in here!"

Whack! The split lengthened, "STOP!" she yelled again, smacking the wall. The whacking ceased.

"Got it!" responded Brunette-Construction-Oriented-Friend-Prone-To-Exaggerating-His-Skills, "Sorry about that!"

"Grrrr," Brunette-Self grumbled as she returned to the living room and back to Craigslist to start looking for linoleum remnants.

Brunette-Construction-Oriented-Friend-Prone-To-Exaggerating-His-Skills came out to put the jigsaw away and offer another Status Report, "We've got the old floor taken out now, just putting down the new flooring."

"Great, thanks," she said absent mindedly, sending off an email inquiry on a patch of linoleum she'd just located.

Whacking commenced from the bedroom for quite some time, and then ended abruptly with a string of swear words streaming from the mouth of Blonde-Spouse-Captain-Construction-Catastrophe. He emerged from the bedroom and quickly shut the door behind him, "Where is the caulking gun and caulk?"

"In the laundry room, why?" Brunette-Self asked, suddenly suspicious.

"Oh, no reason," he rushed as he side stepped her and hastily made his exit toward the laundry room.

Blonde-Spouse-Captain-Construction-Catastrophe grabbed the caulking supplies and disappeared outside. When he came back in, he put them away and grabbed the staple gun and finishing nails and hurried back into the bedroom, again quickly closing the door behind him and in the face of his following brunette wife.

Brunette-Self returned to the couch amid the distant sound of the staple gun being fired repeatedly. After an hour, the two men came out of the bedroom and announced they were done. Brunette-Self came in to assess the work. The two had done a nice job, outside of the split linoleum in the bathroom, the carpet looked professionally installed.

"Nice job, guys, thanks," she said, turning to the boys, "Now I've got a linoleum remnant I need you two to pick up to replace the newly damaged one in the bathroom."

Looking relieved, the two departed to pick up the remnant. Brunette-Self sat back down on the couch, glad to have the floor repaired and the carpet replaced. Brunette-Teenage-Son-And-Self-Designated-Peanut-Gallery-Of-Sarcastic-Commentary started to put his room back in order. A nagging feeling kept hounding Brunette-Self, until she gasped in realization and set out outside in search of the answer to why her Blonde-Spouse-Captain-Construction-Catastrophe had needed the caulking supplies.

On the exterior wall of the bedroom of Brunette-Teenage-Son-And-Self-Designated-Peanut-Gallery-Of-Sarcastic-Commentary she found several nails protuding from the siding of their home, covered in dripping caulk.

Upon their return from their errand, Brunette-Self had confronted Blonde-Spouse-Captain-Construction-Catastrophe regarding the large nails now protruding through the wall of their boys bedroom, to which he responded, "I had to nail the floor in at an angle along the wall, and I realized I went all the way through the wall."

"Why didn't you pull them back out?"

"Well, I set the hammer down to look at the damage and knocked it through the last part of the open floor and down onto the ground underneath the house. So we just used the staple gun to tack down the last piece and then the carpet pad and remnant and left the hammer under the house. So, I caulked the outside tips of the nails so rain water couldn't get in to damage the wall," he finished.

"Why didn't you just crawl under the house and get the hammer to pull them out?" she demanded.

"Because there are spiders down there and it's dark!" he whined.

"FINE." Brunette-Self stormed off and back to the usual hardware-superstore-with-the-super-helpful-salesforce-and-the-super-high-percentage-rate-of-interest to buy a new hammer and some linoleum glue, and to talk someone about how to fill the holes in the wall.

4-29: "The Luggage Lounger"

Brunette-Self and the Blonde-Spouse-Insane-Inventor were cruising the local yard sales when they happened upon a set of rolling luggage, a large collection of various sized belts and a group of folding lawn chairs.

"How much for the lot of this?" Blonde-Spouse-Insane-Inventor asked the homeowner.

"Oh, how about $3?" she answered.

The two sealed the deal and Blonde-Spouse-Insane-Inventor loaded them into the car. When the two were done for the day, they headed home. Blonde-Spouse-Insane-Inventor took his treasures to the backyard and started to work. He sawed off the metal legs of the lawn chairs with a hacksaw. He then attached the bottom of each folding chair seat to the top of the luggage, strapping it on to the top with the belts he had bought.

"What's all this?" Brunette-Self had asked, bemused.

"Oh, this is what I call 'The Luggage Lounger!'" he said, beginning his presentation, "You know, for when you're stuck at the airport in the security line? You can just pop open your 'Luggage Lounger' and kick back in ease while everyone else gets sore feet!"

"And those?" she asked, pointing to the large trunk and the small carry on bag.

"Ah, those!" he said, pointing first to the trunk and then the carry on, "The 'Luggage Lounger' comes in 3 sizes: the original 'Luggage Lounger,' the 'Party Trunk,' and the 'Carry on Compact.'"

While she thought Blonde-Spouse-Insane-Inventor had a good idea, Brunette-Self didn't think airport security would agree.

4-30: Swiss Cheese Swarm

Brunette-Self and Brunette-Teenage-Son-And-Self-Designated-Peanut-Gallery-Of-Sarcastic-Commentary (BTSASDPGOSC) were in a full blown war over who got the last slice of swiss cheese.

"You already had more than your fair share!" argued Brunette-Self.

"But I need to build strong bones!" shot back BTSASDPGOSC.

"Why don't I just go to the store and pick up some more?" interjected Blonde-Spouse-Conflict-Coordinator.

"Okay," the two agreed in unison.

Mr. Blonde-Spouse-Conflict-Coordinator took Blonde-Spouse-Diminutive-Duplicate to the store. Mrs. Brunette-Self and BTSASDPGOSC continued making their sandwiches, hurling each other an occasional dirty look. The two blonde's absence continued for a significant time, prompting the two hungry and brawling brunettes to eat their sandwiches without the cheese. After what seemed to be forever, the two blondes finally returned from the store with four large paper bags full of groceries.

"I thought you were just getting swiss cheese?" started Brunette-Self, annoyed at the length of their absence.

"I did," responded Blonde-Spouse-Conflict-Coordinator, as he opened the lid of the deep freezer and dumped the first bag of swiss cheese into it, "I figured four bags worth should keep you two from arguing for awhile."

It would take three months to exhaust the supply of swiss cheese, and the two brawling brunettes never argued over swiss cheese again as the two were now completely sick of eating it—forever.

Blonde-Spouse-Conflict-Coordinator attributed this to his successful intervention in their argument.

Brunette-Self attempted to give the swiss cheese away after the first month, however no one on their block had been willing to take any of the cheese, given Blonde-Spouse-Conflict-Coordinator's past history with freezer foods.

Brunette-Self sent Brunette-Teenage-Son-And-Self-Designated-Peanut-Gallery-Of-Sarcastic-Commentary to school with several packages of the swiss cheese, thinking teenage boys would eat anything. This was disproven, as the teenage boys and her son's school had also caught wind of Blonde-Spouse-Conflict-Coordinator's abuse of foodstuffs.

Desperate to get rid of the cheese, Brunette-Self had attempted to post them on Craigslist, only to discover she had been blocked from posting ads given the pet wheel incident.

Finally, in desperation, she sent the two kids a neighborhood away from their home to leave the cheese with 'adopt me' notes on the doorsteps of strangers.

5 A NEW BEGINNING

5-1: Hanging Pictures

Brunette-Self finished painting the wall and trim. The paint was dry and Brunette-Self was finally content with the color choice, having painted the wall six other colors before the current one. She washed the brushes and rollers and pans, and put all the painting supplies away. Brunette-Self laid out the pictures on the floor in an arrangement that took four or five prior attempts to achieve. She sat down to take a coffee break.

Blonde-Spouse seized the opportunity and grabbed the hanging nail and hammer in one hand and the largest picture in the other.

He walked over to the wall and held the picture up to it, "This look straight to you?"

"Um, Honey," she began, "I was going to use a laser level to hang those, but first I wanted to measure and mark where I wanted the holes to go, that way everything fits."

"Nah, I got it," replied Blonde-Spouse. He held the picture to the wall, slid it down the wall a half an inch and leaned forward until his tipped head touched the glass in the middle of the frame. Holding the picture against the wall with his head, he reached up and placed the point of the hanging nail against the wall. Blonde-Spouse held the nail tip against the wall and brought the hammer up to the nail head and carefully aligned the two while he looked down at his feet and held the frame to the wall with his head.

"Snicker doodle, Sugarplum, stop--" said Brunette-Self, as she observed her Blonde-Spouse pull the hammer back to blindly swing it at the nail and his other hand.

Her words went unheeded and unheard as the hammer connected with his thumb and he screamed and jerked away from the frame, dropping the hammer onto his foot and sending the frame crashing to shatter on top of the hammer and his foot.

"Ow! Ow! Owieeeeeeee!" Blonde-Spouse whined, grabbing his foot and hopping around.

Unswayed, he cussed at the hammer and went over and picked up another frame. Stooping to pick up the hammer and another nail from the box, Blonde-Spouse approached the wall. He placed the new frame against the wall, this time tilting his head up and holding it there with his chin.

Brunette-Self attempted again to offer her helpful-after-the-fact advice, only to be cut to the quick by surly Blonde-Spouse. He successfully hung the second frame, and proceeded to alter his method a third time: This time, he held up the frame with one hand and put his finger on the wall directly above it and set the frame back down. He discovered the ineffectiveness of his decision the moment he attempted to reach for the hammer and another nail, both still sitting on the floor. He turned and stared at his finger for quite some time, then removed it and back slowly away from the wall, his eyes never wavering from "the spot" he had "marked with his finger."

Brunette-Self, just relieved he spared another frame, decided to allow him to continue testing his method. Blonde-Spouse grabbed the hammer and another nail and drove it into the freshly painted wall. He did not hang the frame on the nail and instead grabbed another frame and another nail and returned to the wall. He repeated the position the picture and finger move a second time, this time driving the nail in without having to move his finger too far away.

Blonde-Spouse missed the nail and hit his finger, throwing down the hammer and grabbing his hand, "Ow! Ow! Owie!"

Brunette-Self sighed and resolved to keep both herself and her helpful-after-the-fact-advice to herself, while Blonde-Spouse repeated his nail driving procedure until each frame had a nail driven for it without further injury. He then started to hang the pictures to match the layout on the floor.

On the third frame hanging, it became immediately apparent his "positioning" had been off by a large margin. The third frame nail was underneath the bottom of the second frame, already hanging lopsided on the wall. He removed the second frame and replaced it with another picture, this one much smaller. Grinning, he hung the third frame. The top two frames were two inches apart, while the second and bottom frames were now more than a foot apart. The Blonde-Spouse discovered similar overlap and distance issues with the remaining frames. He managed to get all but two of the frames of the arrangement on the wall, the first having been destroyed on top of his toe and the second omitted because "it doesn't fit."

Blonde-Spouse stood back to admire his work. Each and every picture in the arrangement was lopsided to varying degree. He put on his thinking cap while he assessed the problem, "Eureka!" he declared and grabbed the box of nails and hammer.

"Oh, crap," muttered Brunette-Self.

Blonde-Spouse then started to straighten each frame, placing a nail at the base of the side sliding up along the wall. He attempted to hammer in the first nail, to help "hold the picture straight." Blonde-Spouse missed both the nail and his thumb, landing the hammer directly into the middle of the frame and shattering the glass. He yelped but swung the hammer again, this time missing both the frame and the nail and slamming a hole into the drywall.

"That's it! You're cut off!" yelled Brunette-Self as she sprung up and ripped the hammer and nails from his hands.

Blonde-Spouse left the room, shooting sulky looks over his shoulder. Brunette-Self removed the frames, swept up the glass, vacuumed the carpet, pulled the nails and puttied the holes driven by Blonde-Spouse. She looked at her freshly painted wall, now polka dotted with white putty and cried a little inside. She then wandered back to the laundry room utility closet to retrieve the paint supplies, she knew it would be a long day of painting it all over again tomorrow.

5-2: The Munchkin Magnet Mat

Blonde-Spouse and Brunette-Self were visited by friends who have a toddler. The toddler reminded them both how they had let their child-proofing skills lapse since their youngest was now school age. The two were kept busy helping their harried friends run down the youngster and keep him from harm and were exhausted by the time their guests departed.

The evening had gotten the wheels in Blonde-Spouse-Insane-Inventor's head, and he was busy scrawling plans for his next revolutionary invention by the time bedtime arrived.

"You go on to sleep, I've got some more work here," he said, and pecked Brunette-Self on the cheek.

"Ok, but remember it's after 10 so no loud noises--sound ordinance," she replied hopefully as she gave him a hug in return.

Brunette-Self woke the next morning to an empty bed. Concerned Blonde-Spouse-Insane-Inventor had been up all night with full access to the power tools, she wrested herself from sleep and went in search of the coffee pot and to do a damage assessment. To her imminent relief, she found the coffee pot but no damage. Brunette-Self was so relieved, she failed to notice Blonde-Spouse-Insane-Inventor was also missing and had been all evening.

She was on her third cup of wake up coffee when he barreled through the front door, causing her to jump and wear the remaining half a cup.

"Sorry, sorry," he muttered, "You've got to see this! I've created the perfect invention to help tired parents keep track of their busy kids! I call it 'The Munchkin Magnet Mat.' Here, let me demonstrate."

Blonde-Spouse-Insane-Inventor laid the box he was carrying down and removed the family Twister game mat. He had super glued strong magnets all over each of the dots on the mat. He reached into the box and pulled out a doll that belonged to Blonde-Spouse-Diminutive-Duplicate, turning the doll so Brunette-Self could see it was wearing a cloth diaper covered in haphazardly sewn on halves of the magnet pairs he'd glued onto the Twister mat.

"You put the cloth diaper cover over your kids diaper, then you put the child down to sit on one of the dots. The child is then magnetically 'stuck' to the mat, which leaves the parent free to cook dinner or whatever while the child safely plays on the floor."

Brunette-Self began envisioning an entire product line of baby and toddler sized copper bracelets that would spring up in response to 'The Munchkin Magnet Mat,' but chided herself for entertaining the thought and turned her attention back to Blonde-Spouse Insane Inventor, "So, how do you lift the kid off the magnets?"

The Blonde-Spouse-Insane-Inventor looked perplexed for a moment, then stood on the mat and attempted to pry the doll off the magnets. The doll would not budge. He tried again. Still, the doll would not yield.

"Try taking the doll out of the diaper?" offered Brunette-Self and her helpful-after-the-fact-advice.

"Oh, hey!" he exclaimed, "Great idea! So, I guess I can build so more magnet diapers, one for each dot on the mat. Then the parent can elect where they strap the kid down!"

"Wow," Brunette-Self responded into her hands.

5-3: The Munchkin Muter

After the failure of 'The Munchkin Magnet Mat' (5-2: The Munchkin Magnet Mat),

Brunette-Self was hopeful Blonde-Spouse-Insane-Inventor would again retire his invention drafting board. She was promptly disappointed.

Blonde-Spouse-Insane-Inventor soon began working on his next 'Top Secret' invention that would revolutionize the world. His work took him away from the home a few hours, which Brunette-Self took full advantage of with a good book.

She did not glance up from reading when Blonde-Spouse-Insane-Inventor entered the room, until he cleared his throat. Brunette-Self took a deep breath, marked her place in the book and turned her attention to Blonde-Spouse-Insane-Inventor.

He was wearing what looked like her fuzzy earmuffs with an erector set coming off the top like industrial antennae on a mutant bug.

"Dare I ask?" she said, annoyed her favorite pivoting adjustable earmuffs were now completely destroyed.

"Glad you did!" started the spiel of Blonde-Spouse-Insane-Inventor, "I proudly call it 'The Munchkin Muter.' See, you just 'flip the switch and it covers the pitch!'"

He reached down to his belt where a box was attached by several wound spools of string. Brunette-Self recognized it as part of the accessories responsible for movement in the erector set belonging to Brunette-Teenage-Son-

And-Self-Designated-Peanut-Gallery-Of-Sarcastic-Commentary. Blonde-Spouse-Insane-Inventor flipped the switch and the industrial antennae attached to the top of her ear muffs began to move, pulling each ear muff up and away from his ears. As the pulleys moved the arms and earmuffs up, they also wound up the hair Blonde-Spouse-Insane-Inventor. Blonde-Spouse-Insane-Inventor was unaware of this mishap until it began to pull his hair, to which he reacted to by attempting to pull off the earmuffs and pulling his hair even more. The additional pain drove him into panic and he vehemently pawed at his head and screamed.
Brunette-Self walked over, reached out and turned off the switch.

"Thank you," he cried, as she steered him to a chair to assess the dreadlocked earmuffs now wound upon his head.

"Go get me the scissors, please," she said, turning to Brunette-Teenage-Son-And-Self-Designated-Peanut-Gallery-Of-Sarcastic-Commentary.

The boy complied, and she began to cut the mess off of Blonde-Spouse-Insane-Inventor's head. By the time the gadget was free, the head of Blonde-Spouse-Insane-Inventor resembled an intricate tangle of blonde dreads and bald spots. Brunette-Teenage-Son-And-Self-Designated-Peanut-Gallery-Of-Sarcastic-Commentary, wanting to keep his title, piped up, "Hey look!

Dad's suffering from Male Pattern Blondeness!"

Brunette-Self tossed the hair and 'The Munchkin Muter'" into the trash and started to work clipping off the remaining defiant strands of hair from Blonde-Spouse-Insane-Inventor's head, trying her best not to smirk at Brunette-Teenage-Son-And-Self-Designated-Peanut-Gallery-Of-Sarcastic-Commentary's comment, at least when Blonde-Spouse-Insane-Inventor was looking.

5-4: Bumper Pads

Two quick successive failures of his past inventions prompted Blonde-Spouse-Insane-Inventor to put away his idea board and don his Blonde-Spouse-Safety-Superintendent hat. The visiting toddler had reminded him that the corners of the furniture were fairly sharp and had bruised more than one shin in the house over the past few years.

Blonde-Spouse-Safety-Superintendent journeyed to the local shipping store, where he bought out their supply of bubble wrap and masking tape. He returned home with his mountain of bubble wrap and tape to a delighted Brunette-Self and Blonde-Spouse-Diminutive-Duplicate, who mistook the wrap as a gift for the two of them to pop and play with. Both were let down when Blonde-Spouse-Safety-Superintendent smacked their hands away, advising them both the bubble wrap was purchased for a practical use.

Intrigued by what Blonde-Spouse-Safety-Superintendent would consider a practical application for a mountain of bubble wrap, Brunette-Self stuck around to help.

"No, No," he said, shooing her away, "Go and read a bedtime story to munchkin. I've got this, no worries."

Brunette-Self didn't buy into his assurances and insisted, only to be thwarted by Blonde-Spouse-Diminutive-Duplicate with a book in hand and a pleading expression upon her face. Caving in to pressure, Brunette-Self took Blonde-Spouse-Diminutive-Duplicate to her room to read her a story. The child had selected a rather long chapter book to delay bedtime, of course, so Brunette-Self spent nearly an hour reading to her while her attention kept redirecting itself to the other room every time she heard the ripping sound of the masking tape.

Kissing Blonde-Spouse-Diminutive-Duplicate good night, Brunette-Self took quick leave and returned to the living room. Every piece of furniture in the room had every edge covered in a layer of bubble wrap cemented onto it with tons of masking tape.

"Why?" she asked, wearily. She knew she really didn't want an answer, but rhetorical questions were beyond his scope of understanding--so was sarcasm.

"Bumper Pads!" declared Blonde-Spouse-Safety-Superintendent, "no more bruised shins! No more bumped elbows! And if you get frustrated, you can pop the corners!"

5-5: Swimming Pool Setup Setback

Blonde-Spouse-Diminutive-Duplicate got a rather large children's inflatable pool a few months early for her birthday. Since her birthday is in August, Brunette-Self and Blonde-Spouse decided to give it to her a few months early so she could enjoy it through out the summer.

The pool was composed of a large round pool liner with an inflatable ring on the top that raised the sides of the pool up as it filled with water. Because the pool had no sides, it was vital it be set up on level ground. So vital was this step, the entire outer lining of the pool was covered in warning signs regarding this very important factor. Somehow the ample warning escaped Blonde-Spouse, who selected a sloped part of the backyard to set it up and fill it. The two ladies were in the house getting into their bathing suits, so they were not present for this location selection.

When the two returned to the backyard, they found Blonde-Spouse inside the pool on the hill. The 900-gallon pool was now half full of water and was sporting a large bulge in the wall facing the downhill side. Blonde-Spouse was trying to heave up the sagging wall, so the water would "get under the floating ring and bring the wall up like it's supposed to do." The wall bulged further out in response to his attempts to lift it up. Frustrated, Blonde-Spouse kicked the wall and lost his footing. Both of his legs shot out from underneath him as he slipped on the slick pool liner floor, plunging him underwater. The slope carried him downhill along the bottom of the pool and into the wall. The collision with the wall forced the ring below the water line, and sent 900 gallons of water and sputtering Blonde-Spouse spewing over the side and across the backyard.

"Classic, Dear," Brunette-Self said, reaching for her mental notebook.

"Daddy, I should have gotten to swim first!" said an upset Blonde-Spouse-Diminutive-Duplicate.

Once he regained his footing, Blonde-Spouse and Brunette-Self freed the remaining water from the pool and relocated it to a level place in the yard. By the time the water had filled the pool, the sun was starting to set and Blonde-Spouse-Diminutive-Duplicate began to cry. Brunette-Self and Blonde-Spouse raped the house of every candle they could find and the family went for a candlelight swim.

5-6: Swimming Pool Safety

Blonde-Spouse-Safety-Superintendent felt the pool they bought Blonde-Spouse-Diminutive-Duplicate was unsafe. He determined that the pool required some special safety features and started rummaging around in the shed. Brunette-Self rolled her eyes and left him to his insanity. Blonde-Spouse-Safety-Superintendent came in and herded the family outside to the pool, where he began his safety first presentation.

First, he pointed to a rope tied to a rubber duck neck also tied to a pulley on an odd contraption he'd installed at the side of the pool. A small wooden plywood platform on which rested two 5-pound weights was held hovering above the pool's edge, elevated by a pulley system he had rigged around a tall Shepherds Hook plant hanger from the garden. A locking pulley sporting a spring release lever was on the rope supporting the platform from the Sheppards Hook, with another rope attached to the spring release lever and the neck of the floating rubber duck in the munchkin's pool.

"This is the Emergency Spill Device," Blonde-Spouse-Safety-Superintendent announced with authority, "If you are drowning, you simply pull on the duck and it will release the pulley and the platform rope will make it come down on to the inflatable floating ring on the pool's edge and cause the water to spill out quickly.

Here, let me demonstrate."

Blonde-Spouse-Safety-Superintendent pulled the duck and released the platform, which came crashing down on the ring and punctured a hole in it. The platform teetered, dropping both 5-pound weights onto Blonde-Spouse-Safety-Superintendents toes.

After several minutes of flooding the yard with pool water, hopping and grabbing each foot consecutively, swearing a blue streak and falling over because he didn't put one foot down fast enough to pick up the other, Blonde-Spouse-Safety-Superintendent regained his composure.

"I can patch that," he said as he indicated the now deflated ring.

"Ughmf," Brunette-Self mumbled into her hands.

Second, Blonde-Spouse-Safety-Superintendent directed the family's attention toward two rows of firewood stacked around the base, "These are to remain here all Summer to shore up the walls on the slightly downhill side."

Brunette-Self debated reminding him that had already moved the pool to the only level spot in the backyard, but decided against it. Instead she directed her attention back to Blonde-Spouse-Safety-Superintendent as he stepped into what remained of the pool water.

"These bricks are lined all over the bottom of the pool to weigh it down in case the wind blows," he said, pointing to the bricks he had laid along the bottom. She didn't have the heart to tell him the water in the pool held it down.

Blonde-Spouse-Diminutive-Duplicate began to cry. Brunette-Self leaned down and whispered in her ear that she would be getting a brand new 'Daddy Safety-Free' pool that day. This news brightened Miss Blonde-Spouse-Diminutive-Duplicate, who smiled and thanked Blonde-Spouse-Safety-Superintendent for all of his hard work.

Brunette-Teenage-Son-And-Self-Designated-Peanut-Gallery-Of-Sarcastic-Commentary and his Equally-Sarcastic-Blonde-Friend offered to clean up the mess created by Blonde-Spouse-Safety-Superintendent.

Brunette-Self convinced Mr. Blonde-Spouse-Safety-Superintendent to go with them to the store, knowing full well he would be completely distracted by shiny things and would miss both the clean up and the purchase of a new pool for Blonde-Spouse-Diminutive-Duplicate.

5-7: Carpentry Chaos

The fronts of the kitchen drawers were held on by a screw-through handle knob and a few tacking nails. Brunette-Self had been fairly diligent about checking to make sure the knobs were screwed on tightly, as Blonde-Spouse had a tendency to turn them like door knobs whenever he opened a drawer, thus unscrewing them.

Brunette-Self made the mistake of lapsing this diligent tightening one week, when Blonde-Spouse came out with the knob and drawer front in his hands.

"It just came off," he declared, baffled.

"Oh, don't worry, Snickerdoodle, I'll fix it. Just set it down on the table, ok?" Brunette-Self soothed.

Blonde-Spouse disappeared back into the kitchen with the drawer and knob. A neighbor came by and Brunette-Self stepped out to visit with her. The two were deep in conversation when a whacking sound emerged from the front door.

"Well, I'd better let you go and see what he's up to," Brunette-Self said and turned worriedly back toward the front door.

"Oh, yes you'd better!" laughed the neighbor and waved goodbye.

Brunette-Self followed the sound of the whacking into the kitchen, where Blonde-Spouse was driving 4 inch nails through the front of the door front in his usual fashion (reader is referred to the Chronicle 1-14: 'HAMMERTIME' for further details.)

"STOP!" she screamed, and reached out and took the hammer out of his hands mid-swing.

"Why?" he hollered back, annoyed.

"I asked you to just set it on the table, NOT DESTROY THE FRONT OF THE FINISHED

PIECE BY NAILING IT TO DEATH! The drawer is held on by the knob, which you keep unscrewing because you treat them like doors not drawers!"

"Oh"

Brunette-Self kicked him out of the kitchen, pried off the nails and assessed the damage. Blonde-Spouse had driven nails completely through the drawer front and drawer frame, splitting it in four places and along each side. Brunette-Self put a note on the calendar for payday reminding her to buy wood paste to cover the holes, and new paint for the cupboards. She knew she would have to repaint each and every cupboard in the kitchen again so the paint would match. Thankfully, Fellow-Virgo-Friend-And-Brunette-Neighbor came to the rescue with both, and repaired the drawer. Brunette-Self also noted it was time to step up the tightening schedule.

5-8: "The Coffee Caddy"

Yard sales always brought out the creativity in Blonde-Spouse-Insane-Inventor, and this time he returned home with an old golf bag on wheels, a used lawn sprayer and some flexible clear plastic surgical tubing.

"What are you going to do with those, Daddy?" asked a curious Blonde-Spouse-Diminutive-Duplicate.

"Shush, it's a surprise for Mommy," whispered Blonde-Spouse-Insane-Inventor.

The two disappeared to the shed, also known as the "Idea and Labor Lair (ILL.)" As the two entered ILL, Brunette-Self went to count the Vacation Fund Jar, just in case.

After quite some time and new gray hairs of worry appeared upon the head of Brunette-Self, the two Maestros-Of-Mayhem returned with what appeared to be the golf caddy covered in a tarp.

"Sit down and close your eyes!" the Maestros-Of-Mayhem said in unison.

Brunette-Self closed her eyes, "Let me know what I can look."

There was a rustle of plastic as the tarp was removed from the caddy, "Ok, look now! Surprise! Surprise! We call it 'The Coffee Caddy!'"

The two Maestros-Of-Mayhem had modified the lawn sprayer, replacing the nozzle and hose with clear plastic tubing. The lawn sprayer was set down into the golf bag. Grinning from ear to ear, Blonde-Spouse-Insane-Inventor turned to Blonde-Spouse-Diminutive-Duplicate and then declared, "Pump me up."

Blonde-Spouse-Diminutive-Duplicate began to pump the lawn sprayer. A dark brown liquid worked its way up the tube and into the mouth of Blonde-Spouse Insane Inventor. His brow furrowed and he ripped the tube out of his mouth, spitting and spraying the hote coffee all over Brunette-Self. He then made gagging noises and stuck his tongue out, trying to wipe the taste off of his tongue.

"Too hot?" offered Brunette-Self.

"Yuck, I should have used a new sprayer! Pesticide aftertaste is the worst!"

Brunette-Self ran to the phone to call 911.

5-9: Electrical Safety

Following his usual pattern, Blonde-Spouse temporarily learned from his invention mishap (5-8: "The Coffee Caddy") and went into Blonde-Spouse-Safety-Superintendent mode. Brunette-Self caught him in the living room, squatting in front of an electrical wall socket. She could hear a hissing sound muffled by his body, and she walked over to him.

"What are you doing?" she asked.

"I thought I would protect munchkin from sticking forks into the light sockets like I did when I was a kid," he said, turning to look over his shoulder at her, "So I'm fixing the unused outlets so she can't get zapped."

"With what?" asked Brunette-Self, thinking these childhood shock experiments might explain a few things about her Blonde-Spouse.

"Insulation foam." announced Blonde-Spouse-Safety-Superintendent.

BrunettBrunette-Teenage-Son-And-Self-Designated-Peanut-Gallery-Of-Sarcastic-Commentary sprung up from his chair and departed for the fuse box.

"You know you can buy plastic plugs to cover those," responded Very-Angry-Brunette-Self.

"But this will also insulate against drafts!" he defended.

5-10: Solicitor Stopper Sign

Brunette-Self was returning home from the neighbor's house when she spied Blonde-Spouse taking a sledgehammer to something in the front yard. Wondering what her plants ever did to him, she wandered over and discovered he was hammering in a wooden post, splintering and squishing the top while he forced it through the ground in the clover patch that had replaced the front lawn.

"What's that for?" she inquired, not wanting to mention he could have used the post hole diggers in the shed.

"Oh, this is to keep solicitors away from our house."

"What is it?"

"It's a sign," he replied, giving her a withered look.

He traded the sledgehammer for the hammer and a few large nails and picked up the sign. Holding it against the wooden pole with his head, he hammered in the nails. Brunette-Self strained to read the sign but it was blocked by his midsection. Finally, he stepped back to reveal a crooked handwritten sign that read "Nobody Lives Here."

"Cute," she commented sarcastically and went inside the house, leaving a beaming Blonde-Spouse to admire his handiwork.

5-11: Making Liquid Soap

Blonde-Spouse faced a mountain of dirty dishes two days before pay day. He was unwilling to wait to wash them the two days before pay day and the family was broke.

"It'll cake on so bad we'll need a blow torch," he informed Brunette-Self.

"Well, why don't we rinse them off and wash them with shampoo.? Then we can stack them in the sink and then rewash them on Friday when you get paid?" Brunette-Self suggested hopefully.

"Nah, that'd be too much work. I have an idea," he said, and left the room.

"Great," snapped Brunette-Self to the empty room.

Blonde-Spouse returned shortly thereafter, carrying a knotted sock with what appeared to be several bars of soap inside of it, wrapped in steel wool.

"We don't need to get physical about this, Honey Buns!" shouted a startled Brunette-Self.

"Silly woman, it's to wash the dishes with!" he laughed, and set to work.

By the time he'd hopelessly scratched the third dish, he threw the bar/sock/steel wool sponge into the sink in frustration.

Brunette-Self sighed and left him to his blondeness, deciding to practice the piano.

She was in the fourth measure of "Phantom of the Opera" when she heard the whirring of the mixer. Brunette-Self stopped playing and darted around the corner into the kitchen only to be assaulted in the face and body with flying soap chunks and water.

"Crap! Crap! Crap!" yelled panicked Blonde-Spouse, randomly pushing buttons on the mixer, speeding it up and increasing the radius of soap chunk splatter. The head of a beloved ceramic bird that belonged to Brunette-Self's great grandmother shattered on the shelf as a soap chunk assassinated it. She cried out in horror and lunged for the mixing bowl, pulling the plug out of the wall.

The entire kitchen was covered in soap chunks and water. The Scottie dog began to lap up soapy water puddles on the linoleum.

"You will be picking up after her the next few days," shuddered Brunette-Self, knowing a Scottie-Dog-With-An-Explosive-Diarrhea-Bout was imminent, "and you'll be picking up this kitchen! What were you thinking? Didn't you learn anything from the chicken chopping incident?"

"The bars of soap weren't working so I decided to make liquid soap out of the bars, like you do when you make your essential oil soaps. Besides, I thought we'd agreed we'd never bring the chicken thing again."

"To make liquid soap, you shave the soap into a pan of water and melt it, you Goofball! And we agreed that it would never happen again, which was why we agreed to not bring it up again." she retorted, now in front of her headless ceramic bird, grieving.

"Oh."

Scottie-Dog-With-An-Explosive-Diarrhea-Bout was quarantined for the next week in the master bathroom with the floor covered with puppy housebreaking pads and the bathroom fan running at all hours.

5-12: Travel Size Slip 'N Slide

"Come check this out!" insisted Blonde-Spouse-Insane-Inventor, tugging on the arm of Brunette-Self, "Your going to love it!"

"I doubt it," muttered Brunette-Self under her breath.

"What?"

"I said, 'I'll love it,'" lied Brunette-Self.

Blonde-Spouse-Insane-Inventor then drug her outside to the driveway and around to the back of the van, "I call it the 'Portable Slip 'N Slide!'"

He opened the back hatch of the van and Brunette-Self saw a rolled up tarp lying across the back. With a sweeping gesture, Blonde-

Spouse-Insane-Inventor unfurled the plastic tarp. The tarp tumbled off of the back bumper and flopped onto the driveway. He had tied two ends of the tarp to the clothing hangers in the back of the van.

He reached into the van and behind the plastic tarp and removed two jugs of water, which he poured out onto the tarp attached to the interior ceiling of the van by the rope and clothing hanger hooks. Water splashed down the front and back of the tarp, wetting the van interior and the driveway.

"Sorry about that," he said, crawling up to stand on the bumper.

"Hon---" she began, only to be cut short by his resounding "Whee!" as he jumped to sit on the tarp. The tarp instantly gave way to his weight, his rear end connecting with the hatch latch on the floor of the van.

"Oompf," came out of Blonde-Spouse-Insane-Inventor's mouth, as he hunched over with his hands going protectively to his groin and raising his legs in the air to put himself into a protective curling position. His ride was not over, however, the motion of his legs caused his rear end to slip off of the bumper. Blonde-Spouse-Insane-Inventor's eyes grew large and his mouth opened in surprise as he slid down the tarp. Again the tarp gave way under his weight, sending his rear end on a collision course with the driveway. The tarp did not stretch in response to his fall, and the top tore from its tie down on the clothing hanger hooks in the van, ripping them from the ceiling and sending tarp, rope and hooks down over the head of the moaning Blonde-Spouse-Insane-Inventor.

"What did we learn?" inquired Brunette-Self, nearly peeing herself with laughter.

"I should have used bungee cords instead of rope so the tarp would give," replied the blue tarped and whining Blonde-Spouse-Insane-Inventor. Brunette-Self shook her head and went inside to get the ice pack.

5-13: Electrical Repair

Blonde-Spouse and Brunette-Self were at the store, when he saw the rubber cement and began throwing several cans into the shopping basket.

"Got a big paper mosaic project coming up?" joked Brunette-Self.

"No, I need it to do some repairs." he said, with an air of great mystery.

She looked quizzically at him, "Like what?" Brunette-Self still had not learned to not ask him rhetorical questions.

"Don't worry about, I got this."

"Ah," Brunette-Self gulped and began to worry.

The two went home and Blonde-Spouse

Drifted into the laundry room with the Rubber Cement. Captivated, Brunette-Self pursued him. He grabbed a damaged extension cord out of the "Broken Box" and started to coat the tear in the cord and exposed wires with Rubber Cement. Brunette-Self reached out and stopped his hand as he began to plug it in to the outlet to test it.

"Why?" she asked.

"The wires in the extension cord are coated in rubber, so I thought I would use rubber cement to seal them up and make it safe to use again."

"Look, shiny!" she yelled and pointed into the kitchen, trying to distract him.

"Where?!?" he joyfully shouted, running down the hall. Mission accomplished.

Brunette-Self unplugged the cord and threw it into the "Broken Box" along with the jars of rubber cement. She was just closing the closet door on their hiding space when he returned.

"The light must have changed," he said, dejected, "No shiny."

"That's okay, Snickerdoodle," she replied, patting him on the shoulder, "We'll go find another one."

5-14: Cleaning the Refrigerator

As Brunette-Self was in the middle of preparing spaghetti sauce for canning, Blonde-Spouse-Super-Spotless decided to tackle cleaning the refrigerator. He removed all of items, placed them in an ice chest and dumped all of the ice from the freezer on top.

He took out all of the shelves and drawers a few at a time and washed them well in the sink, setting them out to dry on the tablecloth he'd laid out on the table. Brunette-Self, realizing her counter space was quickly disappearing, put her sauce back to simmer and retired from the kitchen.

Once Blonde-Spouse-Super-Spotless had removed and washed every shelf and drawer, he left momentarily and returned with the power washer.

"Hon, not a good idea," said Brunette-Self, stopping him from destroying their kitchen, "Try a sponge and a bucket instead."

Grumbling, Blonde-Spouse-Super-Spotless put the pressure washer away and returned with a sponge and a bucket. Brunette-Self busied herself watching a DVD on the computer. She was just getting to the good part when she heard him start swearing loudly.

Sighing, Brunette-Self paused her movie and went in to the kitchen. Blonde-Spouse-Super-Spotless was standing in a rather large puddle of soapy water.

"Did you knock the bucket over?" she asked as she reached for the mop to hand it to him.

"No, since you wouldn't let me use the pressure washer I had to rinse it somehow, so I filled the bucket full of water and heaved the water in it as quickly as I could into the fridge and slammed the door. Obviously, I wasn't fast enough," he replied.

"Ah," Brunette-Self replied and stifled a smile and returned to her movie.

The Blonde-Spouse-Super-Spotless finished mopping up the mess and wiped down the inside of the refrigerator. He then carefully replaced the drawers and shelving and started to put the food away.

"Hey, Honey?" yelled Brunette-Self, still engrossed in her movie, "Would you please put my spaghetti sauce on the bottom shelf? I'll warm it up again tomorrow morning and let it simmer again before I can it. Thanks!"

A moment later, her movie was again interrupted, this time by the sounds of screaming. She went into the kitchen to find Blonde-Spouse-Super-Spotless covered head to toe in spaghetti sauce and standing in another pool, this time red. A quick glance around the kitchen revealed the splatter had hit most of the cupboards and some of the walls.

"Oh, no!" she mumbled, then regained her composure, "You okay?"

"It burns!" he whined, turning and running for the bathroom shower, leaving a trail of spaghetti sauce in his wake.

"Great, he got it on the carpet now," she grumbled and started to wipe off the cupboards.

"Oh, no!" she exclaimed, as soon as she realized the sauce had stained and she would have to repaint the cupboards AGAIN.

Her stomach sank as she realized he'd also hit the walls and as she remembered his trail through the house. She wished she could afford a cleaning service, but instead went to rent a carpet steamer.

When she returned, he had moved on to organizing the canned fruits and vegetables in the pantry. Thinking he'd be fairly safe stacking cans, she cleaned the carpets with the help of Brunette-Teenage-Son-And-Self-Designated-Peanut-Gallery-Of-Sarcastic-Commentary.

Blonde-Spouse-Super-Spotless finished his task and promptly disappeared to take a nap.

Later that evening, Brunette-Self went to the pantry to collect some canned vegetables for the casserole. She opened the cupboard doors, and was rather impressed with how neatly Blonde-Spouse-Super-Spotless had stacked the cans. This sense of happy contentment was shortlived, however, as she mistakingly grabbed a can of green beans and discovered Blonde-Spouse-Super-Spotless had lost a few support pins for the shelves during his work and had propped the shelves up with—stacked cans.

Brunette-Self managed to scream for help before being buried in canned goods. Her cries were not heard by Blonde-Spouse-Super-Spotless, who continued to snore on the couch. Thankfully, her cries brought Brunette-Teenage-Son-And-Self-Designated-Peanut-Gallery-Of-

Sarcastic-Commentary, who ran in to unbury her and rush her off to the emergency room to be checked out.

Blonde-Spouse-Super-Spotless awoke a few hours later to a hastily scrawled note written by Brunette-Teenage-Son-And-Self-Designated-Peanut-Gallery-Of-Sarcastic-Commentary,
"Had to rush Mom to the ER, she says, well, she says a lot of things but I can't repeat them. Anywho, she says if you are going to use canned goods as shelf supports kindly label them FIRST."

5-15: Suburban Survivor

In order to preserve the sanity and shield them from the dire medical consequences of reading such a long chronicle of momentous blondeness, the author has taken a short hiatus by submitting instead to the reader a briefing from the diary of Brunette-Self, names have been altered to protect the innocent and guilty alike:

Suburban Survivor

THE CAST: 3 adults, 2 kids, 2 cats and a dog.
THE LOCATION: Suburban Backyard
THE RULES: No internet, No TV, No sneaking into the house in the middle of the night to go to bed in our real beds (using the modern toilet is excluded, for obvious reasons).

THE WINNER: Will be the last one who does not succumb to "the lavishes" of the civilized world, temptingly calling from 40 feet away!

Day 1: Set up, Urban Foraging & Urban Hiking

Blondie and son set up two 10'x10' tents, one 10'x12' gazebo, a smoker and a BBQ. I still can't believe it all fit, with room to spare, in our small backyard. They then gathered firewood from the back of the shed and from the local store, along with smoker wood.

My-Blonde-Friend and I departed for urban foraging and hiking. Our first stop on the hike was a nearby garage sale, in which we killed an ornately painted Russian style Rooster ceramic for her Grandfather. Our second stop, urban dwelling shopping, led my friend to put an offer on the condo just down the road from our house and they accepted. Our third stop, ye old watering hole and food source, the local Dairy Queen. A delicious iceream treat later, we explored the outer ranges of the wild at the park by the river. Finally, we ended our 'grueling' hike at the grocery store, where we spent $80 gathering foodstuffs, selecting beverages, and hunting the elusive game of the meat aisle.

Blondie and son took to the task of getting the BBQ and smoker coals ready, while my friend, myself and my daughter (our self-appointed Supervisor and Quality Assurance Coordinator/Taste Tester) began the daunting task of compiling 30 chicken and beef kabobs. My son shucked the corn. Corn almost becomes popped corn with Blondie Hubby puts it into the empty marinate pan directly above the smoker coals without water. Large flames follow. Quickly extinguished by water from the kitchen tap (although the garden hose is right there, he cannot bear himself to "rough it' that much!).

Delightful dinner finished off with rounds of Smores. Our daughter so covered with chocolate, marshmallow and graham crackers that The Council must vote that the youngest will require the modern amenity of a shower. Blondie Hubby then voluntarily offers to disqualify himself by giving her a shower (and taking one himself).

By 9 pm, two humans are kicked off Suburban Survivor (but allowed to stay for the fun), three humans to go and three pets to go.
By 10:30 pm, my son disqualifies himself by appearing out the backdoor with a CD player and CDs. The cats are disqualified the minute they start whining for their kibble bowls--reminded of them when he opened the door--and are put inside for the night.

Two humans, one pet still in the race for the title of Suburban Survivor. Dog is disqualified at nearly midnight when she started woofing and had to be taken in for the night. The finals, two of us left: My-Blonde-Friend and myself.

Day 2: Rude Awakenings

Somewhere around 4 am, I woke with a start to an alarm going off. Not my cell phone alarm? CHECK. Not my car alarm? CHECK. Neighbor's house alarm? UCK. Someone's teenage son is getting g-r-o-u-n-d-e-d. Said son also does not know TURN OFF CODE so we are subjected to the alarms, soon to be mixed with SIRENS, and then…blessed silence about 25 minutes later. Ahhhhhhh. Downpour begins. Resist the urge to stay "f-it to the cold and the rain and go in and sleep in my nice warm bed. MUST RESIST."

About 5:30 am, woke to find myself in tears and biting down on the ear of daughter's teddy bear. Soon to be deceased Blonde Hubby mutters something like "You know, they have therapy for that."

Also realize that Blonde Goofball and son did not set up tent on level yard, have Charlie horses in both legs as I've been unconsciously using my legs to keep me from rolling down the slope to the other end of the tent in my sleep. Resisted urge to smack my husband. It was hard.

About 6:50 am, wake to whiny daughter who is cold and also wet (apparently Blondie did not fully get her tent window zipped up). I stood up and noticed my friend's bed is empty. Thought to myself, "Maybe she's making breakfast inside?"

Oh, inside. How I missed it so. Went in to change my daughter into warm dry clothes and make coffee. Hmmm, no friend? Did a quick bedroom check to see who snuck inside in the middle of the night. Son's room, empty. Daughter's room, empty. Our room, AHA! CHEATER! A sleeping friend.

WHOOT! WHOOT! I WON! And then, promptly disqualified myself by entering this into my online journal.

We now resume the reader to the regular chronicles, please stand by.

5-16: Stackable Humans

Blonde-Spouse-Insane-Inventor traced around Blonde-Spouse-Diminutive-Duplicate while she laid on top of cardboard. He cut it out in her shape. When he completed her silhouette, he then had the Brunette-Teenage-Son-And-Self-Designated-Peanut-Gallery-Of-Sarcastic-Commentary down on another large piece of cardboard and repeated the process. He had Blonde-Spouse-Diminutive-Duplicate trace his outline on yet another piece of cardboard. Finally, Blonde-Spouse-Insane-Inventor had Brunette-Self stand against a piece taped to the wall and traced around her silhouette.

"Why are you doing this?" Brunette-Self asked, rather dismayed.

"It's a surprise!" he declared.

Blonde-Spouse-Insane-Inventor then departed for his workshop, ILL (5-8: The Coffee Caddy.) Brunette-Self tried to peek in on him, but he met her at the door and shooed her away. Giving up, she went back into the house.

Two days later, Blonde-Spouse-Insane-Inventor approached the family and asked them to follow him outside. The family walked across the street and looked back at their house. Life-size photocopy cut-outs of the entire family stood in the window.

"Even the pets? Where are the pets?" asked Blonde-Spouse-Diminutive-Duplicate.

"Not yet," began the Blonde-Spouse-Insane-Inventor sales pitch, "They'll be marketed as accessories. I give you 'Stackable Humans!' Tired of waiting in commuter traffic? Then I've got the answer for you: simply use 'Stackable Humans' in the car for the commuter lane! Feeling lonely? Pull out your 'Stackable Humans' and have a party! Need some home security while your on vacation? 'Stackable Humans' can stand in your home to give the illusion someone is there! Also available in child size and elderly family member, best used for situations involving senior discounts or children's rates. You can even use 'Stackable Humans' in your garden! Yes, 'Stackable Humans' will scare those varmints away! 'Stackable Humans' come in all ethnicities, ages and genders. Act now and we'll include the optional family pet! 'Stackable Humans' store easily in the closet, under beds or in other narrow spaces."

"'Stackable Humans,' Babe, really?" asked Brunette-Self sarcastically.

"How come you don't have 'Stackable Girlfriends,' Dad?" asked BTSASDPGOSC, "You know, for that lonely geek on the go?!?"

"Because they already sell the inflatable kind."

5-17: A Trail To Bedtime

Brunette-Self was on her way to put away clean clothes the bedrooms when she noticed a trail of Skittles along the carpet. As she rounded the corner she bumped into Scottie-Dog, who was busily disposing of the Skittles trail ahead.

Brunette-Self put down the clothes and went in search of Blonde-Spouse-Diminutive-Duplicate. She found her in the living room playing with her dollhouse. Brunette-Self sat down to confront Blonde-Spouse-Diminutive-Duplicate.

"Why did you leave a trail of Skittles?" she asked Blonde-Spouse-Diminutive-Duplicate.

"I didn't. Daddy did."

"Why?"

"I don't know, ask Daddy." she replied, giving her mother a withered look.

"Fine. Thank you."

Brunette-Self went in search of Blonde-Spouse and found him in the backyard attempting to measure out edging for a flower bed with a 12 inch ruler.

"Honey Bunny," she began, "Why the Skittles trail? The dog enjoyed them quite a bit, by the way."

"Oh, I was trying to bait munchkin to bed, did it work? Was she in bed?"

"No, she was in the living room playing with her doll house. The Scottie-Dog thanks you, though. So, could you please not do that again? You could end up staining the carpet."

"Well, what if I use M and Ms? They melt in your mouth, not in your hand. If they don't melt in your hand, they won't melt on the carpet," he replied, placing a finger on the edging to mark his spot and moving the ruler for the next foot.

"Would you like the measuring tape?" she said, pointing to his ruler, "And please, no more candy trails because chocolate hurts the dogs."

"Nah, I've only got a few feet more to measure...I think...wait. Oh, you messed me up! Now I have to start over again!"

Brunette-Self went inside, grabbed the measuring tape and tossed it out the back door on the grass next to Blonde-Spouse. She then went and told Blonde-Spouse-Diminutive-Duplicate it was time to pack up the dollhouse and go to bed.

5-18: Landscaping Letdown

Blonde-Spouse, seeking a day in the wilds and sunshine, offered to take the kids and collect rocks for the retaining wall. The three departed midmorning and left Brunette-Self to herself.

She enjoyed her leisure time by taking a nap. The ringing phone interrupted a great dream. Brunette-Self tried to bat it away, but the ringing persisted.

Annoyed, she answered, "Hello?"

"Hi, Honey," came the voice of Blonde-Spouse, "We're, ah, stuck. Do we have AAA still?"

"No."

"Uh, well, could you help me find the number for the tire store nearest to where we're at and call them and tell them to come out here? Ok? Thanks, Bye," Blonde-Spouse disconnected the call.

"Wonderful," mumbled Brunette-Self to herself and went back to sleep.

A half an hour later the phone rang again, "Well, did you get the number?"

"No."

"WHY NOT?"

"Because you never told me where you were, Dear."

"Oh. We're at milepost 27," Blonde-Spouse said and hung up again.

Nearly an hour passed before the phone rang again, and this time he sounded very upset, "Where the #$^& are they?!?"

"I haven't called them."

"WHAT?!?"

"Milepost 27 means squat unless you tell me what road you are on."

"You know, you could have mentioned this when we last talked," he spat accusingly.

"Well, Dear, I would have but you hung up on me without saying good bye."

"We're on Highway 12. Will you call them now?"

"Yes."

Brunette-Self went online and found the nearest tire repair store to their location and gave them a call. She requested they call her for payment, given Blonde-Spouse's propensity to lose things she had confiscated his debit card.

It was nearly two hours before the phone rang again, this time the voice belonged to The-Friendly-Tire-Repair-Store-Staff-Person-Who-Could-Not-Contain-Her-Laughter, "Hello, I'm calling to take a payment on your van."

"Ok," sighed Brunette-Self, pulling out her debit card, "What's the damage?"

"That will be $3,468.52, Ma'am."

"$3,468.52! What for?!?"

"Well, um--" began The-Friendly-Tire-Repair-Store-Staff-Person-Who-Could-Not-Contain-Her-Laughter, "All four of the tires were completely popped, so they had to be replaced in the field before the vehicle could be towed back to the shop for repair…"

"Repair?" interrupted Brunette-Self.

"The responding driver had to assist your husband in removing several pounds of rocks from the back of the vehicle. Your husband overloaded the vehicle and hit a large dip in the road, popping all four tires and damaging your rear and front axles," laughingly explained The-Friendly-Tire-Repair-Store-Staff-Person-Who-Could-Not-Contain-Her-Laughter (who could no longer resist and had finally succumbed to her giggling).

"How long to complete the repair?"

"About a week" she chortled.

"Really?"

"Afraid so."

"Would you let them know I'm on my way down to pick them up? Here's that card number…"

5-19: Another Solicitor Stopper Sign

Elections were coming up and the neighborhood community "No Solicitors" sign had been largely ignored, as the residents hid behind locked doors and drawn drapes from the clipboard, pamphlet and propaganda touting army of political candidate recruiters on the other side of the door, hoping to litter the occupants with brochures and claim a piece of their front lawn for their signs.

Annoyed by this onslaught on his front door, Blonde-Spouse Solicitor Stopper composed another sign, thereby putting the family forever on the Terrorist No Fly List:

We believe in Government and our household thereby resembles Congress:

One Republican and One Democrat live here. The two parties will never agree, just like marriage. Please try back in 4 years, however note that unless you are a corporate lobbyist we'll be unavailable to you until just prior to our reelection campaign.

5-20: King of Clerical Errors:
A Contagious State of Blonde

Brunette-Self had long suspected Blonde-Spouse-Blondeness was, well, quite frankly, contagious. In fact, she secretly believed he should come with a warning label:

Caution: Blondeness Contagion Active (BCA): Please seek shelter of the nearest brunette as soon as possible.   If you experience symptoms of BCA: forgetfulness, extreme sudden attraction to shiny objects, inability to open or close doors or perform simple tasks, or otherwise find your head flipping consistently to one side seek immediate medical attention or risk severe consequences.

To best illustrate this belief, Brunette-Self humbly offers the reader the following examples of Blondeness Contagion in Action:

Example One:

Blonde-Spouse went to the Department of Motor Vehicles (DMV) to obtain his license. Everyone in his immediate vicinity fell victim to his BCA and forgot to take a number. This angered several DMV patrons once they realized they had spent more than an hour waiting in the lobby without a number. Because BCA strikes silently, they were unaware of which direction to retaliate toward, and thus grew snappy with each other.

Blonde-Spouse, after having his Brunette-Self pulled number called, promptly infected the DMV staff person. She misspelled his name -- twice. Once she finally had his name corrected, she kept printing his picture onto the identification card of the ever impatient individual who proceeded him in line and who had been waiting for their identification to print so they could go home. Blonde-Spouse and Brunette-Self had arrived fairly early that morning, about an hour before the DMV opened, and did not leave with his license until nearly 4 pm that afternoon. Moreover, Brunette-Self discovered when they arrived home that the DMV staff person had misspelled his name a third time.

Example Two:

Blonde-Spouse went to the bank to deposit $200 in cash. It should have been a very simple transaction, considering the hair color of the teller waiting on him. BCA would thwart this simple transaction, and would bring with it two days of sequential bank errors that would cost the couple nearly that much in overdraft fees.

The BCA infected teller deposited $100 in cash into another account belonging to an individual with a similar name to Blonde-Spouse. Brunette-Self then immediately disputed the incident. It was the end of the day before the teller discovered the other $100, which had slipped below her counting drawer, however, not before the bank had denied two charges and assessed two over draft fees. The teller then deposited the found $100 into the other similar name account, and two more charges came through the couple's account and bounced with two more fees charged. Their account was now severely overdrawn.

Brunette-Self called the bank, and was incorrectly charged an additional fee for talking to a live person. The BCA infection was becoming an outbreak, now infecting nearly every bank employee within breathing distance of the Blonde-Spouse deposit. The account was placed on hold while yet another call to the bank led to a money trace. Somehow, the computer system was now infected with BCA and not only did not hold the account, but put all four charges through not once, not twice, but five times. Each time the charges were put through by the computer, they were rejected and another overdraft fee was assessed.

The couple was now a $1,000 overdrawn. Brunette-Self, watching her account dwindle faster than a 401K on Wall Street at the end of 2008, urgently called the bank and was charged another fee for talking to a live person. The bank finally was able to locate the money and return it to the account, were it was immediately eaten up by overdraft fees. It took another three calls to correct all of the fees.

Example Three:

Blonde-Spouse decided to simplify his working life by signing up for direct deposit for his paycheck. Payday arrived and the deposit did not. Blonde-Spouse called the bank, the bank responded they hadn't received it. Blonde-Spouse called the employer, who verified they sent it. Blonde-Spouse decided someone must be holding it hostage in cyberspace and turned it over to Brunette-Self.

Brunette-Self, with the aid of a half hour conference call between a human resources person and the bank branch manager, finally located in the paycheck in a trust fund belonging to the bank customer with similar sounding name. Shortly thereafter, Brunette-Self switched banks.

Example Four:

Years before Blonde-Spouse met Brunette-Self, he had been assaulted by a customer at a restaraunt where he had worked for several years. Blonde-Spouse missed out on perfect job and was advised BCA responsible for clerical error entered into state patrol database making Blonde-Spouse the perpetrator not the victim.

Correction of the BCA induced clerical error took nearly 8 months, an attorney and a private investigator to locate the now retired prosecuting attorney and retired police officer to verify clerical error, which then could be corrected.

Example Five:

Brunette-Self, attempting to get a copy of their marriage license, discovered BCA has induced yet another clerical error changing their wedding date from 5/1/2004 to 5/4/2001. Brunette-Self noticed that right next to this error, the cleric had even entered the correct year of their marriage license being issued by the county. Brunette-Self has still been unable to get the county to correct this database error.

Example Six:

Blonde-Spouse had an ex-girlfriend that clerical errors cause to move in to the couple's home nearly every four months. This clerical error is across both state and federal databases, which makes filing taxes difficult every year. Ex-girlfriend is deceased, but this does not seem to matter to government employees.

It takes Brunette-Self hours every few months of phone time 'kicking out the ex,' only to have her 'sneak back into their lives like a cyberghost love affair.' Brunette-Self feels if dead ex is so bent on haunting them she should ante up some bill money.

Example Seven:

Blonde-Spouse signed the couple up for automatic bill pay. The first month, a clerical error caused the couple to make three car loan payments, three insurance payments, and three payments each to the phone and utility companies.

Brunette-Self leaves the reader to ponder these and determine for themselves whether or not BCA should be considered a Super Bug.

5-21: Cretin Costume, Highlighter Pens and Halloween

Blonde-Spouse remembered his promise to Brunette-Self (Chronicle 4:20: "My Near Death Experience" by Blonde-Spouse) and set to work on his costume so he could take Blonde-Spouse-Diminutive-Duplicate trick-or-treating for the holiday. It was decided the two would go out and leave Brunette-Self to be the candy dispenser, er, the one who handed out candy to the trick-or-treaters approaching the family door. The two blondes were already on the Brunette-Self Ca-Ca List, having been caught drawing on their hands with yellow highlighter pens. Blonde-Spouse had weakened his position further by painting Blonde-Spouse-Diminutive-Duplicate's fingernails with a permanent black marker to make her costume "more gothy." A highly annoyed Brunette-Self was currently repainting Blonde-Spouse-Diminutive-Duplicate's fingernails black with actual nail polish, having spent quite some time scrubbing off the marker.

The two looked up from nail painting when Blonde-Spouse cleared his throat, he stood before them turning this way and that, "What do you think of my costume? I call it 'The Cretin Costume.' "

Brunette-Self took in Blonde-Spouse, who was wearing clothes he normally wears: a tee shirt on inside out and backwards over a long sleeved flannel shirt, also on inside out and backwards; mismatched colored socks and shoes on the wrong feet.

"I don't see anything different, Dear," she volunteered snottily.

Blonde-Spouse looked indignant and pointed to his chest. Attached to his chest with a large rubber duck diaper pin, was a note:

Please Help Me: I am Blonde!
If Found, Please Direct Me to the Nearest Brunette.
Brunette instructions on other side of paper.

Brunette-Self stood up and walked over to Blonde-Spouse Cretin Costume, flipping up his note and looking on the other side, "There's nothing written on there."

"Well, there's where you come in! You've got to write the instructions!"

Brunette-Teenage-Son-And-Self-Designated-Peanut-Gallery-Of-Sarcastic-Commentary sauntered in and hungrily eyed the candy bowl.

"Hey, kid, you want to hang out here and hand out candy to the little kids that trick-or-treat? You've got to promise to actually save some for the kids, though, ok?" Brunette-Self asked him.

"Sure, Mom," replied Brunette-Teenage-Son-And-Self-Designated-Peanut-Gallery-Of-Sarcastic-Commentary as he grabbed the bowl and plopped down in front of the computer, "Besides, your better off giving those 'Brunette Instructions' in person."

Brunette-Self donned a quick costume and headed out for trick-or-treating with Blonde-Spouse-Cretin-Costume and Blonde-Spouse-Diminutive-Duplicate-Gothy-Girl. The trio went up and down a few blocks, Blonde-Spouse-Cretin-Costume diligently gathering "Donations for the Brunette Wifey PMS Stash Fund." Because his shoes were on the wrong feet, he quickly started complaining that his feet hurt and maybe they should turn for home soon.

Brunette-Self talked him into going into the haunted house on the corner first, thus ending their trick-or-treating on a 'big finale.' The trio wandered through the haunted house, scared by moving scarecrows and ghosts. They approached the garage and the "last big scare" of the haunted house: a mummy hiding in a coffin up against the wall in the garage--a mummy who was about to jump out amongst the dry ice fog and black lights to scare them and then direct them to the treat table.

As they entered the garage and fully into the black light, Brunette-Self noticed Blonde-Spouse-Cretin-Costume and Blonde-Spouse-Diminutive-Duplicate-Gothy-Girl were covered in highlighter doodles and writing. The black light exposed the previously "invisible" highlighter graffiti, which included the words "nana nana boo boo" on Blonde-Spouse-Cretin-Costume's forehead and "Mom will never know" scrawled across the forehead of Blonde-Spouse-Diminutive-Duplicate-Gothy-Girl.

"So, um, you guys put those highlighters away, didn't you?" inquired Brunette-Self, setting the two up.

"Oh, yes! Of course we did! You told us not to write on ourselves with them! We put them away, just like you said to do," responded the two in feigned wide-eyed innocence.

"Uh huh. Busted!" replied Brunette-Self, spinning the two around by their shoulders to face their reflections of the mirror behind them.

As she spun the two around to reveal their guilt to them, the hiding mummy saw the writing on their faces and broke into hysterical laughter, thereby giving himself away as he fell out of the coffin. Tripping on his tattered bandages, the mummy stumbled and crashed into the stunned blondes and sent the three to the floor. The mummy turned out to be the father of the household, and he was so tickled over the incident he gave Brunette-Self a six month supply of PMS Candy Stash. He sent the two 'naughty blonde children' home with no candy. Pouting, the blondes let Brunette-Self lead them back home.

5-22: Arabica Affliction

Brunette-Self was brewing some coffee and she handed the water pitcher to Blonde-Spouse, "Please fill this up with some water?"

Blonde-Spouse dutifully took the water pitcher and walked right past the sink and down the hall with it, disappearing into the master bathroom. Grumbling to herself, she filled the carafe instead and started to brew the coffee.

Content the coffee was merrily perking along, Brunette-Self followed Blonde-Spouse down the hall to the master bathroom. Blonde-Spouse had placed a 5-gallon bucket into the bathtub. He'd placed a metal grill grate from an old BBQ on the top of the bucket, and had set one of Brunette-Self's Arabica coffee plants on the grill. Blonde-Spouse had turned on the shower and was trying to aim the stream of water into the top of the plant.

"What are you doing, honey? Flushing the organic fertilizer out of the soil?" she asked.

"Nope," he said, glancing up from his work, "I'm sifting water through the root ball of the coffee plant so the water will be pre-caffeinated, thereby making it much stronger than regular tap water! See, it's already turning brown with coffee!"

Brunette-Self followed his pointing finger down into the bucket with her eyes, "You mean the water that is now dirty because you ran it through the soil?"

"No, that's pre-coffee!" he defended.

"Well, I already took the liberty of brewing a new pot, have at it," she replied.

Blonde-Spouse took off down the hall to retrieve a fresh brewed cup of coffee. Brunette-Self disassembled his strainer and hid the bucket and grill, and moved the plants to another room.

5-23: Watering the Woodwork

Brunette-Self was enjoying the first real stretch of sunshine the area had had all Spring, as she lazily sunbathed in the stream of sunshine pouring in her living room window. She laid back on the couch and watched the prisms hanging in her window shoot rainbows throughout the room.

Her revelry was rudely interrupted by the sound of raindrops hitting the windows, "No more rain!"

Glancing up at the window, she noticed the rain was falling but the sun was still shining. Getting up from the couch, she went outside to dance in her favorite kind of wacky weather. She was spinning slowly in a circle with her head down and hands outstretched, and laughing when the sun disappeared again.

The shadow of Blonde-Spouse blocked out the sun and drew her gaze up to the roof of the house, where he shouted down at her, "Is it getting the windows and the sides of the house or do I need to have you turn it up more?"

"Is what getting the sides of the house and windows?" she asked, confused.

"The water. I'm trying to wash the house, so I set the sprinkler up here on the roof. What I need to know is it hitting the sides of the house or do I need to have you turn up the water more?"

"Uh, Honey, I think the water hitting the sides of the house is bouncing off the car parked here in the driveway or off the driveway--not sure which. But, I think I have a better way you can wash the house instead."

"Well, I don't want to have to sit and hold the hose. Does it involve holding the hose?" he inquired hopefully.

Sighing, she replied, "I guess not, although that would be the best way. If you must I guess you can set it down to water the yard and the side of the house at the same time."

"Ok," he said, lifting the sprinkler off the roof and trying to walk back to the ladder. The hose got stuck and he gave it a tug. It freed unexpectedly and he lost his footing and ran down the roof of the house trying to regain his balance. He caught both feet up in the hose, sending him belly flopping onto the roof of the house. Blonde-Spouse's body then slid down the roof face first toward the gutter and he managed to grab a hold of the gutter on his way over the edge of the roof. Blonde-Spouse now dangled by the gutter with the sprinkler sending sprays of water in every direction. He kicked and tried to free his feet from his hose ankle shackles in order to gain footing against the house.

"Hon, just let go already," yelled Brunette-Self, seeing Blonde-Spouse's feet dangling only two feet from the ground.

Her words were too late, the gutter gave way under Blonde-Spouse's weight, sending Blonde-Spouse, the hose, sprinkler and the gutter down into the flowerbed and on top of her highly valuable prize ornamental maple tree.

Brunette-Self smacked her forehead instead of smacking Blonde-Spouse.

5-24: Keyless Entry

Brunette-Self had read Blonde-Spouse the Riot Act more than once over his horrific habit of losing everything important: his car keys, his wallet, his drivers license, his parked car, his winning lottery ticket, bills; once even losing the only keyless entry and keys set in a snow bank during a snowball fight. She had tried in vain to train him for nearly six years to put these things in one location so he didn't always lose them. To his credit, Blonde-Spouse really did attempt to retrain himself to do this. And thus, brought forward his new "Keyless Entry" invention.

Blonde-Spouse-Insane-Inventor announced it one evening over dinner, "I have a new invention."

"Dare I ask?" inquired Brunette-Self, reaching for the antacids she knew she'd need later.

"Oh, nothing grand. Just a keyless entry for the car. You know, because I'm always losing my car keys. You're always yelling at me for it because they've got special computer chips in them for the alarm and ignition kill switch so they get expensive."

"Yes, reprogramming the entire system every time you lose the stupid things does get expensive," Brunette-Self sarcastically agreed.

Her sarcasm was lost on Blonde-Spouse-Insane-Inventor, "Follow me and come check this out!"

He led the family out to the car parked in the driveway. Brunette-Self glanced in the driver's window and noted the alarm was active. She then spied the keys and the only keyless entry remote sitting in the drivers side seat.

"Sh--," she muttered under her breath and made a mental note to cancel her appointment for the next day, she knew she would be spending it in the waiting room of the local dealership.

"See, I put them in the car so they won't get lost! I armed the alarm so no one could steal the car, either," he announced proudly.

"So, how do you get the car keys out, Dad? You rolled up the windows," commented Brunette-Teenage-Son-And-Self-Designated-Peanut-Gallery-Of-Sarcastic-Commentary.

"Well, Mr. Smarty Pants," retorted Blonde-Spouse-Insane-Inventor, "That is why I rolled up the windows, so no one could reach in and take the keys. But, what the thief doesn't know, is I've attached the keys to this clear fishing line. I just pull on this piece sticking out of the top of the window here, and it will pull the keys right to me!"

Blonde-Spouse-Insane-Inventor gave the fishing line a tug, jerking the keys 'magically' off of the seat and sending them flying through the air, where they collided with the window and slid up the glass, stopping as they reached the top of the closed window, "Oh, no."

"Forgot to roll the window down enough to get the keys out, didn't you, Dad?" smirked Brunette-Teenage-Son-And-Self-Designated-Peanut-Gallery-Of-Sarcastic-Commentary.

"No! It would have made them too easy to steal that way!" hollered back Blonde-Spouse-Insane-Inventor, still tugging with all of his might to pull the keys through the open slit of the window. He gave the fishing line one final violent tug, setting off the car alarm and snapping the fishing line. The keys plummeted to the ground while the siren went off and the car headlights turned on and off repeatedly.

"Real, nice, Dear," said Brunette-Self angrily, "Flipping NICE."

Ignoring the screaming Scottie dog howls, she stormed back into the house to call AAA for an alarm disarm and a tow to the dealership the next morning, glad, at least, the alarm would only sound for a few minutes. She was also very glad she had decided to get another membership.

5-25: Weatherproofing

The-Neighbor-Next-Door had a flurry of activity at their house. Blonde-Spouse and Brunette-Self, out in the yard, noticed the movement and went to find out what all the excitement was about. The-Neighbor-Next-Door told the two he had the utility company come out and weatherize his home for the winter. Brunette-Self thought this was a fantastic idea and obtained the phone number for the program from their neighbor. Blonde-Spouse, however, decided to get a head start on the weatherization. He set to work while Brunette-Self and The-Neighbor-Next-Door chatted over a cup of coffee in the driveway. The two were so engrossed in their conversation that they hadn't noticed he was missing until he returned, covered in dust and smile of accomplishment.

"Come see what I did," he said, leading her away from The-Neighbor-Next-Door.

"Talk with you later, have a great day," she said over her shoulder as she was drug away.

"First, I dealt with the heat loss coming from the windows by insulating them," he started, pointing to the window nearest the two.

The window appeared to be covered in clear silicone caulking on top of which he'd pushed on saran wrap. Blonde-Spouse had "sealed the edges of the saran wrap insulation" by running duct tape along the edges of the doors and window sills to "seal out drafts." Blonde-Spouse did not take into account opening or closing the windows or doors, and he proceeded to rip off the duct tape (and the paint) on the front door as he continued the weatherization tour inside.

He directed her toward the water heater, where he had wrapped it at least two dozen times in bubble wrap, "to better insulate it." He indicated he had done the same with the furnace and heat registers in the floors.

"Come check this out!" he declared, grabbing a flashlight. Blonde-Spouse pulled Brunette-Self out of the back door and over to the crawl space entrance under the house. He opened the door and pushed her head in and thrust the flashlight in underneath her chin, "I wrapped all of the heating ducts underneath the house with all of those old blankets we had, now the ducts will stay warm in the Winter!"

A confused and very sad Blonde-Spouse-Diminutive-Duplicate came out the backdoor, "Momma, where are all of my stuffed animals?"

"Oh, Honey, you didn't," started Brunette-Self, turning to Blonde-Spouse.

"Well, I ran out of blankets and I needed to insulate the crawl space above the ceilings!"

Brunette-Self took Blonde-Spouse-Diminutive-Duplicate shopping at the local thrift store for a new supply of stuffed animals.

5-26: Printer Paper Perplexed

Blonde-Spouse came home from work and announced his Blonde-Boss was offering the family seven cases of printer paper.

"Wow, that's exceedingly generous," declared Brunette-Self, immediately suspicious. She remembered that Blonde-Boss had once locked herself in the walk-in freezer because the thought it was the elevator.

"Oh, she accidentally ordered too many boxes and now she can't get into her office," replied Blonde-Spouse.

"Well, this is regular printer paper, right? Not dot matrix paper?"

"What's the difference?"

Rather than beating her head against a brick wall explaining the difference, she simply replied, "Just ask her if it's dot matrix printer paper. If she says 'Yes' then say 'No thank you.'"

"Okay dokey, will do."

Blonde-Spouse returned home from work the next evening, toting a case of printer paper, "There's six more in the van," he said, directed toward their Brunette-Teenage-Son-And-Self-Designated-Peanut-Gallery-Of-Sarcastic-Commentary, "and she says "No Take Backs," he directed toward Brunette-Self.

Thinking his boss must have held up the local office supply store, Brunette-Self was already thinking of all the things she could print on that paper. Excitedly, she tore open the first box to find -- dot matrix printer paper.

Brunette-Self still cannot decide if Blonde Boss was infected with a scorching case of BCA (Chronicle 5-20: King of Clerical Errors: A Contagious State of Blonde) or a suffering from "Diabolical Deceptive Ditchiness."

5-27: Coat Hanger Cup Holder

Blonde-Spouse-Insane-Inventor decided to purchase gigantic coffee travel mugs that did not fit in either vehicle's cup holders. He brainstormed and disappeared into ILL (Chronicle 5-8: The Coffee Caddy) for several hours.

Brunette-Self was nearly done cooking dinner when he reappeared, "I have a solution to the gigantic coffee travel mug holder issue."

Blonde-Spouse-Insane-Inventor led her outside to the van and opened the door for her. She got in and sat down in the passenger's seat. Before her were two large coffee cans with two holes punched in the top of each rim. Blonde-Spouse-Insane-Inventor had cut two wire coat hangers and slipped them through the holes, turning the coat hangers up to hold the hanger to the coffee can. He had hung the coat hangers onto the air vents of the van dashboard.

"Now put your full coffee travel mug in the can, Honey," said Blonde-Spouse-Insane-Inventor.

Brunette-Self set the travel mug into her coffee can cup holder, cutting both of the backs of each hand with the cut wire of the coat hangers in the process, "Ouch!"

"Oh, that's going to leave a scar or two," said Blonde-Spouse-Insane-Inventor, clucking his tongue. He took of his old tee shirt and wrapped it around both of her hands like cotton handcuffs. While both were engrossed in stopping the bleeding of Brunette-Self's hands, the coat hanger strained under the weight of the gigantic coffee travel mug. The holder gave way and sent the can crashing to the ground. Both occupants of the van and the van's interior were drenched in hot coffee with sugar and cream.

"I really am sorry, Dear," apologized Blonde-Spouse-Insane-Inventor, while the two waited in the emergency room to be seen for burns and gashes, "at least you'll have two scars to commemorate the moment forever?"

Blonde-Spouse was also treated for a concussion.

5-28: Rechargeable Rotisserie

Brunette-Self was unpacking the trunk of the car for the family's weekend camping trip. Blonde-Spouse-Insane-Inventor had come rushing out of ILL before they'd left home and stashed something in the trunk, so Brunette-Self was removing every item with extreme caution. When she got to the bottom of the trunk, the only remaining item was a cordless handmixer with one modified beater consisting of the metal skeleton of an umbrella. The umbrella skeleton had been shortened so that when opened, it's radius was about 6 inches.

"Why a handmixer, Snickerdoodle?" asked Brunette-Self, holding up the drill and long bit.

"That's my rotisserie!" announced Blonde-Spouse-Insane-Inventor, as he dumped another load of wood on top of the fire, "You said you always wanted to cook a roast or chicken out here over the campfire in a dutch oven, but you never do because it wastes so much wood. So, I invented the Rechargeable Rotisserie, for the griller on the go!"

"Oh, I've got to see this!" she said, and took a seat by the campfire.

Blonde-Spouse-Insane-Inventor went over to a second ice chest he'd managed to pack without the knowledge of Brunette-Self. He opened the lid, bent over and removed a plastic wrapper. Handing the wrapper off to Brunette-Teenage-Son-And-Self-Designated-Peanut-Gallery-Of-Sarcastic-Commentary, Blonde-Spouse-Insane-Inventor held the mixer and long beater above his head, laughed maniacally, and plunged the umbrella beater into the ice chest as hard as he could. A sickening thunk could be heard muffled by the ice chest.

He turned the mixer on for a moment and then lifted the "Rechargeable Rotisserie" out of the ice chest to reveal he'd impaled a 12-pound turkey with it. He staggered with the weight of the turkey, finally eliciting additional assistance from the esteemed Brunette-Teenage-Son-And-

Self-Designated-Peanut-Gallery-Of-Sarcastic-Commentary in getting it over to the fire.

Blonde-Spouse-Diminutive-Duplicate stood by with a clean paint brush and a bottle of olive oil dumped into a camping pan. Blonde-Spouse-Insane-Inventor turned on the mixer and the turkey began to spin wildly. Blonde-Spouse-Diminutive-Duplicate decided she wanted nothing to do with it, and handed the brush off to her brother. With great care, Brunette-Teenage-Son-And-Self-Designated-Peanut-Gallery-Of-Sarcastic-Commentary dipped the brush into the oil, turned his head and held it out to the wildly spinning turkey. Oil flung all over the campsite, cars, camp kitchen, camping gear, tents, campers and the campfire; the last responding by exploding into a raging inferno.

"Well, there went all of tomorrow's wood," sighed their Brunette-Teenage-Son-And-Self-Designated-Peanut-Gallery-Of-Sarcastic-Commentary, as he and Blonde-Spouse-Diminutive-Duplicate prepared to gather more wood.

They left Blonde-Spouse-Insane-Inventor with the campfire and a dismayed Brunette-Self, his spinning turkey top and his Rechargeable Rotisserie still whirring madly away as they departed to find more wood.

"Hey, Hon--" began Brunette-Self as she noticed with each spin the turkey was getting further and further away from the mixer and closer to the fire.

"Yes, Dear?" asked Blonde-Spouse-Insane-Inventor, looking up from his rotisserie at her. As he glanced away from the mixer his hand moved slightly downward. The mixer tipped slightly toward the ground, giving the spinning turkey the necessary force to rotate right off of the end of the beater. The turkey completed one full turn before landing squat in the middle of the campfire. The flames roared up and fed on the turkey like a pack of rabid wolves.

"Well, I'd give that turkey a perfect 10 for the acrobatic dismount," snapped Brunette-Self, now painfully aware the turkey-fed fire just became a beacon to every black bear and mountain lion in a 100 mile radius.

She bit her tongue rather than share this realization with Mr. Blonde-Spouse-Insane-Inventor, whom she knew would use the opportunity to create a tin can 'Bear Camp Infiltrating Alarm System' or something similar and open every can of food they had to do it.

"Damn it," cursed Blonde-Spouse-Insane-Inventor, "it was working, too!"

"Well, Sweetie, it's probably for the best," soothed Brunette-Self, "it would have taken several hours to roast that turkey anyway and those batteries are only good for an hour or so."

"Well, I already thought of THAT," he snapped and ran over to the van, pulling an extension cord out from underneath the front seat, "I came prepared."

5-29: The Fire Pit Moat

The turkey bear beacon bonfire (Chronicle 5-28: Rechargeable Rotisserie) got Blonde-Spouse-Safety-Superintendent to thinking about forest fires and fire safety.

The family retired that evening, stuffed full of marshmallows and hotdogs, and left Blonde-Spouse-Safety-Superintendent to put out the coals before bed. He sat in the dark, thoughtfully staring at the coals. Brunette-Self had a sense of foreboding but realized she'd done a great job of isolating that campfire in the middle of a clearing filled with only dirt and rock and that the tree line was at least 50 feet away. The fact she and the kids had locked the firewood in the car overnight with the food for safe keeping and that key was safely in her pocket kept Brunette-Self from tossing and turning in panic.

The next morning, the family woke at dawn and unzipped the tent. Blonde-Spouse-Safety-Superintendent was trying to pick the lock on the car door. He seemed relieved to see her, "Can I have the keys, please? I'd like to brew some coffee."

"Sure, Babe," she said sleepily, handing him the keys, "Were you up all night?"

"I was," he replied, pointing to the campfire, "but I think you'll like what I've done here. Go check it out."

Mr. Blonde-Spouse-Safety-Superintendent had spent all evening digging a six-inch deep trench and had lined it will all of the plastic garbage bags. He had duct taped the bags together, end to end. There were two 5-gallon buckets full of river water sitting next to the campfire.

"What is all this?" she asked.

"Fire Pit Moat!" he said, picking up first one and then the other of the 5-gallon buckets and pouring the water into the trench, "it will catch any sparks popping off of the fire!"

Blonde-Spouse-Diminutive-Duplicate came running up after having used the porta-potty, stepped into the moat, lost her footing and almost swan dived on top of the campfire coals. She was caught just before she fell by Brunette-Self, who replied to Blonde-Spouse-Safety-Superintendent, "I think we've identified a safety issue."

"Well, I'm tired now so I'll deal with it when I get up from a nap," he snapped and he then disappeared into the tent.

Brunette-Self brewed some coffee to wake up and enjoyed a cup while her chair straddled the moat. Brunette-Teenage-Son-And-Self-

Designated-Peanut-Gallery-Of-Sarcastic-Commentary and Brunette-Self spent the rest of the morning pulling out the bags, refilling the trench and taking a trip into town to buy more garbage bags and firewood.

5-30: FAMOUS LAST WORDS

Blonde-Spouse-Slogan-Buster had always loved mass media advertising slogans. Far too often, unfortunately, he took them literally or completely out of context (Chronicle 1-21: Car Maintenance Mistakes, and 2-3: Attack of the Advertising Icons.) Often, he would combine his extensive knowledge of advertising slogans with humor, and this would lead Blonde-Spouse-Slogan-Buster into a great deal of trouble.

Such was the case with the border patrol one afternoon while the family was attempting to enter Canada. The border patrol officer had just spoken to Blonde-Spouse while he sat behind the wheel in line, the officer had turned to leave when Blonde-Spouse turned to Brunette-Self and joked, "I'm hungry, maybe we should run for the border." All the officer heard was "run for the border." The family spent most of the rest of that day in a retaining room.

After the border patrol incident, Blonde-Spouse had been more diligent about combining his humor and ad slogan knowledge. However, one afternoon he and Brunette-Self had to attend a memorial service at a local church, where his combination proved to nearly cost him his life. When his humor and ad slogan knowledge combine in disaster, Blonde-Spouse-Slogan-Buster goes into panic mode and starts spouting more slogans without thinking, often digging a deeper hole for himself in the process.

Thus, Chronicle 5-30: Famous Last Words, (aren't you glad it's nearly over?) began:

The two were already in trouble before they went into the church for the service. The minister and his pregnant wife stood at the door, greeting people as they came in the building.

Blonde-Spouse-Slogan-Buster, thinking he was funny, remarked to Pregnant-Wife-Of-Minister, "Nothin' says lovin' like something in the oven."

"Excuse Me?" said Body-Builder-Church-Patron, standing nearby as he puffed up in anger at Blonde-Spouse.

"I'm just saying she's answered the question, "Where's the beef?'"

"I'm going to pound you!" yelled Body-Builder-Church-Patron with clenched fists.

"Have it your way."

"Right now!" Body-Builder-Church-Patron demanded loudly.

"Just do it!" said a panicked Blonde-Spouse-Slogan-Buster.

"I mean it!" said Church-Patron.

"Reach out and touch someone!" he yelled.

Body-Builder-Church-Patron had grabbed Blonde-Spouse-Slogan-Buster by the scruff of the neck, causing him to panic further.

"I'm going to kick you're ass!" he yelled, throwing Blonde-Spouse-Slogan-Buster down the church steps and onto the sidewalk.

"Please don't squeeze the Charmin!"

"Why won't you just shut up?"

"Because you're worth it!"

Body-Builder-Church-Patron started hitting Blonde-Spouse-Slogan-Buster, the sound of his fists hitting his face punctuated only by the occasional panicked Blonde-Spouse-Slogan-Buster mutterings, "Snap! Crackle! Pop!"

Brunette-Self apologized to Minister and Pregnant-Minister-Wife and explained that it was panic mode that kept him spouting off ad slogans. The couple immediately forgave him and even laughed a bit at his antics.

Brunette-Self managed to call off Body-Builder, and take her bleeding Blonde-Spouse-Slogan-Buster to the emergency room.

"Why do you do this to yourself, Snickerdoodle?" she asked as the nurse cleaned up his face and put ice on his eye.

"No More Tears," he said, wiping her cheek with his hand, "If I've only one life, let me live it as a blonde!"

ABOUT THE AUTHOR

In her former career, Jax Hix was a scientist who published scientific research, science fiction stories and poetry. She is still a geek and lives in Washington with her Blonde Spouse, Human and Furry Children and many plants. Jax has been writing, drawing, and performing music since early childhood. She would like to someday grow up to be the weird cat lady on the block. Jax is obsessed with coffee and detests shoes. She is prone to ramble and suffers from an unnatural obsession with bubble wrap and lineoleum. She also loves to run with scissors and other sharp objects, but never in front of the kids. When she is not busy embarassing her children, she writes. She recently completed Golden Deer Sun and White Bear Moon (children's book) and Chronicles of My Life With a Blonde (comedy fiction). Her nonfiction book, Suburban Farming, will be available in 2012. She continues to write novels and annoy her children, which she feels is every parent's duty.

LEGAL DISCLAIMER & EXCEEDINGLY SMALL PRINT

VERY IMPORTANT SMALL PRINT COMING UP!
Grab a magnifying glass, you're going to want to read this! This book was written with fake names (Blonde-Spouse, Brunette-Self) to protect Blonde Spouse in any future potential employment endeavors...this book breaks all of the rules because it can. Now, for the small print:

Situational Disclaimer:

IF YOU ARE A BLONDE FEMALE: The pictures are here to help with the story, if you get confused, please hand the book to a Brunette to read it to you. Just kidding! This book is for you, FINALLY someone is ripping on the men!

IF YOU ARE A BLONDE MALE: Put away your Sporks and Bic lighters, you lynch mob, you've had the luxury of the world picking on your women counterparts for far too long, everyone gets a turn...and this one's yours. No? You're going to lynch mob me anyway? Look! Shiny! Over there! Go get it!

IF YOU ARE MARRIED OR OTHERWISE DIRECTLY INNVOLVED WITH A BLONDE: You have my deepest sympathies. I think we should form a support group.

IF YOU ARE THE ACLU - Look! Over there! Congress just told me I couldn't do something stupid to hurt myself because I didn't know any better - Go get them! Protect my right to kill myself stupidly!

IF YOU ARE ANY OTHER ATTORNEY REPRESENTING A BLONDE FOR POTENTIAL LAWSUIT: I'll save you the trouble...I'm already broke. Seriously. Broke. Why do you think I wrote the book? BROKE. Ok? This is not the author you are looking for *end Jedi mind trick.*

IF YOU ARE A BOOK BANNER: Wow, thanks for the compliment! Thank you for assuring college freshman decades from now will be assigned my book as homework...my descendents thank you.

FOR THE REST OF YOU EASILY OFFENDED TYPES: It's a JOKE, GET OVER IT. Can you imagine how much happier our world would be if more people could laugh at themselves in addition to others? Stop supporting the happy pill drug companies and open your mouth and let it pour out - laugh** - live. Buy my book, enjoy it. Do your duty as human beings to make the world a better, happier place. Tell your friends to buy it. Tell the friends of your friends to buy it. Give it for as a gift for any celebration, laughter heals. For that matter, smuggle one or two copies into the waiting room of your doctors and dentists for others to find. JUST BUY MY BOOK, PLEASE. I'm broke! Thanks!

**Some restrictions apply. Must have a sense of humor. Not for faint of heart. Author not liable for any medical conditions or other maladies that occur from failure to follow instructions or from hysterical response to book stimuli. Offer void in Hawaii and Mars.

So, that's it. The book is over now. Please go find something productive to do: go outside, hug someone—probably better get permission first for that one, go dancing, go watch television, torture your friends by buying them a copy of this book. Pretty, pretty please? It's for a good cause, really. The author could use that sale to actually go on vacation. Wouldn't that be cool? She'll send you a postcard.